RIDING THE BLACK SHIP

JAPAN AND TOKYO DISNEYLAND

Harvard East Asian Monographs, 173

Riding the Black Ship

Japan and Tokyo Disneyland

Aviad E. Raz

Published by the Harvard University Asia Center
and distributed by Harvard University Press
Cambridge (Massachusetts) and London
1999

Printed in the United States of America

The Harvard University Asia Center publishes a monograph series and, in coordina-
tion with the Fairbank Center for East Asian Research, the Korea Institute, the
Reischauer Institute of Japanese Studies, and other faculties and institutes, administers
research projects designed to further scholarly understanding of China, Japan, Viet-
nam, Korea, and other Asian countries. The Center also sponsors projects addressing
multidisciplinary and regional issues in Asia.

Library of Congress Cataloging-in-Publication Data
Raz, Aviad E., 1968–
        Riding the black ship : Japan and Tokyo Disneyland / Aviad E.
Raz.
        p.   cm. -- (Harvard East Asian monographs ; 173)
    Includes bibliographical references and index.
    ISBN 0-674-76893-0 (cloth : alk. paper)
    ISBN 0-674-76894-9 (pbk. : alk. paper)
    1. Tokyo Disneyland (Urayasu-shi, Japan)   2. Amusement
parks--Social aspects--Japan.   3. Popular culture--Japan.   4.
Japan--Civilization--American influences.   I. Title.   II. Series.
    GV1853.4.J32 T657 1999
    791'.06'852135--ddc21

                                                    98-43028
                                                       CIP

Index by the author

♾ Printed on acid-free paper

Last number below indicates year of this printing
08 07 06

Acknowledgments

Without the encouragement and assistance of many individuals, this book would never have come to fruition. I am particularly indebted to my instructors at Tel-Aviv University, Israel: Haim Hazan, who saw the anthropologist in me, and Jacob Raz, who initiated me into the study of Japan. I am also indebted to Norman Denzin, whose knowledge and guidance have been invaluable throughout this project. I owe special thanks as well to John Van Maanen, who introduced me to the academic club of Disnoids. Yehuda Shenhav has taught me that organizations are an object worthy of ideology critique. Among the many Japanese scholars who helped this study, I wish to thank Miyata Noboru, Kazufumi Manabe, Takigawa Yoshito, and, above all, my sponsor at the "Institute for the Culture of Travel," Kanzaki Noritake. I wish to thank Helen Hardacre and the Reischauer Institute of Japanese Studies at Harvard University, who kindly offered me a post-doctoral fellowship. Professors Andrew Gordon and Merry White read the first draft of the manuscript and provided helpful comments. Christine Yano, Timothy George, and Kim Kyu Hyun have given me encouragement and assistance. I am also very grateful to John Ziemer for his friendly and effective editorial guidance. Funding for my research in Japan was provided by the Japan Foundation, and for that, needless to say, I am extremely grateful. The research has also benefited from funding generously provided by the

Ben-Gurion Scholarship, Ministry of the Sciences, State of Israel; and by The Curiel Center for International Studies as well as the Horowitz Institute, both at Tel-Aviv University. A special grant from the Faculty of Humanities and Social Sciences, Ben-Gurion University, funded the preparation of graphic material.

On a more personal level, my thanks go to Odano Yasuko, Goto Hiroyo, Miyazaki Shuji, and Tanaka Satoshi, who sacrificed many nights watching field videos and going through the manuals. Otsubo Ryuta introduced me to the world of part-timers' training as well as to Shinyōen Buddhism, which for him are inseparable. Idit and Erez Paran helped us to get settled in Tokyo, and Idit introduced me to people who were extremely important for this study. The time my family spent in Tokyo would have been totally different without the help of Idit and Erez. I am also greatly indebted to the many OLC employees and TDL imagineers, who must remain anonymous, for agreeing to meet with me and discuss their personal thoughts.

My greatest debt of thanks is to my wife, Ayala, and my children, Or (Oru) and Yoav (Yoabu). They have done so much to help that it is impossible and useless to try and detail everything. I thank Ayala for giving up her own plans in order to give precedence to mine. I am grateful to Or and Yoav for their resilience and courage in leaving their familiar surroundings and adapting to a new place, a new language, and new friends.

A.E.R.

CONTENTS

Maps, Tables, and Figures

ABBREVIATIONS

CS	customer satisfaction
DL	Disneyland
OJT	on-the-job training
OL	office lady
OLC	Oriental Land Company
QC	quality control
TDL	Tokyo Disneyland
ToDo	Tokyo Dome
WDW	Walt Disney World
WDP	Walt Disney Productions

Riding the Black Ship

Japan and Tokyo Disneyland

INTRODUCTION

On April 10, 1996, the main exhibition hall of Makuhari Messe—East Asia's largest convention and exhibition complex—was packed with *sarariiman* (salarymen), housewives, and "office ladies," all anxious to view the latest tourist attractions. Golden Week—a national vacation (April 28–May 6) for company employees—was imminent, and it was time to decide where to go. Around 150 exhibitors awaited visitors to this *Tabi* (Travel) Fair sponsored by the Japan National Tourist Organization. Prefectural tourist associations, acclaimed hotels (like the Okura hotel chain), and *ryokan* (Japanese traditional inns) catered to the enthusiasm of tourists for the upcoming Golden Week. One booth, however, stood out. Equipped with a life-size traffic light and a children's-size convertible, painted in pastel colors and staffed with guides in checkered suits to match, Booth F-212 boasted a big English sign proclaiming: "Toon Town is open!" Tokyo Disneyland's booth proudly presented its "new land" amid the traditional "lands" of Kyoto and Osaka prefectures and the islands of Hokkaidō and Kyūshū.

Tabi Fair '96 vividly captured the extent to which Tokyo Disneyland (TDL for short) has been assimilated into the Japanese leisure market. Taking advantage of the nostalgic yearning for the "home country" (*kuni*), many booths displayed traditional crafts, costumes, housing, and foods. Visitors could watch a "genuine" craftswoman producing pottery or taste milk from Hokkaidō. The word *tabi* (journey) in the fair's title carries with it a sense of *furusato* (hometown) nostalgia, of returning to one's old hometown (see J. Robertson 1989, 1995). *Tabi*, the traditional journey, is not *kankō* (tourism), with its modern connotations.[1] *Tabi* has, however, become bracketed, modernized, and camouflaged by a thriving industry of domestic tourism. It has become a "fair." In a sense, TDL (pronounced *tidieru* by the Japanese), which opened in 1983, has been naturalized as a "homeland" (*kuni*), somewhere to make a journey (*tabi*) to time and time again.

The presence of TDL at Tabi Fair '96, however, was not just an affirmation of belonging and cultural legitimacy. It was also part of TDL's marketing strategy, which claims that resorts—diversionary outings for skiing, fishing, hiking, and domestic tourism in general—constitute its real competition, rather than the "conventional" amusement parks. Indeed, the other booths featured a wealth of resorts, parks, and various "foreign lands." Niigata prefecture had a showcase for its Russian Village, Kitakyūshū city boasted Space World as one of its attractions, the Okura booth advertised a hotel in Huis Ten Bosch (formerly Oranda Mura, Holland Village) near Nagasaki. The Fujikyūkō Railway Company was distributing flyers for its latest diversionary outing—Fujikyū Hairando near Mount Fuji, which boasts the world's largest (Guinness record) roller coaster. Although not as successful as TDL, these attractions represented the opening up of the Japanese leisure market since the 1980s. Tabi Fair '96 thus also stands for Japan's ongoing transformation, since the 1980s, into a post-industrial society—a stage the United States entered about 40 years ago.[2]

Tabi Fair '96 also serves to illustrate the socioeconomic context of TDL in contemporary Japan. In 1995–96, when this study was conducted, TDL had existed for thirteen years. No longer the American implant considered too adventurous by the Japanese media, now it is as if TDL had always been around. It is taken for granted as a popular destination for school excursions, hospitality tours, *hanabi* (fireworks) parties in the summer, and New Year's (*shōgatsu*) celebrations. TDL has matured, synthesizing its own organizational culture. Makuhari Messe, which hosted Tabi Fair '96, is also where TDL conducts job interviews for part-timers.

Socio-anthropological studies usually begin in the field. This, however, becomes complicated in the case of TDL, since it is a displaced field—a field that has been exported, or perhaps imported. In looking at TDL, one in fact looks at how Disney has traveled to Japan, how a significant piece of American business, ideology, and fantasy has been remade in Japan. On the face of it, this may seem to be a case study in cultural imperialism. My main argument is, however, that TDL reveals the opposite—namely, the active appropriation of Disney by the Japanese.[3] This book, therefore, is a case study of TDL in terms of its own organizational complexity and as part of the wider activity of leisure in Japan, as a segment in the relationship between the imaginaries of "Japan" and "America," and as a means of viewing social-scientific theories of globalization.

To study TDL, one first has to look at the original Disneyland. The Magic Kingdom with its various paraphernalia is unique as a popular culture phenomenon in that its popularity has endured for over 50 years and shows no sign of fading. Disney's global success has made it something closer to a secular religion than a producer of entertainment. It is America's national baby-sitter, mythmaker, and re-creator of history. For managers and businessmen, Disneyland is the Sistine Chapel of service culture: an American model for training and managing people. In referring to Disney, scholars employ neologisms such as "Disneyfied," "the Disney version," "Disney realism," "Distory" (Disney history), and "DisneyTalk." It would be difficult to find any other institution of popular culture so reified as a cultural force. Indeed, for many Disneyland is more than just an organization, it is a national shrine. Its ideological representations of American history, commodified nostalgia, utopian space, post-modern consumer society, and audience control have been the subject of much sociological discussion. Taking these questions to Tokyo entails a whole new context of inquiry.

TDL is a big organization and a big success—a bigger success than its American precursors. In 1996 it had 12,390 employees, about 2,000 regulars and 10,000 part-timers. TDL is the largest employer among Japan's diversionary outings. In the same year, TDL was visited by slightly more than sixteen million people. This makes it the most successful theme park in the world. In terms of the Japanese market, the number of visitors to TDL more or less equals the number of visitors to all the rest of the parks in Japan, and its yearly revenues exceed those of the rest of the parks combined. Annual attendance at TDL has risen steadily, to about 17.3 million in 1997, despite Japan's five-year economic recession. More than 200 million guests have streamed through the park's gates since they first opened, a demonstration of TDL's unflagging appeal in a country in which most fads fizzle out in a matter of months. Per capita expenditure among visitors to TDL is higher than that at any other Disney park and reached an average of U.S.$74 per visitor in 1997. The venture has been such a success that Walt Disney Company announced in 1997 it would enter a licensing agreement with the Japanese company that owns TDL for a $2.6 billion ocean theme park to be called DisneySea. The new park will be built on a landfill, and Disney predicts it will attract more than 10 million visitors a year.

TDL is owned and operated by a Japanese company, Oriental Land Company (OLC), which is a partnership between Mitsui Real Estate Development (Mitsui Fudōsan) and Keisei Electric Railway (Keisei Dentetsu). OLC was licensed by Disney in return for 10 percent of admissions earnings and 5 percent of food and souvenir sales. Since 1983 TDL's marketing strategy has basically remained the same—to claim that it is a 100 percent copy of the American original. This brings us back to the common view of Disney as a symbol of cultural imperialism. My aim, in contrast, is to look at TDL "from below," from the point of view of its adaptation and consumption.

The socioeconomic context of TDL's success is obviously only part of the larger picture. Disneyland, as Walt Disney said, is always changing—it is a multifaceted show, designed to be photogenic from all perspectives. "The Disney smile," the photogenic hallmark of the show, can be taken as a symbol of the park's various facades and contexts. We begin with a simple question: how to interpret the Disney smile? Like Clifford Geertz's famous "wink," this smile entails multiple readings. The Disney smile is at one and the same time a muscular spasm, a learned behavior conveying friendliness, and a disciplined conditioning. Like everything Disney, the smile has an "onstage" facade (the inviting facial expression), a "backstage" (the training), and an "offstage" (the smile as an image of commodified mass culture). The smile can be read differently by its various audiences: the cast members, the visitors, the trainers, the sociologists. Reading the Disney smile in Tokyo, one takes all these perspectives and projects them on a new facade. How does the Disney smile work in TDL? Does it require similar training? Does it generate similar reactions from cast members, visitors, and commentators? The Disney smile, the image of production, has a counterpart image in terms of consumption, which is the audience's laughter. This laughter is also the site of polysemic readings, ranging from marketing research to ideological critique.

In this study, I focus on the relationship between the smile and the laughter, between TDL and its audience. Onstage, or the show, is just the beginning. One must go backstage, and then take a step backward and view the smile in such larger contexts as popular culture, the service industry, and leisure organizations. Deciding on the vantage point is not a simple task, and trying to exhaust all possible viewpoints might prove impossible—almost like trying to ride all the attractions. The ethnography presented in this study is divided into three parts, each of which contains both description and theoretical discussion. At some point I will say something about the attractions, about employees, managers, engineers, and visitors. Stephen Fjellman (1992: 17) has argued that "there is no best, coherent way to see Walt Disney World." The same goes for TDL, and evidently for each of Disney's worlds.

TDL will be studied here within three broad contexts: the show, the organization, and the discourse of popular/consumer culture. The first context (Part I of the study) focuses on the onstage spectacle. It examines specific attractions, designs, and elements to ask how Disneyland was modified as it moved to Japan. Part II focuses on the backstage. It considers the "Japanization" of Disneyland (as well as the "Americanization" of OLC), examines such topics as the personnel system and the translated manuals, and compares regular employees (seishain) and part-timers (junshain). This part also analyzes and critiques the "service culture" of TDL as a Taylorist system (that is, a workplace that exemplifies the stringent principles and methods of scientific management, originally advanced in the United States by Frederick Taylor, at the beginning of the twentieth century). In order to examine how "Japanese" the implementation of this organizational culture is, I compare TDL to a local amusement park in Tokyo. Part III deals with the popular/consumerist discourse of TDL by discussing the phenomenon of "Disney socialization" in Japan and comparing Disney and parallel Japanese examples of popular culture, such as *manga* (comics) and *animē* (animation). The main actors considered in this context are specific groups of "Disney fans," among them office ladies (and the related consumption of Disney as cute, *kawaii*), the repeaters, school pupils on excursions, and *onoborisan* (a derogatory term denoting "country people" who "come up" to Tokyo). By focusing on reception, on the visitors' point of view, I attempt to describe how TDL has become a kind of "secular ritual," a "post-modern leisure pilgrimage" worked into everyday life.

Reading through these three contexts, one first moves inside as onstage (Part I) turns into backstage (Part II) and then moves outside again to view TDL within the larger context of popular culture (Part III). This book is something like the ultimate TDL ride—first going through the surface spectacle, then behind the scenes and into the organization, and finally soaring above and zooming out to capture its borders. It does not guarantee to deliver the keys to the Magic Kingdom, but at the very least it promises a better view of it. My theoretical guideline throughout this ride is to do an ethnography "from below." Many previous studies of Disney's worlds have focused on a cultural reading of the onstage while neglecting its production (by workers) and reception (by visitors and customers). This study is the first to combine all three viewpoints. In a similar manner, many previous discussions of Disney abroad have centered on the "modernizing" role of Disney as an imperialist text and its political mission within a world-systems perspective (most notably in Latin America). This approach often neglects the "native's" point of view, since it reproduces those subjected to cultural imperialism as passive and silent. This ideological view might image TDL as a "black ship"—an exported, hegemonic model of American leisure and pop culture—that "conquered" Japan.

As we will see, however, this black ship is an elusive metaphor with multiple meanings. To begin with, it refers to the black ships of Commodore Perry, which have become an image of forced Americanization and the coerced opening of Japan to foreign influence.[4] TDL was nicknamed *kurofune* (black ship) by its Japanese competitors in the amusement business, who cast it as the shock troops of American capitalism. Some of the more critical Japanese observers accused TDL of spreading around Japan a smoke screen of infantile happiness and false consciousness. TDL was also the black ship of leisure that opened up the Japanese market for theme parks and local foreign lands. Yet it also was the Japanese who imported Disneyland for their leisure, translating and editing it to project a Japanese national identity and consuming it in unique ways. The historical black ships of Commodore Perry are actually featured in a TDL show called "Meet the World," an optimistic historical narrative of Japan, apparently made by and for the Japanese. The black ship of TDL is thus also a symbol of Japan's appropriation of the Other. This multifaceted black ship figures in this book's title precisely because of its seductive elusiveness. The black ship is a historical symbol, an ideological facade, a ride, and a hyperbole. This study, conducted aboard the black ship, is a journey for real among many imaginaries.

Theoretical Considerations

"We just try to make a good picture. And then the professors come along and tell us what we do."

—Walt Disney (cited in Schiller 1973: 78)

Disney and its worlds have been subjected to much analysis. I begin this section by reviewing the literature on Disney, focusing on the parks since my case study concerns one of them. I list the major perspectives from which Disney has been studied, with particular reference to studies of TDL (which are, however, rather scarce in English). Then I introduce the broader theoretical perspectives confronted in this study, namely globalization, cultural imperialism, and consumerism.

Disney studies can be subsumed under three headings: those concerned primarily with onstage, those dominated by the backstage, and those seeking to locate Disney within the larger context of (popular, American, post-industrial, leisure) culture. The three parts of this book follow a similar schema; together they are meant to provide a multifaceted view of the complex organization called TDL. These three research domains (as well as the book's parts) are interrelated. There is a particularly strong link between the first domain (onstage) and the third (the broader cultural analysis). The analysis of the show is also a cultural analysis, and these two overlapping fields are separated here for heuristic reasons only.

Fjellman's (1992) thorough study of Walt Disney World (WDW) can be regarded as an archetype for the first and third domains. It illustrates almost all the themes of onstage research and their organizing cultural theses. Chapters 2–5 in Fjellman's work, for example, deal with the construction of history at WDW by making a tour of Frontierland, Liberty Square, the American Adventure at the World Showcase (EPCOT), and various parts of Future World. The emerging historical narrative is summed up by Fjellman (1992: 59) as a "Norman Rockwell view of history—Distory, if you like." History at WDW was also discussed by David Johnson (1981) as a distillation of one version of the United States and its view of the world. It was designed—according to yet another reading—to soothe park visitors by leaping back across two world wars and the Great Depression to colonial America, the nostalgic American West, and the turn-of-the-century Victorian echoes of Main Street USA (Wallace 1985). Mary Yoko Brannen (1992) similarly reads a narrative of Japanese history in the TDL attraction called "Meet the World," to which I return in my onstage reading.

Another dominant onstage theme taken up by Fjellman is space. The Disney theme parks have been considered by many as utopian urban/leisure spaces (see also Moore 1980). Chapters 10–12 in Fjellman (1992) take the reader through WDW's transportation, energy, waste disposal, and water control systems and analyze them as a model of technological utopia. The theme of Disneyland as a modern form of utopian space was originally proposed by Louis Marin (1977) and was later developed by many others, notably Mark Gottdiener (1982), J. C. Wolfe (1979), and Sharon Zukin (1991). Yoshimi Shun'ya (1996) uses this perspective to discuss TDL as a "utopian space of amusement," a bound world where no external reference point exists. Chris Rojek (1993) considers the Disney parks as utopias of rational recreation, a theme I return to (through the backstage) in discussing TDL as a Taylorist system. Finally, many authors have drawn the connection between the park and consumerism. Main Street (where the Victorian-style buildings are actually fronts for shops) and EPCOT's World Showcase (where the pavilions are in fact a world's fair of souvenir stands and restaurants) are the regions most frequently referred to as essentially concerned with consumption (see Wakefield 1990; Eco 1986; Wasserman 1983). Fjellman (1992: chaps. 13–15) pays a similar visit to Fantasyland to discuss the relations between reality and artifice in the late capitalist world of commodities. The general idea behind the organization of Fjellman's book is obviously that each "land" deserves and requires a different cultural analysis. For Gottdiener (1982), in contrast, all Disneyland's lands are signifiers of capitalism. Frontierland signifies predatory capitalism, Adventureland—colonialism/imperialism, Tomorrowland—state capitalism, New Orleans Square—venture capitalism, and Main Street—family capitalism. Disneyland is therefore "the fantasy world of bourgeois ideology" (Gottdiener 1982: 156).

A second category of Disney research focuses on the backstage, with Disney as an organization. One of the first books to deal with Disney as an example of a highly effective American corporate organization was by Richard Schickel (1968). Another early book, by Anthony Haden-Guest (1972), contained a section on the training given at Anaheim through the Disney University, as well as a discussion of other forms of company indoctrination. More recently, several sociologists have dealt with the indoctrination of Disney values, language, and stories as means of corporate control (Van Maanen & Kunda 1989; Van Maanen 1991; Smith & Eisenberg 1987; Boje 1995). Among business journalists, Disney is considered the Sistine Chapel of service culture. Its "strong organizational culture" is praised and revered by business-minded authors who write "in search of excellence," like Peters and Waterman (1982) and Deal and Kennedy (1982). The Disney approach to training is especially admired (see Blocklyn 1988; Eisman 1993). The tremendous success of TDL has similarly spawned a thriving genre of "how does it really work" books in Japanese (e.g., Komuya 1989; Tsuromoki 1984; Tadokoro 1990; Awata & Takanarita 1984; Kano 1986; and most recently, Lipp 1994). Many of these books explain the success of TDL in terms of its human resource management and service manuals. This Japanese genre is a faithful mirror-image of its American counterpart. There have been no studies of the responses of TDL employees to their indoctrination in the "Disney way." This will be attempted in Part II of this book.

The third category of research generally seeks to locate "things Disney" (parks, films, characters, merchandise) in the larger field of cultural consumption/production. There are, for example, several neo-Marxist and feminist critiques of the Disney texts. José Piedra (1994) and Kay Stone (1975) explore the issue of gender in Disney films and cartoons. Ariel Dorfman and Arman Mattelart (1975) have written the classic critique of Disney as an imperialist text in Latin America (more recently, see Cartwright & Goldfarb 1994 for a cultural critique of Disney's health education films for Latin America). The image of Mickey Mouse alone has generated three papers: Stephen Jay Gould (1979) studied the sociobiological appeal of Mickey's round face, and Elizabeth A. Lawrence (1986) as well as Robert W. Brockway (1989) followed with cultural accounts of the changing design of the famous mouse. A new theoretical market for Disney was opened up by Baudrillard (1983), who described Disneyland as the archetypal simulacrum and a model of the postmodern: "Disneyland is presented as imaginary in order to make us believe that the rest is real, when in fact all of Los Angeles and the America surrounding it are no longer real, but of the order of the hyperreal and simulation" (Baudrillard 1983: 25).

Baudrillard's view is not without flaws. His theory of the "simulacrum" can be seen as a theory of cultural imperialism; it certainly shares the latter's blind spot, namely, ignoring the audience. As Michael Billig (1994: 165–66) convincingly argues, for Baudrillard,

> the masses are described as an undifferentiated, undifferentiating entity. . . . Ordinary lives are dismissed, theoretically sacrificed. These lives do not matter. . . . Regarding Disneyland, Baudrillard comments that "you park outside, queue up inside, and are totally abandoned at the exit" (1983: 23). In another sense, it is Baudrillard who totally abandons visitors. Disney's customers leave the park—they have done their brief job as anonymous extras in the narrative of the critic. But it doesn't have to be like this.

For Baudrillard (1983, 1988a,b, 1993), the post-modern is dominated by models of the real without origin or reality. For him, therefore, "America is a cinematic society. . . . A Disneyland where the cinema and TV are our reality" (Baudrillard 1988a: 56, 104). As Michael Eisner put it at the opening of the Disney-MGM Studios, the new theme park represents "the Hollywood that never was and always will be" (cited in Birnbaum 1989: 153). Hollywood—and the Disney films and parks—propagated the hyperreal by creating a "cinematic society" where "the real" (which exists only as long as it is screened) is actually the image, the advertisement, the simulation (Denzin 1992; Jameson 1991). Incidentally, the Disney term *cast members* (denoting frontline employees) highlights the cinematic structure of the parks.

Similar analyses have been written about TDL. Donald Richie (1991: 41), the famous critic of Japanese cinema, wrote that "looking at Tokyo, one sometimes wonders why the Japanese went to all the trouble of franchising a Disneyland in the suburbs when the capital itself is so superior a version." To be sure, the hyperreal is as pervasive in Tokyo as it is in Los Angeles. This has been the motivating premise behind recent discussions of post-modernism and Japan in works edited by Masao Miyoshi and Harry Harootunian (1988, 1991), which unfortunately do not mention TDL. Disney and post-modernism, however, are the subject of a more recent anthology (Willis 1993) titled *The World According to Disney*, whose contributors later published a treatise on WDW, composed by a collective forum called "The Project on Disney" (1995). Eric Smoodin (1994) recently edited a book entitled *Disney Discourse*, in which one chapter (Yoshimoto 1994) does the inevitable by discussing TDL and post-modernism.

Globalization: Cultural Imperialism or Local Adaptation?

At first glance, Tokyo Disneyland is a physical and social copy of Disneyland—a clone created six-thousand miles distant and perhaps something of a cultural bomb dropped on perfect strangers. . . . TDL is perhaps a glimpse of the coming world culture, a commodified, mechanized and highly standardized mass culture built on the Coca-Colonizing forces of western, particularly American, consumer values. . . . The apparently asymmetric transfer of meaning systems gives way to an empire of signs ruled by those who produce and export the world's most desirable goods and services. . . . In many respects, the Disney corporate logo of the globe with mouse ears is hardly an idle boast. (Van Maanen 1992: 9)

John Van Maanen thus aptly summarizes the view of Disney as a global project of cultural imperialism (a view he then seeks to subvert). In a similar manner, this study seeks to re-examine social-scientific theories of globalization in the context of TDL. The view of globalization as cultural imperialism (mainly of American popular culture) has been dominated by the competing perspectives of either the modernization thesis (now considered outdated) or the more recent world-systems theory. Both perspectives presume a unilateral structure of Western hegemony whose culture is imposed on some silent recipient(s). In this study, however, TDL represents a case study where the acculturated— the Japanese—are not passively dominated but rather make an active and manipulative use of Western culture (i.e., Disneyland). Moreover, TDL has not simply been shipped to some cultural periphery, but stands at the core of a first-world economic superpower. By focusing on the active role of the Japanese in importing, modifying, and consuming Disney, this study undermines the taken-for-granted premise that a Disney park is the same everywhere and hence a model of cultural imperialism.

Globalization can be imagined as a black ship: a traveling armada spreading cultural homogeneity and consent. This is how it has been imagined within modernization and (later) world-system theories.[5] Such a view hinges on a perspective of *asymmetry*; its key conceptual pairs are center (or core) and periphery (e.g., Shils 1975; Wallerstein 1974) and metropole and satellite (e.g., Andre Frank 1967). Such asymmetries codify cultural imperialism as an all-embracing reality (see also Robertson & Lechner 1985; Tomlinson 1991).[6] Tokyo Disneyland, however, is an example of cultural flow within the core. Moreover, if Disneyland is a black ship, then it is the Japanese who are riding and steering it, not the Americans. "Riding the black ship" is therefore offered here as a new metaphor for the transnational flow of culture. It is meant to capture the dynamic and bilateral nature of cultural exchanges between first-world cores such as Tokyo and Los Angeles. I hope that it conveys a sense of how the global/local dichotomy can be overridden, how "black ships" can float over such dichotomies, or, in other words, how the local can appropriate, domesticate, and steer, as well as travel with, global forces such as leisure, post-industrialism, and consumer and service culture.

TDL provides a framework for reversing, even collapsing, the dichotomies between globalization and localization, cultural imperialism and cultural consumption, and the familiar and the exotic. The discourse of globalization as cultural imperialism can be reversed by showing how TDL has been "Japanized," as I attempt to do throughout the three parts of the book. Part I discusses how the onstage has been changed: how specific attractions, scripts, shows, and facades have been modified or even created, and how "Japan" enters the park through local holidays and festivities. Part II, the backstage view, reveals many Japanese aspects of work, management, and labor relations in TDL. Part III analyzes groups of repeat visitors and asks what Disney does for them, how it fits their own cultural expectations and constraints.

A logic of reversal and transformation underpins the whole structure of TDL. Its onstage is visibly "American," and the cast members operating it seem to be happily following American manuals. The onstage has, however, been meticulously "Japanized," and interviews with cast members reveal their dilemmas and frustrations in dealing with these dual expectations. The backstage, which is clearly populated by Japanese personnel following Japanese organizational conduct, has for its part been deeply influenced by American methods. TDL as a whole is a reversal of the social order, in which adults are given social license to be children again, and the work ethic changes into a playful leisure time (not so, however, for TDL's workers). TDL can therefore be seen to play a role similar to that traditionally found in Japanese festivals (*matsuri*). According to the famous Japanese ethnographer Yanagita Kunio (1964: 201–2), the *matsuri* is a utopian form of culture in which all social divisions dissolve in the ecstasy of communal celebration. The inherent reversal of TDL, a trompe l'oeil of facades within facades, is arguably at the heart of what TDL is: an American in Japan and a Japanese view of America. TDL is essentially an image processor. Within it, two imaginaries ("America" and "Japan") look at each other, and this entails a double-mirror effect: the effect of the hyperreal. Baudrillard's simulacrum is arguably more alive in TDL than in America.

This reading of the flow of culture in TDL follows other recent theories of globalization. For at least a decade, images of "domestication," "hybridization," "pidginization" and "creolization," in which local socie-

ties actively assimilate external influences, have become central metaphors in the study of globalization (e.g., Hannerz 1989; Wilson & Dissanayake 1996; D. King 1991; Der Derian & Shapiro 1989; for the specific
case of Japan, see R. Robertson 1987). These approaches could be
grouped under the term *glocalization*, which denotes the combination of
global and local. In their introduction to the journal *Public Culture*, Arjun
Appadurai and Carol Breckenridge (1988: 5) frame the issue this way:

> Today's cosmopolitan cultural forms contain a paradox. As forms, they are
> emerging everywhere; films, packaged tours, specialized restaurants, video-
> cassettes and sports spectacles seem to be drawing the world into a dis-
> turbing commercial sameness. But as vehicles for cultural significance and
> the creation of group identities, every society appears to bring to these
> forms its own special history and traditions, its own cultural stamp, its own
> quirks and idiosyncrasies.

In other words, the paradox of the flow of culture is that "black
ships" can turn into "rides." This metaphor also suggests that by focusing
on local adaptations, the bleak alarmism of the black ship model can
often be animated by the more colorful and playful themes characteriz-
ing the (usually ingenious) local practices of consumption. Although
studies of cultural interaction and adaptation are proliferating, it is pre-
mature to claim that theories of world systems and cultural imperialism
are outdated. A recent textbook on the "sociology of the global system"
(Sklair 1991), for example, defines five types of theories of globalization:
imperialism, modernization, world systems, Neo-Marxist, and "modes
of production." Although I disagree with Sklair's classification, I mention it here as a telling example of the neglect of the possibility (or perhaps the theoretical plausibility) of cultural adaptation. Neo-Marxist
and functionalist accounts of globalization, developed in the context of
third-world countries (usually in Africa and Latin America), seem to
have gained the status of theory, whereas more complex conceptualizations of local adaptations (often developed in the context of East Asia,
particularly Japan) are more modestly defined. In the final analysis, both
"cultural imperialism" and "cultural adaptation" really occur, and the
global is complex enough to accommodate both. Nonetheless, I agree
with Ulf Hannerz (1989: 66) that it is the theorization of cultural

adaptation that forms "the largest task now confronting a macro-anthropology of culture." However, given that much of the strength of anthropology hinges on its contextual and situational grounding, it is still not clear how and whether a macro-anthropological theory of globalization can be developed.

Theories of cultural imperialism are well and alive in the literature devoted to Disney productions around the world, especially in the context of Latin America. Researchers such as Dorfman and Mattelart (1975) and more recently Cartwright and Goldfarb (1994) have vociferously attacked the imperialist attempts of Disney to "modernize" its Latin American customers. These attacks on "Disney discourse" illustrate a blind spot common to many studies of cultural imperialism. What is often missing from such attacks is an empirical focus on reception, or the relationship between text and audience (see also Fejes 1984; Ang 1996). This relationship, as John Tomlinson (1991: 44) argues, "must precede any advance in our approach to cultural imperialism." However, as J. O. Boyd-Barret (1982: 193) pointed out, few critiques of cultural imperialism address it: "Individual capacity for psychological compartmentalization and rationalization is underestimated (by cultural imperialism) to an extraordinary degree. Much more attention needs to be given to the processes by which individuals and groups interpret, translate and transform their experiences of foreign cultures to relate to more familiar experiences." Or as Hannerz simply puts it: "To be more completely persuasive, arguments about the impact of the transnational cultural flow would have to say something about how the people respond to it." A recent example of audience research focused on the global reception of the popular American television series *Dallas*. Tamar Liebes and Elihu Katz (1990) conducted part of their research on *Dallas* in Japan (where *Dallas* failed), and I will discuss their findings in the concluding chapter.

Audience research on TDL can expose the process of cultural importation as a multilateral negotiation of meanings between equally dominant global powers. The selective replication and rearrangement of Disneyland in Tokyo can be seen as an example of a post-imperialist process that suggests a story different from that suggested by other forms of globalization. It is a story of how TDL—a reflection of global consumer culture (Featherstone 1991; Jameson 1991) in late capitalism, a stage at which national borders have supposedly become permeable (Harvey 1989)—was reconstructed to project an ethnocentric, Japanese worldview. Indeed, Japanese scholars have recently suggested that the formerly seductive and all-embracing view of "internationalization" (*kokusaika*) is gradually undergoing a change of image in Japan. Iyotani Toshio (1995) has stated that "the positive image those terms [*world* and *international*] once evoked lost its luster when the bubble economy of the 1980s collapsed. Instead, a prolonged recession, mounting numbers of unemployed, and an unstable political situation combine in an ominous brew, one that could possibly even feed a new wave of nationalism."

Japan as a Consumerist Society

My theoretical point of departure is to seek to understand globalization by situating TDL within the local context of Japan in late capitalism. This perspective has no predefined set of theoretical constructs. Rather, it seeks to ground its analytical concepts in an ethnography "from below" (see Denzin 1978; Strauss 1987). Japan's leisure and consumer society provides an intriguing backdrop for the study of TDL. Previous studies have shown that consumption plays an important role in Japanese life, shaping tastes, desires, lifestyles, and ultimately identities (Fields 1983; Befu 1983; Ivy 1988, 1996; Skov & Moeran 1995). This effect has been particularly well illustrated in the context of consuming "things Western" (especially American) which are "re-made in Japan" (Tobin 1992). Some have even claimed that consumerism is one of the sources of the newly developed "soft individualism" in contemporary Japan (Yamazaki 1984). The role of consumerism in Japan has also been studied in the context of tourism (both domestic and overseas) as a means of self-discovery (Moeran 1983; Graburn 1983). TDL, it should be noted, is presented as an opportunity for international tourism within Japan.

TDL's success should therefore be examined against the backdrop of Japan's growing leisure and consumer society. Popular culture, consumerism, and leisure activities are as much an inherent part of society in Japan as they are in the West (Powers & Kato 1990; Linhart 1988). The Japanese have been speaking of the "leisure boom" (*rejā-būmu*) in their country since at least the end of the 1970s (Linhart 1988: 273). In fact, the surge in popular culture after Japan's postwar economic success (Plath 1964; Kato Hideo 1959) should be seen as part of the larger, continuous history of popular Japanese culture since at least the Edo period. Japan was one of the first nations to develop a pre-industrial popular culture, which was not reserved for the aristocracy alone but directed to the lower strata as well (Longstreet 1988; Walthall 1986). The traditional *yūkaku* (amusement quarter) and the more recent *sakariba* (Linhart 1986) are urban zones traditionally dedicated to popular culture and leisure activities. Since 1973, the Economic Planning Agency of the Japanese government has systematically surveyed the leisure behavior of the Japanese and issued the results semiofficially in the *Handbook on Leisure* (Yoka kaihatsu sentā 1973–91). The Japanese leisure market has been opened up by TDL (see Leisure Industry Data 1993, 1994). While continuing to dominate the market, TDL has spawned many new theme parks and created a boom of "foreign lands" or *gaikoku mura* (Ito 1995)— consumerist embodiments of the "global village."

Many studies of the Japanese leisure market have characterized it as more structured than its Western equivalent. Consumerism and age, for example, are significantly linked in Japan. According to Millie Creighton (1994: 94), "In Japan consumerism is less a way of 'finding oneself' and more a way of *linking selves* to others." In Japan, age cohorts tend to be more coherent in terms of behavior (White 1995: 260). Life-stage activities—such as school completion, marriage, childbearing, workforce participation, and retirement—are particularly predictable. Media people and marketers have used this age-governed system to generate and refine further age gradations and definitions of generations in terms of the consumer market (Skov & Moeran 1995: 56). Successful marketing campaigns have produced annual events (such as Valentine's Day) and shaped new age categories. Adolescence, for example, has only recently emerged as "a marked stage in the cultural conception of the Japanese life course" (White 1995: 255). Marilyn Ivy (1993) notes that the Japanese media have created a "consumption definition of the middle class." And Laurel Anderson and Marsha Wadkins (1992) argue that the "new breed" (*shinjinrui*) is also a consumerist creation. *Shinjinrui*, which now stands for all those born since 1960, is also a negative term used by the *sarariiman* or *kyūjinrui* (the old breed) generation, the postwar baby boomers who are today's section managers and trainers of the *shinjinrui*.

As in the West, the proliferation of consumer culture in Japan has entailed the glorification of youth. The culture of *kawaii* (cute), dominant throughout the 1980s, resulted in hoards of office ladies (single women, usually between 20 and 26) affecting similarly childlike clothing, accessories, and speech (Kinsella 1995; Allison 1996). Many office ladies live at home with their parents as long as they are single, use their income primarily for shopping and consumption, and attract massive marketing efforts. These activities in turn reinforce their image as easygoing, leisure- (and husband-)seeking "moratorium people" (Iwao 1992: 165; Risu 1980). In Part III, which deals with the reception and consumption of TDL, I use a life-span perspective to show how TDL gets worked into the everyday life of various age groups, from children to youths, adolescents, "office ladies," the *shinjinrui*, the middle-aged (most notably parents), and the elderly. TDL will therefore be discussed in the context of everyday life, off stage as it were, as providing a window to the age structure of Japanese consumer culture, which involves both "uni-age style" and subcultures, protest and subjugation, opportunities and social control.

Methodological Considerations

This study is the result of participant observation at TDL between May 1995 and May 1996. I paid for the many visits from my pocket and often wandered around the park like any other visitor. At other times I was chaperoned; I participated in five of TDL's official guided tours, as well as in eight unofficial tours guided by OLC employees. Each guided tour took about four hours, and they were conducted in various seasons (summer through winter) and together covered all of TDL's lands. I took guided tours with both Japanese- and English-speaking guides, in order to record the differences, if any, in the park presentation. I have also talked to many visitors and workers. In order to examine the reception of TDL by its visitors more systematically, I videotaped the rides and discussed them with six Japanese key-informants. These discussions followed the methodology of focus-group research (Morgan & Spanish 1984). The focus group included a male manager from a big service company, a female professional interpreter, an office lady, a female secretary, and two male graduate students, one in sociology and one in anthropology. Occasionally some of these persons brought his or her children to watch the video with us and express their thoughts. Although the group as a whole was characterized by a white-collar, middle-class inclination, each group member had his or her personal biases. It was convened once in a month between December 1995 and May 1996, for a total six times.

As a result of a small ad in the Tokyo classifieds, I was able to conduct interviews with current and former OLC employees. I interviewed 30 OLC employees: 21 part-timers (ten of them worked in Foods Division, but I managed to interview at least one employee from each of OLC's major divisions, including Attractions, Merchandising, and Personnel) and nine regular employees (keiyaku-shain and seishain). In addition, I interviewed three of TDL's American employees and eight employees of Kōrakuen, an amusement park in Tokyo. Informal interviews were held in cafes and restaurants, lasted between one and three hours, and were usually taped. Formal interviews were conducted in the office and were usually not taped. The language used in these interviews (both formal and informal) was Japanese. TDL's American employees were interviewed in English. All the workers currently employed in TDL requested anonymity, and their names have consequently been changed or omitted altogether. Where necessary, I have slightly altered some of the identifying details of their jobs in TDL. Additional information was collected through telephone conversations with employees reluctant to be seen with me in public. With some of the regular employees of OLC and Kōrakuen, I established a regular e-mail connection, which was used to exchange information even after I had left Japan.

The interviews, observations, and the textual analysis of company guidebooks provided the basis for a double comparison: one between TDL and the American Disneylands, the other between TDL and Kōrakuen. This double comparison cuts through the book and provides its macro methodological framework. By comparing TDL both to its American originals and to a Japanese counterpart, the study aims to trace the interplay between "America" and "Japan" in the onstage, backstage, and consumption of TDL. The comparison between TDL and the American Disneylands can throw into relief how Disney has been modified in Japan. Additional comparison, though more limited in scope, will be made with Disneyland Paris. My knowledge of organizational life in the two American Disneylands is based on secondary sources written by American journalists, sociologists, and service professionals, as well as by current Disney employees and ex-managers. This literature is vast and often self-serving. I have tried to do as much cross-comparison as possible in order to present an up-do-date and authoritative description of these complex organizations.

The second comparison, between TDL and Kōrakuen, can expose the American "core values" of the former. This comparison is based on firsthand ethnographic research. Kōrakuen, one of the biggest and arguably the first amusement park in Tokyo, was selected for several reasons. First, Kōrakuen has a reputation—and a historical record—of being a pioneer in the amusement business. Its personnel department has close relations with that of TDL, and Kōrakuen managers may have advised OLC managers when the latter established their organization. Second, TDL has no doubt "stolen" many visitors who would otherwise patronize Kōrakuen. This competition has a fertile spawning ground of images of and references to TDL among Kōrakuen trainers and managers. The competition with TDL is arguably one reason for Kōrakuen's recent strategic changes and its attempts to create new attractions that are less family-oriented and more focused on young adults.

Additional interviews were conducted with Japanese scholars and journalists whose names are mentioned in the book. These interviews were conducted at various stages of the fieldwork and covered issues related to Disney. There were no particular criteria for choosing these people, only the fact that they had expressed an interest in a Disney- or TDL-related issue. In addition, I made a special effort to interview people who worked in the fields of media and marketing. I also conducted interviews with Disneyland repeaters and self-acclaimed "Disney fans," who were either met casually or introduced to me. The fact that I had two children in a Japanese kindergarten opened up to me relatively hidden fields of ethnography where one would not usually expect to find Disney, such as nursery-school sports activities, local children's festivities in the community, and school excursions.

Japanese personal names are presented in this study in the Japanese order, with the family name first. Anglicized versions of company names are given where these are commonly used, and the titles of organizations and their internal sections in romanized Japanese will be given as required. The OLC materials I read or watched for this study can be subsumed under two categories: public and company-owned. The first category contains all the literature that is in the public record, from sociological research through business interviews to media programs and advertisements. A shelfful of books in Japanese offers to unlock the secrets of TDL's success. For the most part, these are journalistic accounts focusing on "human resource management" and economic data. The second category consists of corporate texts, mainly manuals and guidebooks, but also newsletters and press releases. The manuals in particular are strictly company property in the eyes of OLC. Most are not to be removed from company premises. The TDL and OLC manuals cited in this work were received, for the most part, from my part-timer respondents. Japanese texts were read and translated with the help of several of the Japanese key-informants, who crossed the lines and became my research assistants. I tried and failed to obtain permission from OLC to reproduce TDL materials. The official response, signed by an employee of OLC's Publicity Division, stated that materials produced for guests (such as guidebooks or passports) are to be used only in the park and that the other uses are prohibited. The same prohibition was made in regard to an OLC advertisement for employment and manuals and other company publications.

This study is full of details about TDL, perhaps numbingly so. But the number of details, as Fjellman (1992: 19) aptly noted in the methodological introduction to his study of WDW, "is part of the message. The message is about cognitive overload, but it is also about the possibilities for active recognition and response." There are many wonderful details at the parks—"lots of things to notice, each one of which somebody thought to put there" (Fjellman 1992: 19). The details are the traces of the visible and invisible hand of Disney.

Traveling with Disney

"I love it!" asserts anthropologist Stephen Fjellman at the outset of his treatise on WDW (1992: 16). Unfortunately, I cannot repeat his assertion with such unrestrained enthusiasm. I first came to TDL as a student of globalization as well as a student of Japan. My idea was to become a "nomadic theorist" and follow the travels of the familiar Disney to see how it becomes exotic in Japan. I wanted to exoticize Disney in order to familiarize Japan. As Walter (1988: 18) notes, "the word 'theory' is from the Greek *theoria*—to see the sights or to see something for yourself" (cited in Perry 1995: 35). This was my intention: to take the globalization ride in TDL and see for myself. Although TDL looks like a hollow copy from a distance, I thought that it could also be a doorway into "Japan." I was attracted to TDL as something that enables us to talk about "Japan"—the elusive, contemporary, high-speed "Japan"—without essentializing it. That is, TDL has the potential to be a springboard for studying "Japan" without reproducing the Japanological "effect of the real"—the professional commitment to unwrap, recover, and interpret the *essence* of Japan, an act that inevitably recasts Japan as the Other. However, it took time, social contacts, and a certain assimilation of life in Japan before I was able to see the "Tokyo" inside of Disneyland.

When I arrived in Japan, my first inclination was to look for a job in TDL, since I knew OLC was hiring foreigners. As it transpired, there were two problems. First, since I was invited to Japan as a Japan Foundation Doctoral Fellow, my visa status was "cultural activities" (*bunka-katsudō*), which legally prohibits one from working. I tried to explain to the officials that by working at TDL I would be fulfilling my mission of engaging in "cultural activities." It was a long, hilarious, and, of course, futile talk. Second, I later discovered that all of OLC's foreign cast members were contract employees from Disneyland in California. No job interviews for foreigners were conducted in Japan. I therefore remained an outsider, both to the organization I was studying as well as to the larger society in which I was living with my Israeli family. I was also an outsider in the sense that I was researching and writing in two languages that were not my own. Like Disney, I was an implant in Japan, conducting an adventurous (and certainly expensive) endeavor. This state of mind is no doubt reflected in my study. As Perry (1995: 43) asserts, "the nomadic theorist who emerges from this mode of representation is disrespectful of boundaries and resistant to categorization; with the concomitant scattering of theoretical identity, theory is hybridized, mongrelized, customized, made promiscuous, invested with voice."

A Short History of OLC and the TDL project

OLC, which owns and operates TDL, is a partnership between two companies: Mitsui Real Estate Development (Mitsui Fudōsan) and Keisei Electric Railway (Keisei Dentetsu). Mitsui owns 48 percent of OLC, and Keisei 52 percent (Koren 1990: 158). But Mitsui, with its vast political and economic influence, has been by far the more active partner (on the history of Mitsui, see Roberts 1973). OLC was formed in order to reclaim a part of Tokyo Bay near Urayasu City in Chiba prefecture. According to Edo Hideo, chairman of Mitsui Real Estate Development and senior member of the Mitsui corporate group, the decision was made in January 1958. In an interview in *Business Japan* (Mino 1984: 19), he is cited as saying:

> There was a lot of internal and external oppositions, but since our purpose was to catch up with Mitsubishi Estate Co., we went ahead with it. The project was exactly in line with Japan's high economic growth. Yawata Steel, Tokyo Electric Power, Idemitsu and other major enterprises built plants in the already reclaimed area. It was transformed into a modern industrial zone. As a result, Chiba prefecture, previously poor and deficit-ridden, became wealthy overnight.

Chiba prefectural authorities agreed to the landfill plan in 1960 but requested that the reclaimed land be used for a major recreational facility. Landfill began in 1962 after Takahashi Masatomo, later the legendary chairman of OLC, obtained the consent of local fishermen. During this early period of its activities, however, OLC was connected to two scandals. My brief description of these two scandals draws on the thorough discussion found in Kano Yasuhisa's aptly titled 1986 book *The True Story of Tokyo Disneyland*.

The first of these scandals was connected to one of the OLC founders, Tanzawa Saburō. Called the "Bushu Railway affair," this scandal exploded in July 1961 when the media reported that several businessmen had bribed politicians in order to get permission for a railway project. The key persons in this affair were later found to be the (then) president of Saitama Bank, the minister of transportation, and the president of the Daiei Movie Company. Although Tanzawa was found innocent, his involvement in this scandal was a "black rumor" (Kano 1986: 39) that followed him as well as OLC. In 1964 Tanzawa sold all his OLC shares to Osano Kenji, one of the richest men in Japan and widely associated with the "dark world" of Japanese politics, who was later found guilty of perjury in the Lockheed bribery case (Kaplan & Dubro 1986: 397). The financially troubled Tanzawa had to sell his shares at the low price of 700 yen per share. Osano sold the shares the next year (1965) to the business firm Nichimen for 1,200 yen per share (Kano 1986: 40). Nichimen thus became a major shareholder in OLC. It consequently sent four directors, including one of its vice presidents, to work in OLC. The vice president's first demand was that Nichimen be given two-thirds of the construction work for the reclamation of Area A, the first landfill zone. The problem was solved when Keisei and Mitsui bought Nichimen's shares, thus regaining control of OLC. Later on, Nichimen withdrew altogether from OLC.

In the second scandal, which transpired during the landfill, OLC became embroiled in a political controversy over the area's development. The official accusation revolved around an improper application procedure, but there were also rumors that Mitsui board members, who had close connections with the ruling Liberal Democratic Party, had attempted to gain governmental permission to change the restrictions on usage of the land-filled area. In November 1967, a Diet member from the Kōmeitō (the Sōka Gakkai supported–party) publicly criticized the Ministry of Construction for its handling of the Urayasu reclamation. Four firms—Mitsui Real Estate, Keisei Railway, OLC, and Asahi Real Estate—were accused of rapidly reclaiming land without permission. "Reclamation without permission" was allegedly the responsibility of Chiba prefecture, which had not followed the proper application procedure in dealing with the Ministry of Construction. Following this criticism, the minister of construction promised a strict investigation. The result was a long delay in gaining permission for the reclamation of Area C. When the next minister of construction finally gave permission in March 1969, he removed 77.55 hectares (235,000 *tsubo*, 1 *tsubo* equals 3.3 square meters) from the 247.5 hectares (750,000 *tsubo*) of the original area designated for landfill. Since this area was necessary for the large-scale plan of the park, OLC could not give it up. Its continuous lobbying bore fruit only five years later, in 1974, when the Ministry of Construction permitted a further landfill, "to be used as a green tract of land" (Kano 1986: 48).

From 1966 to 1974, while these two affairs were taking place, OLC representatives were screening tourist, leisure, and recreational facilities around the world in search of a model. In 1974, they approached Walt Disney Productions (WDP). So did Mitsubishi, Mitsui's archrival, about a project on land near Mount Fuji. Ron Cayo from Disney visited Japan in 1974 to look at both proposals. Over the course of the negotiations, Mitsubishi dropped out mysteriously. Koren (1990: 59) argues that this was the result of government pressure.

The atmosphere surrounding the negotiations between WDP and OLC was uneasy. In 1977, OLC president Kawasaki Makoto resigned. This was a blow to the negotiations since Kawasaki—a top executive at Keisei —was an eager supporter of the Disneyland project. The reason given for his resignation was the difficult situation of Keisei after the first oil crisis in October 1973. Edo Hideo, chairman of Mitsui Real Estate, is cited in Kano (1986: 58) as saying that "with Kawasaki's resignation and the internal difficulties in Keisei—which was the initiating force behind our negotiations with Disney—the ball landed in Mitsui's field. . . . We were obliged to go on with it, although we lacked the will from the outset." Mitsui Real Estate Development, as its name implies, was a conventional real estate and construction company with no previous experience of handling theme parks. It built Tokyo's first skyscraper, the 36-story Kasumigaseki building, and later constructed more high-rise buildings in Shinjuku. In addition to its unconventionality, the TDL project demanded more and more investments. Kano (1986: 59) points out that the estimated construction cost for TDL grew from 50 billion yen to 120 billion. The biggest problem was obtaining a bank loan of over

100 billion yen. According to Kano (1986: 60), OLC's new president Takahashi Masatomo saved the day. He negotiated with the governor of Chiba prefecture directly, pulling strings in order to change the status of the reclaimed land. This enhanced the land's mortgageable value, thus making it easier for the banks to approve the loan. Chiba's governor was also eager to help out, since the Disneyland project meant good business for the whole prefecture. Edo Hideo (cited in Mino 1984: 19) said that the "Chiba governor pleaded with us to proceed with the project." Takahashi was thus able to change the status of 210.6 hectares (638,200 *tsubo*) designated for leisure facilities and 102.96 hectares (312,000 *tsubo*) designated for a green tract into land designated for "business and dwellings." The Chiba Municipal Office issued a memorandum permitting the selling of some land (which would remain after the completion of the park) for dwellings, if the administrative situation demanded it. Furthermore, Kano (1986: 101) argues that Chiba prefecture agreed to a lease contract; Chiba would own the land until OLC paid it back "when it had the revenues." Edo (cited in Kano 1986: 61) recalled that "since it was now possible to sell some of the real estate, the total price of which was estimated to be 200 billion yen, we received our requested loan."

Having secured financial backing for the project, Mitsui resumed the negotiations. Now OLC had to face Disney's demands. In Japanese fashion, OLC sent fifteen negotiators to Disney's two. Disney's representatives were Ron Cayo (a lawyer) and Frank Stanek,[7] who was then with World Disney Imagineering (a Disney department that conceives and designs parks and attractions). For the Japanese, a huge investment was at stake. Disney was optimistic about the profit potential. Disney's CEO Michael Eisner was confident that licensing would result in a big payoff. Disney, however, was then in the middle of building EPCOT, and presumably nobody there thought about investing actual money in Tokyo—only later was it realized that this had been a mistake. The Mitsui representatives in OLC, who originally wanted housing on the site, remained unenthusiastic. Their contract with Chiba said that if the leisure project did not succeed, the land could be sold off at a profit. "Ron Cayo," writes Koren (1990: 60), "thought that Mitsui was just waiting for the deal to collapse." The Japanese media, in addition to being skeptical about Mitsui's real motivations, were unanimous in predicting the project's failure. Tsuboi Hajime, president of Mitsui Real Estate at the time, said that "TDL's particular character as an enterprise is that it is next to impossible for us to make it profitable" (Koren 1990: 158). The talks were almost called off many times.

Takahashi, who became vice president of OLC in 1975, was again a key person in realizing the deal. To judge from media interviews of Takahashi as well as OLC employees' opinions, Takahashi appears to have been the visionary behind the contract, a person who wanted a large-scale project that would leave his mark on Japan. When talks broke down in 1977, Takahashi stepped in and used all his connections and influence to bring the two sides together. Carden ("Card") Walker of the Walt Disney Company told Ron Cayo that he should demand 10 percent of the entrance fees and 5 percent of the sales revenue from goods. Takahashi said 5 percent of both, because "amusement is a tough business" (Kano 1986: 85). According to Kano (1986), Walker won. The deal was that in return for its licensing and ongoing advice and expertise, Disney would receive 10 percent of admissions fees and 5 percent of the revenues from food and souvenir sales.[8] The same numbers were also reported by Edo (cited in Mino 1984: 19), who wryly added that "including various other payments, royalties reached 20 million dollars in our first year. . . . We are contributing greatly to the elimination of Japan-U.S. trade friction." The Ministry of Finance had set the maximum duration of a foreign rights–licensing agreement in Japan at 20 years. Disney insisted on a 50–year deal and settled in the end for 45 years.

The official history of TDL, as commemorated in the *Tokyo Disneyland Diary* (issued in 1995) begins only in February 1974 with "Mitsui and Keisei approaching Disney." Almost fifteen years of landfill and the surrounding political and economic turmoil are elided, as are the troublesome negotiations with Disney. The *Diary* briefly mentions that in July 1977 OLC issued an invitation for sponsors (Japanese companies sponsoring specific park attractions), as though the company was already certain about the positive outcome of the negotiations with WDP, which resulted in a contract signed only in April 1979. Two months later, WDP-Japan was established. In 1980, over 100 OLC managers went to Disneyland to learn how to run the park, and 200 Disney people came to work on site in Japan. "Park procedures are all laid out in volumes of

Disney manuals," said Ron Cayo to Koren (1990: 62), "and strict adherence to these has been a big part of the project's success." Construction began in December 1980. In October 1981, the first fifteen sponsors were chosen. The building of attractions commenced in April 1982, in May the recruit center was opened, and in September the top of Cinderella's Castle was laid. In November 1982 the opening date was announced. On April 15, 1983, TDL's grand opening took place, as planned. A little over a month later, on May 23, TDL had already been visited by a million "guests."

PART I

ONSTAGE

CHAPTER I

America in Tokyo: The Remaking of Disneyland in Japan

The vast bulk of Disney studies have concentrated on Disneyland (DL) and WDW, rather than on TDL and Disneyland Paris. The main reason for this, as Bryman (1995: 63) notes, is that the parks in America have existed longer and have been more accessible to sociologists writing in English. Moreover, the common belief is that the basic structure of the parks has been globally replicated in the Japanese and French "copies." To be sure, all parks comprise the same four basic lands, a castle, and a Main Street funnel, and many of the rides are similar. However, the globalization preconception ignores the differences, which exist even between the two American parks. DL, now considered by Disney imagineers as the "first generation," was built during the early 1950s on a 160-acre orange grove outside Anaheim, south of Los Angeles. The Magic Kingdom (the original part of WDW) was constructed at the end of the 1960s on 27,400 acres of reclaimed swampland in central Florida. A number of writers have discussed the differences between DL and WDW. Both Umberto Eco (1986) and Blake (1972) suggest that DL's smaller scale produces more coherence and a greater sense of excitement. Noting a difference in the visiting population, Francaviglia (1981: 153–54) suggests that "DL was envisioned and designed as an international ambassador of Yankee ingenuity and national nostalgia, and California visitation was indeed highly cosmopolitan. . . . Whereas WDW is directly linked to the transportation corridor from Boston-Washington to Miami, and is visited by people seeking more of a Florida vacation."

TDL was primarily modeled on WDW (the "second-generation" park). However, it differs from both WDW and DL. Located in the Tokyo Bay area, near Maihama, about 20 minutes by train from the central Tokyo station, it is owned by a Japanese company and operated by Japanese personnel. It has six themed lands (according to the official count)—World Bazaar, Adventureland, Westernland, Critter Country, Fantasyland, and Tomorrowland, all clustered around Cinderella's Castle (see Map 1 for an overview of the park). The recent addition of Toon Town brings the number of themed lands to seven. TDL, at 46 hectares, is about 1.5 times the size of DL (30 hectares), and about the same as WDW's Magic Kingdom (43 hectares). The surrounding grounds at WDW, however, cover 11,300 hectares; in contrast DL has 73.5 hectares, and TDL 82.6.

The following sections deal with the onstage strategies of TDL. This part opens with the Jungle Cruise, moves on to Cinderella's Castle Mystery Tour, and ends with Meet the World. Each attraction receives a detailed analysis in terms of design, script, narrative, and audience reception. These attractions were singled out because of their relative onstage sophistication. First, each has an elaborate script (spiel, in DisneyTalk). This allows for a more substantial discourse analysis—in terms of both language and ideology. Second, each has a distinct narrative. Although attractions in the "screamer" category may be more popular, they have neither a spiel nor a narrative. Splash Mountain, TDL's most popular ride, is basically a wonderfully designed water-sled. I refer to many of TDL's attractions in less detail in Chapter 2. Furthermore, the three attractions selected for detailed analysis represent three models of recontextualization that take place in TDL. Jungle Cruise is arguably the most American of the three. It is a traditional Disney ride that has changed little over the years. TDL has kept the design and narrative of Jungle Cruise while modifying its spiel. Cinderella's Castle Mystery Tour, in contrast, is unique to TDL. It is a story of Disney heroes and villains written for and told by the Japanese. Whereas Jungle

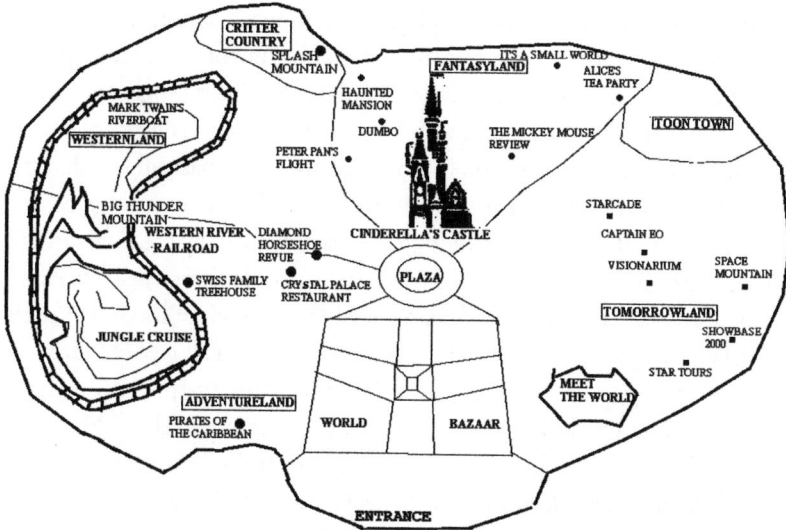

Map 1 TDL park layout: lands and major rides and attractions

Cruise stands for the imported-modified model, Mystery Tour illustrates "Disney made in Japan." Finally, Meet the World represents an extreme case of Japanization. A show on Japanese history, it stands for "Japan" inside Disneyland. The three attractions therefore represent a gradient of cultural flow that applies to all TDL attractions. Other strategies of cultural consumption and their various manifestations in the park are also discussed in Chapter 2.

The Dubbed Spiel: Jungle Cruise

Located in Adventureland, the ten-minute Jungle Cruise is one of the oldest and most popular attractions. It has been replicated in all of Disney's worlds, except Disneyland Paris, as an "E" ticket ride.[1] An early DL guidebook claims that "the Jungle River Cruise is considered by many to be Disneyland's finest achievement. . . . A vicarious exploration for the stay-at-home dreamer" (Sklar 1975–76: 26). Fjellman (1992: 225–26) agrees that "the core of Adventureland is the Jungle Cruise" and adds that "it is one of the most visited attractions at the Magic Kingdom." *Walt Disney World* (1986: 34), the commemorative Disney volume, describes it as "a favorite of armchair explorers, because it compresses weeks of safari travel into ten minutes of fun, without mosquitoes, monsoons or misadventures." TDL's guidebook invites its guests to "venture deep into the mysterious and danger-filled jungle and experience the thrilling perils of the wild." As the three blurbs illustrate and the onstage design reaffirms, Jungle Cruise has been left basically unchanged. One minor difference in the design relates to the surroundings.

In both DL and WDW, Jungle Cruise is flanked by the Swiss Family Treehouse. The tree is called by the Disney people *Disneyodendron eximus* (extraordinary Disney Tree). A total of 800,000 vinyl leaves cover the WDW tree (Fjellman 1992: 226), and 300,000 the DL tree (Sklar 1975–76: 28). The top of the tree affords "a 70 feet vantage point [on Jungle Cruise] from which the twisting waterway is serenity itself" (Sklar 1975–76: 28). In TDL, the Swiss Family Treehouse was built further away from Jungle Cruise, and at 19 meters (62 feet) it is not high enough to afford such a view. The architectural reason for this might be the location of the Western River Railroad Station just beside the entrance to Jungle Cruise, whose queues snake back and forth endlessly (see Map 1).

The TDL Western River Railroad is itself an example of onstage difference and makes for an interesting cultural reading that merits a brief detour from the Jungle Cruise. The Western River Railroad, a "D" ticket ride, offers a train trip around part of Adventureland and the whole of Westernland (see Map 1). Westernland is a Japanese recontextualization of the American Frontierland, a renaming that will be considered below. The Western River Railroad is thus unique to TDL, since the monorails in DL and WDW go around the perimeter of the Magic Kingdom, so that visitors can get off at each of the lands. Brannen (1992: 221) thus argues that

> Perhaps the most obvious visual break in the Disney metanarrative is the course of the railroad; whereas the original DL railroad encircles the entire park, TDL's version cuts off Adventureland and Westernland from the rest of the park.

Brannen (1992: 223) cites a TDL spokesperson's explanation:

> The structural reason for limiting the path of the railroad involved maintaining the sense of fantasy: if it had been constructed around the entire

circumference of the park, the elevation of the tracks at various points along the route would have allowed guests to catch glimpses of the surrounding Chiba area, thereby disrupting their foreign vacation experience.

This explanation thereafter serves to support Brannen's (1992: 219) assertion that TDL "keeps the exotic in a way of distancing the self from the Other, or, in Japanese terms, a way of maintaining the *uchi-soto* dichotomy—the distinction between inside and out."

Although keeping the exotic exotic may well take place in TDL (I refer to this subject more explicitly in Chapter 2), the course of the Western River Railroad may have a technical explanation outside the cultural reading offered by Brannen. One of the imagineers working in TDL told me:

> We don't have the monorail because of Japanese bureaucracy. In Japan, if you have a train that's going only to one station, it's not considered a train. That's what we have. A train that goes to only one station. That's Western River Railroad in Adventureland. It's a ride, not a train. Otherwise, we would have to deal with the Transportation Department, apply for various licenses, and be subjected to various requirements and supervision. This was something we didn't like to deal with. So we cut the bureaucracy by turning the monorail into a ride. That's the practical explanation, and that's the only explanation.

Let us now proceed to Jungle Cruise itself.

> Captain: "Hello Everyone, Good day to you. I am the captain of this ship. I will guide you through this dangerous jungle, but you might not come back alive. So please wave to those behind you and say bye bye, *sayōnara*. Now we are inside the jungle of the Amazon. It rains all year. Here in the Amazon we have a lot of animals and plants. Oops, one alligator came up from under water. . . . Now an elephant comes. . . . It's the most violent in this jungle. . . . Now we're in the river of the Nile in Africa."

The captain (*senchō*) is traditionally a male guide, though OLC is now considering female guides for the Jungle Cruise. The spiel has changed little over the years (Fjellman 1992: 225; note that my use of the word *spiel* hereafter follows the Disney convention, rather than the colloquial denotation of *spiel* as a memorized, meandering locution). As Sklar

(1975–76: 28) describes in the official DL guidebook, "the 'native guides' who pilot the boats keep up a constant stream of chatter, part rehearsed and part ad-libbed, but all in the true spirit of adventure and fun." The adventure hinges on what Fjellman (1992: 225) terms "cute colonial racism," which unfolds through an impossible array of tropical scenes—the Amazon, the Nile, the African savanna, and the Ganges, to name a few. I will return to this first theme later. The second theme, fun, hinges primarily on the pun-filled script. In DL and WDW, typical jokes are "Please remove your earrings, they attract the head-hunters." Or, "Keep your hands and arms inside the boat—these crocodiles are always looking for a hand-out." And, "Gentlemen, if your mother-in-law is still aboard, you've missed a golden opportunity" (Sklar 1975–76: 28). The last was scrapped from the TDL script, probably because it was too offensive for a Japanese audience. Furthermore, the puns had to be completely rewritten.

> Watch out of these crocodiles. . . . Keep your hands inside the boat. To the right, the gorilla and the crocodile are playing "paper, scissors, stone" (*jan ken pon*).[2] What happened between them? Gorilla made a paper (*pa*), alligator made a scissors (*choki*) with his mouse. But the alligator (*wani-chan*) cannot beat the gorilla for long, because he can make only *choki*. . . .
>
> You can see a lot of animals around us. . . . It seems that we have entered the depth of the jungle. The zebra came to eat the plants, the lions are eating the zebra. The vulture is eating the lion's leftovers. It's a tough world. . . . Only the strongest survive in the jungle. . . . To your right you can see the hippos. They're very persistent and have a habit of eating those who watch them. In front, we see Dr. *Shubaitzuwa* [Schweitzer], and he's in some kind of trouble. Those on the right, please watch out, we might crush into the waterfalls! It's dangerous! *Wa!* That was dangerous. Your captain is very busy today. We are now going deeper into the Amazon. There's a hippo coming from our right side. . . . These animals are very violent if you make them angry . . . (taking out a pistol and shooting in the hippo's mouth) I did it! . . . We are now going into the land of the head-hunters (*kubikai zoku*). They seem to be in the middle of some ceremony. They are dancing. (Boat passing underneath the head-hunters' veranda.) Watch out, something is going to hit us from the left. Oh no, I thought left was dangerous, but now something comes from the right as well! They

have spears (*yari*)! They are throwing spears at us! (Going away) This is too much for me.

This fragment illustrates the use of puns in the Japanese spiel. The key word for understanding the pun is *yari*. It first appears in the spiel when the captain says "I did it!" (*yarimashita*) after shooting the hippo. Then it appears again as he warns the cruisers from the spears (*yari da!*). Finally he says "It was too much for me today," *senchō kyō wa yarisugichata*, literally meaning: the captain (*senchō*) did too much (*yarisugichata*) today (*kyō*). First, the linguistic use of *yarisugichata* (the collegial form of *yarisugiteshimata*) gives this utterance a friendly, playful air. Second, it conveys a pun, in the category of *share* (the word also means "decorations"). *Share* has a refined and long-standing tradition in Japanese literature. When *share* is used in *tanka* poems, the result is called *kyōka* (a comic *tanka* poem). An Edo-period *kyōka* written after the arrival of Commodore Perry's Black Ships can be translated as "four steamships, and no one can sleep." *Steamship* (*jōkisen*) was also the name of a Japanese tea company, and the poem therefore humorously describes the black ships as causing insomnia: "four cups of tea (= black ships), and no one can sleep."

The *share* told by the captain is an integral part of the spiel, and there is no ad-libbing. I witnessed one occasion, however, on which the *senchō* made a reflexive remark about his (or the spiel's, to be more precise) *share*. Referring to the headhunters from which the boat has just been saved, the spiel goes: "Their way of life in the jungle is very irresponsible" (*kare da wa janguru de ikagena ikikata o shite imasu, nageyari na jinsei*). The *yari* lurks in *nageyari*. This is not a very good pun. My Japanese companions said it was *dajare*, a "bad pun." When the audience did not react, the captain remarked, "That wasn't such a good one" (*muriyari deshita*—[it was] forcing things; I didn't do so well). Even this last remark had a play on *yari*.

To be sure, not all *share* in Jungle Cruise are based on *yari*. Another example plays on the word *kubi* (head). Further entering into the head-hunters' land, the captain says:

To your right there's the most capable salesman in the jungle, his name is Sam (*Samu*). He holds two heads (*kubi*) that belonged to his employees.

Recently there has been a depression in the jungle, and he often complained to me because he has a lot of debts and he cannot pay them back (*kubi ga mawaranai*) [literally: "cannot turn his head," an expression denoting inability to perform something]. That's why he's selling those heads. As for me, I can turn my head anytime (*kubi ga mawaru*) [meaning, "I am free."]

Share is the hallmark of Japanization in Jungle Cruise, what I term "dubbing the spiel." In fact, it is a creative rewriting and "redecorating" of the English version.

In contrast, the second theme of the cruise, adventure, copies that found in the original DL and WDW rides. As Fjellman (1992: 226) aptly sums it up, "[Almost] all of the human characters in the Jungle Cruise are people of color. . . . All are caricatures that, in the interests of 'normal fun' might reinforce visitors' notions of exotic (and colorful) others. . . . Here we have a middle-class version (of the safari) for those who don't mind being crowded together on shared seat cushions."

This seems to appeal to the Japanese as well. The cute colonialist appeal of Jungle Cruise, however, somehow did not work for the French. The Jungle Cruise has been removed from Disneyland Paris, perhaps "because it . . . reminded visitors of their colonial past" (Van Maanen 1992: 26). Although the Japanese apparently share the American amusement with third-world people, they amuse themselves with their own spiel. Jungle Cruise represents the importation of the American original, whose cultural contents are preserved while its wrapping (spiel) is changed considerably.

Domesticating Disney: Cinderella's Castle

Cinderella's Castle is located in Fantasyland next to Central Plaza (see Map 1). In both WDW and TDL, Cinderella's Castle is "the visual magnet that draws visitors down Main Street USA and deeper into the Magic Kingdom" (Fjellman 1992: 171). However, the WDW Cinderella's Castle has no ride. Inside its architectural shell are a broadcast room, security rooms, and a small apartment—built for the Disney family and used mostly as a changing room by the various Tinkerbells (Fjellman 1992: 271–72). A restaurant—King Stefan's Banquet Hall—is beneath

the apartment. It is named for Sleeping Beauty's father, perhaps an allusion to the fact that the castle in DL is Sleeping Beauty's Castle. There
is no such restaurant in TDL. Below the restaurant, on what is taken by
visitors to be the ground level, is an arched tunnel that forms the entrance to Fantasyland from the Plaza. Large glass mosaics depicting
episodes from the Cinderella story decorate the walls. This is the same
in both WDW and TDL. To the left of the entrance is the King's Gallery, a shop selling such items as clocks, chess sets, and jewelry. In TDL,
in a similarly located shop called the Glass Slipper, artisans (some of
them imported from America) demonstrate glass cutting, glass blowing,
porcelain painting, and damascene (inlaid gold). The Glass Slipper also
carries many themed glass souvenirs, including Cinderella's slipper. Finally, under the Castle are utility corridors through which people and
materials move backstage. This is the same in TDL. As Fjellman (1992:
272) sums up, "Cinderella's Castle is a summary statement for all of
WDW, containing as it does fantasy, food, communication and com-
merce." The same goes for TDL, but there is much more. In TDL, Cinderella's Castle has its own ride, called the "Mystery Tour," priced as a
"D" attraction.

TDL's castle has been turned into a repository of sinister themes
and villains from Disney stories. "Can you conquer the evil forces of the
Disney villains in the Castle?" asks the blurb in the guidebook. The line
for the Mystery Tour starts in the tunnel on the ground level, which was
widened for that purpose. As each group of about twenty visitors is permitted into the anteroom inside the castle, they are greeted by the tour
guide, usually a female, wearing the Mystery Tour uniform, which looks
like the hunter's attire in Snow White and the Seven Dwarfs. In the back of
the anteroom, the ride operator, wearing a costume, stands in front of
the master control panel, which is built into a podium-like stand; a rope
prevents the visitors from crossing into this area. Its switches and LEDs
are titled in English, for example "secret door no. 1" or "elevator #2." One
of TDL's imagineers confirmed that the control panel had been shipped
from the United States. "In TDL," he said, "the Imagineering Department cannot manufacture or engineer anything, since this is done by
OLC and its contractors."

The greetings uttered by the tour guide are part of an elaborate ride narration. While the spiel itself is fixed and rehearsed, there is some space for personal ad-libbing. I first describe one typical ride with a regular spiel, and then discuss possible modifications and the meaning of ad-libbing in general.

> Good day. Please come in! This is Tokyo Disneyland's Cinderella's Mystery Tour. I am the guide of this tour. My name is Satō Akiko. How do you do? It's nice to meet you! Before we start, let me remind you that the owner of this Castle doesn't like cameras. From here, we go deep into the ravines of the Castle. Please follow me, otherwise you'll get lost. Let's go inside.

The spiel opens with "Konnichi wa, irasshaimase!" (Good day, please come in!). This is a hybrid of TDL lingo and traditional Japanese courtesy. *Irasshai* yells of welcome from men (and the more polite *irasshaimase* of women) are traditional greetings uttered by shopkeepers and other service professionals when inviting a customer into their establishment (see also Linhart 1986: 199). This is a *kimarimonku*, the formal phrase fitting the occasion (*kimari* means "fixed," "decided"; *monku* is "words"). *Konnichi wa*, in this context, sounds more friendly, part of a daily face-to-face interaction. TDL manuals have a lot to say about this seemingly trivial distinction. Throughout their training, TDL cast members are requested to say *konnichi wa* instead of *irasshaimase* because the former is said to "create more communication." Whereas *irasshaimase* does not require a reply, accepted conduct demands that a person greeted with *konnichi wa* reply with the same greeting. Cast members who work in merchandising and restaurants are told to "unlearn" the traditional *irasshaimase* and use only *konnichi wa*, which they still, however, use with the traditional "service voice" (a high-pitched female tone sometimes called *koneko-chan*, "kitty's voice"). The spiel of the Mystery Tour combines both *konnichi wa* and *irasshaimase*, perhaps because the guide is about to lead the visitors in. Interestingly, many tour guides did not use the service voice, perhaps because their theatrical performance made it irrelevant.

The following exchange between the guide and her audience is a good example of the TDL "communication" approach to visitors. The guide says *dōzo yoroshiku* and pauses. This would typically be translated into English as "pleased to meet you" (literally, it is closer to "please be nice to me," "please take care of me"; see, among the myriad of other Japanese textbooks, Mangajin 1993: 14). The whole expression is *dōzo yoroshiku o-negai shimasu* (the last two words meaning approximately "I ask you to"). The guide pauses in order to allow her audience to greet her back by completing the expression. If no reply comes, then she utters "*o-negai . . .*" and pauses again. This time the audience never fails to reply correctly. Throughout the exchange, the guide uses a high-pitched voice, which in this context serves as a self-indulgent version of the "effeminate" service voice. Although exchanging similar greetings is common practice for Japanese engaged in introductions, it is usually done formally and uttered independently. The Mystery Tour introduction, in contrast, is done with an air of playful childishness.

This introductory exchange provides a good illustration of the TDL (and Disney) strategy of promoting "communication," which is actually conducted within a prescribed, prearranged spiel. The exchange also illustrates the Japanization of the spiel, an important part of the process of "domesticating Disney." This process assumes a special importance in Cinderella's Mystery Tour, and I discuss it in more detail below. The whole exchange reminded my Japanese discussants of their participation in similar sessions in kindergarten as part of their early etiquette training. Promoting a "mental transformation" from adulthood to childhood is another function of the spiel, as well as of TDL at large. The spiel cleverly transforms the adult audience into children (with the guide as a responsible yet cheerful kindergarten teacher) while at the same time keeping their status unoffended by using a speech level of "ordinary politeness."[3]

A door then slides open behind the guide, and the group steps inside, stopping in the first room. It is still dark.

> Guide: "Come closer so that I feel better—it feels like I am a star surrounded by a lot of fans. (Suddenly the lights turn on.) Now you can see the heroes of Disney, who confronted the forces of evil and cruelty."

She points to the pictures on the wall, which are now visible. They include Pinocchio, Peter Pan, young Arthur (from the Disney film *The Sword in the Stone*) and the prince from *Snow White*, among others. There is a sound of thunder and roaring. On the opposite wall appears the mirror on the wall from *Snow White*. The face of Snow White's witch stepmother, wearing her black crown and red lipstick, appears in the mirror. As the image speaks, its holographic face changes:

> "You say such silly things! Wait until I let you see my castle."
> Guide: "Oh, it's you again! In the mirror of Snow White. . . . Are you a magic mirror?"
> Mirror: "How dare you insult Disney's villains? Did you say cruel? Did you say evil? Now I will show you those villains!"

The guide screams. The pictures of Disney's heroes metamorphose into Disney's villains from such films as *The Black Cauldron*, *Fantasia*, *Sleeping Beauty*, and *Snow White*.

> Mirror: "How do you think these creatures look? They are the real Disney stars!"
> Guide: "How dare you say that? Those villains were beaten by the heroes we saw before!"

A secret door between the walls opens slowly.

> Mirror: "I look into the future—you will go down into the basement with those guys, and I promise to test how you confront the powers of evil" (laughter).
> Guide: "Let's go! I will prove that Good can win over Evil, like Disney heroes did. Everybody, we are going down the stairs, use the handrail and watch your step please."

This expository scene presents the visitors a conflict and a role. The conflict is an ultimate one: Good versus Evil. Being virtually transformed into this Disneyfied reality, visitors are requested to take the role of the Disney heroes, become one with the myth, and be tested against the "powers of evil." The final scene indeed invites the visitors (at least one of them) to take an active role in destroying evil. Having been temporarily beamed back to childhood, visitors are further transformed into Disney heroes in the first room. Seduced into a temporary suspension of disbelief, the group can now proceed. The following minutes are composed of crooked corridors, secret elevators, scary holograms, and a loud soundtrack of roars, howls, and horrendous laughter. The Mystery Tour is notably one of the longest attractions in TDL—about a fifteen-minute walk—and I will not present it in detail here. On first impression, it is something like a journey through a Disneyfied maze of the game of Dungeons and Dragons. There are many rooms, each with its own variation on evil: a dragon, something holographic called "goo" that lives in water, the demonic scene from *Fantasia* screened on the wall, and collections of black magic paraphernalia (crystal balls, old books, skulls). Occasional quarrels between the mirror's voice and the guide provide a driving sense of urgency that propels the group forward. For example:

> Mirror: "How was it? Didn't my cute pets frighten you?"
> Guide: "Don't worry about it. We are very brave."
> Mirror: "Hahaha. . . . Maybe until now."
> Guide: "What do you mean?"
> Mirror: "Soon you will understand."

The group then enters the last room, which is rather large. The mirror's voice explains: "This is the big pot of the magic black ghost" (*burakku gosuto* in Japanese pronunciation). The black ghost, a horned creature standing behind a cauldron, is an audio-animatronic robot.

> Black ghost: "I can make more devils from human bodies, I can make as many as I want. I can make them in the shape of devils" (laughter).
> Guide: "This is an ancient story. The King of Heaven demolished the big pot with the sword of light. After that, evil was destroyed."
> Mirror: "It seems you have too much self-confidence. You know you might never escape this place. *Yosh!* this is the final confrontation. Heaven and hell. You're about to see the power of evil."
> Guide: "That's okay. If something happens with the big pot, we should have courage, and fight back. (Pointing to the pot, which gradually becomes radiant, to the sounds of an ominous soundtrack): Look! This is . . . the legend . . ."
> Black ghost: "Your life is very short. . . . You cannot escape me any more. Wake up, black condor (*condoru*)."
> Guide: "No! Stop it!"

While the audience watches the audio-animatronic skeletons come to life to the sound of a melodramatic soundtrack, the guide takes one of the visitors (usually a child) with her. The lights suddenly focus on them as together they hold up the "sword of light" and aim it toward the pot. The sword radiates, and as the soundtrack reaches its peak, the pot explodes. To the sounds of violins, everybody claps hands. Going out of the room through an arched passage, visitors face a wall rug ornamented with the inscription "Good Conquers Evil" (in English).

Cinderella's Mystery Tour is unique. It exists only in TDL. It is the only "ride" in which visitors walk by foot rather than being transported in small vehicles ("people movers"). It also raises many questions. Where did OLC get the idea? What are Disney's "villains" doing in Cinderella's Castle? And whose story is this? I asked these questions of the people who should know: OLC managers and TDL imagineers. None of the OLC employees—regulars or part-timers—with whom I spoke could answer them. Embarrassed by my reluctance to abandon this line of inquiry, an OLC manager summed it up for me: "Cinderella's Castle is TDL's symbol," he said, "and Mystery Tour is its ride. Take it or leave it." The imagineer with whom I spoke said that the reason why TDL has a Cinderella's Castle is that "it is our third-generation park, and therefore a replica of WDW and not of DL. The Castle was already a part of WDW. It was replicated in TDL. The Castle was built before the park was opened (in 1983), but the Mystery Tour was added only later, in 1986." According to TDL's official Diary (1994–95), the Mystery Tour opened on July 11, 1986: "The Mystery Tour was created especially for TDL. There is nothing like this in any other place. All the villains come to live there. . . . It's a dungeon, not a castle." It was only after taking the Mystery Tour a few times and visiting some of Tokyo's conventional amusement parks, such as Toshimaen and Kōrakuen, that I came up with a possible explanation. The Mystery Tour, I argue, is TDL's version of the Japanese ghost-house (obakeyashiki). Several clues support this idea.

1. Structural similarity: The traditional ghost-house is a covered labyrinth of corridors and rooms, a mystery tour (often made by foot) among various displays of evil creatures and horrors. Cinderella's Castle, with its first-class technological design and sophisticated spiel, leaves the conventional ghost-house far behind. The underlying structures, however, are parallel.

2. Marketing rationale: Ghost-houses are among Japan's most popular traditional amusements. Their history can be traced back hun-

dreds of years to traveling shows (*misemono*). There were also portable *obakeyashiki* shown during festivals. Ghosts, demons, and monsters in general have been prevalent and favorite characters in Japanese popular culture (see Richie 1995; Napier 1996; for major Japanese sources dedicated to the world of ghosts, see Karasuyama 1992; Taiyo 1987). As Napier (1996: 95) sums up, "Premodern Japanese literature contains an enormous variety of demons and ghouls ranging from the river-dwelling *kappa* to the Dream Eater of Buddhist theology. In modern popular culture that tradition lingers in the image of Godzilla, whose descendants have continued into the present day in comics, animation, and live-action cinema."

Popular cultural forms featuring ghosts include manga, television shows, films, and card games. Many manga involve ghost characters, such as *Ghost Sweeper Mikami* or *Hell Teacher Nūbe* (see also Schodt 1986). Among the many *obakemanga* (ghost comics), one of the most popular is Shigeru Mizuki's *Kitarō*, the story of a half-ghost, half-human boy whose father lives inside a large eyeball. The story was turned into a popular television animation series. The famous ghost story *Yotsuya kaidan*, an immensely popular nineteenth-century kabuki play, was made into more than 50 films. Finally, *karuta*, a card game with drawings of ghosts, has been popular since the Taishō period (1913–25). Given the vast popularity of ghosts, OLC managers played it safe when opting for the Mystery Tour. Moreover, the link between Disney and *bakemono* (ghosts) is not so far-fetched. In 1985, about a year and a half before the Mystery Tour opened, the Disney videotape *Scary Tales* was released in Japan. Titled *Bakemono no hanashi* (Ghost stories) in Japanese, *Scary Tales* is a compilation of cartoons including *Lonesome Ghosts* (Mickey, Goofy, and Donald as clumsy ghost busters in a 1937 cartoon); *Donald Duck and the Gorilla* (1944); *Trick or Treat* (1952); and *The Legend of Mr. Hollow* (from *Ichabod and Mr. Toad*, 1958). The tape also features several sequences from *The Skeleton Dance* (a black & white oldie from 1929, the first of The Silly Symphonies) as interludes. This video, which was very popular in Japan according to several of my respondents, might have indirectly inspired TDL's Mystery Tour.

3. Audience reception: On several Mystery Tours, I heard parents telling their bemused children, upon entering the black ghost's room:

"Ara! Oni-san da yo!" (Wow, it's Oni!). The black ghost made its original appearance in an old and somewhat forgotten Disney film, *The Black
Cauldron*. This film is usually unknown to Japanese visitors; I am not
sure how many Americans are familiar with it. Visitors need models to
associate with the black ghost, and many of them turn to the well-known
figure of Oni, who has been variously depicted as a devil, a ghost, and a
demon. Oni can eat humans and transform them into demons, just as
the black ghost threatens to do. Although very powerful, Oni can be
destroyed and killed by swords (for discussions of the vast folklore on
Oni, see Baba 1971; Kawai 1988).

When I offered my idea about Mystery Tour as an *obakeyashiki* to
my Japanese respondents, particularly young TDL part-time workers,
they paused to think about it for a moment and then simply said: "Yes,
that's true." My informants at Kōrakuen were also quick to agree. However, I suspect that calling the Mystery Tour an *obakeyashiki* served other
purposes for them. Some of them regard TDL as an "unfair American
imposter," and the *obakeyashiki* image carried with it a welcome sense of
disbelief, as if it exposed TDL as a 'fake.' *Obakeyashiki* has a sound of the
antique and the colloquial about it, which is completely different from
TDL's image as hypermodern, foreign, and American.

Another explanation of the genesis of the Mystery Tour was sup-
plied by one of the American imagineers working in TDL. "It is a coincidence," he said. "You see, there is a technical explanation to the question of the Mystery Tour. Most of the Castle's interior space was under
ground. There was some space above ground level, but not enough on its
own. The fact that it was under ground inspired the idea of dungeons.
. . . That's how the Mystery Tour was born." Even if this is true, it does
not exclude the cultural explanation proposed here. TDL imagineers
may have suggested the dungeons concept to OLC, which associated it
with *obakeyashiki*. Perhaps there was no conscious thought of *obakeyashiki*
behind the Mystery Tour. However, the visitors' cries of "Oni-san da!"
and the positive replies of my respondents to the idea prove that in Japanese eyes the association exists. TDL also replicates the DL and WDW
attraction named the Haunted Mansion, an "E" ride found in the upper-
left corner of Fantasyland. The Haunted Mansion, filled with "999

ghosts and goblins and ghouls," is perhaps more readily considered—at least in terms of production—as the American cultural equivalent of the Japanese *obakeyashiki*. However, this does not exclude the possibility of yet another *obakeyashiki* in the form of the Mystery Tour. Moreover, audience reception plays a much more important role in the Mystery Tour than in the Haunted Mansion. The ghosts in the Haunted Mansion are distinctively foreign to the Japanese. They sing in English and dance to unfamiliar music (the original Disneyland lyrics are hardly comprehensible). In the Mystery Tour, the mirror, the guide, and some of the monsters all speak Japanese. The visitors travel through the Haunted Mansion in small vehicles. In the Mystery Tour they walk, run, and play an active role in the show. As Van Maanen (1992: 19) puts it, "Little passivity is apparent on this attraction as customers whoop and holler to one another and race wildly through the castle trailing their tour guide." Furthermore, I never heard in the Haunted Mansion remarks similar to those made by visitors to the Mystery Tour in an attempt to make sense of it. The Mystery Tour—with all its Disney villains (*Dizunii no warumonotachi*)—seems much more "Japanese" than the Haunted Mansion.

The Japanization of TDL can therefore take place through the way it is consumed. This is not a trivial assertion; theories of globalization have long discussed the influence of the "imperialist text" without actually considering how it is consumed by those subjected to it. The Mystery Tour offers yet another example of the active role of consumption in subverting the "ideology" of production. Commenting about the "Japaneseness" of the Mystery Tour, Van Maanen (1992: 19) claimed that

> it is hard to imagine a similar attraction working in either DL or WDW. Not only would group discipline be lacking such as to insure that all members of the tour would start and end together, but selecting a sword bearer to do battle with the Evil One would quite likely prove to be a considerable test for the tour guides when meeting with the characteristic American chorus of "Me, Me, Me" coming from children and adults alike.

The defeat of the black ghost / Oni-san is not the end of the tour. There is an epilogue: a medal-awarding ceremony. The group is led through a passage into a smaller room. The way out appears to the left and, for the first time in the castle, daylight is visible. The guide stands in front of the group and invites the ghost slayer to step up.

> Guide: "Tokyo Disneyland's official statement will be given now. Yamada-san! Please step forward and show your face."

Visitors clap their hands as Yamada-san, a schoolboy about the age of ten, joins her.

> Guide: "He did superbly. He gave power to the sword of light. He saved us from the terrible evil. That brave and pure heart we must respect. We make him a knight (*kishi*) of Fantasyland and hero of the Kingdom. We give him the title of star (*sutā no shōgō*) and a commemorative medal (*kinen no medaru*). Sa, Yamada-san, please show everyone your face. (Pausing) The castle is safe now. Here is the medal. Please take off your glasses and bend your shoulders. (Putting the medal over his neck) Everyone, please applaud him who has a brave heart. (Pausing for applause) Thank you. We applaud from the bottom of our heart to each person who fought to the end. Thank you so much. Everybody, one more time: (screaming) *Aku ni katsu!* (triumph over evil!) (Pausing, applause, the guide raises her fist, then bows) I have received my proof. We can now return safely to Fantasyland."

The award, like any ceremony, seems to be accompanied by a strict spiel. To what extent are the guides loyal to the spiel? The question of ad-libbing has been studied in DL as an example of subverting corporate control (see Van Maanen & Kunda 1989). One such award ceremony that I witnessed took place on a Tuesday morning. It was a regular work and school day, and my group consisted of young adults only, mainly romantic couples. When the guide invited the medal winner (a man in his 30s) to step up, the audience (particularly his girlfriend) giggled rather than applauded. Obviously sensing the mood of her audience, the guide said: "[We're] both embarrassed" (*hazukashii no otagai sama*). This did not sound as if it were part of the spiel. When saying "Please show your face to everyone," the guide suddenly paused and added: "Please continue laughing and smiling" (*warai tsuzukete kudasai*). This evoked a burst of spontaneous laughter from the audience, apparently because of the contrast between formal onstage spiel and what seemed to be a slip-page in "backstage instructions." At the end of the ceremony, having performed the last theatrical sequence of *Aku ni katsu*, the guide threw in a final remark: "I like to do this" (*suki de yattemasu*), and then, instead of pausing for the applause as the spiel dictated, added: "Please don't mind me" (*kinishinaide kudasai*), meaning You don't have to applaud. My Japanese discussants insisted that this did not sound like a spiel. Indeed, it sounded like something that was meant to ease the role-distance experienced by the guide in front of her obviously disenchanted audience.

The incident with the adult group represents an extreme case of ad-libbing. However, there were many smaller examples of guides' using a slightly different spiel. In the anteroom's introduction, for example, some guides said: "We start slowly, but please hold on to your valuables, like friends or kids or cameras." Another emphasized the spiel's warning against the use of cameras by adding: "The other day, someone tried to take pictures, and he went to jail." In one case I witnessed, as our group left the medal-awarding ceremony and the castle, the guide called after us: "*sayōna . . .*" her voice fading out as if she were falling down into some deep abyss behind us. This trick was not repeated by others.

When discussing these incidents (some of them I had videotaped) with other TDL visitors, the general opinion was that the Mystery Tour is exceptional because it contains relatively more ad-libbing. Hiroyo, an office lady in her 20s, said that "in contrast to other rides, the Mystery Tour is more fantastic. The guide is like a storyteller. Her role is much more important, and that's why she feels free to ad-lib." Satoshi, a company employee in his 20s, said that "if you compare the Mystery Tour to the Jungle Cruise, it's totally different. In the Jungle Cruise, the boat sails on its own. It will sail on even if the captain doesn't speak a word. But in the Mystery Tour, if the guide doesn't speak, the group will not move. The guide has to keep the group going." There is another important difference between the Mystery Tour and the Jungle Cruise. Whereas the Jungle Cruise spiel is founded on jokes, the Mystery Tour has practically no jokes. It has a serious spiel, sometimes deadly serious. Indeed, the seriousness of the spiel is meant to support the illusion and dynamize the fantastic journey through the castle. When the guide fails to do so, she resorts to cynicism, just like the flight attendant that "has a problem with phoniness" mentioned by Hochschild (1983). I elaborate on the topic of emotive dissonance in the work of cast members in Part II.

Wishful History: Meet the World

Meet the World is located on the outskirts of Tomorrowland just in front of the World Bazaar's eastern exit (see Map 1). In terms of TDL's topography, it is found at the end of a circle whose starting point is the World Bazaar and whose preferred direction of movement is generally westward, or clockwise. This observation is not trivial. The basic topographic design of all the Disney worlds is the same (Birnbaum 1989: 62). All are divided into five lots or zones—Main Street (World Bazaar in TDL), Adventureland, Frontierland (Westernland in TDL), Fantasyland, and Tomorrowland—which radiate from a core area (Central Plaza in DL, Cinderella's Castle in WDW, Central Plaza with Cinderella's Castle right behind it in TDL). In principle, this circular design allows for freedom of movement. Upon entering the park in Main Street (or World Bazaar), one can move either westward to Adventureland, or eastward to Tomorrowland, or forward toward Cinderella's Castle. In practice, however, almost all visitors swarm westward and then continue, more or less persistently, clockwise. Although no arrows or signs in the park encourage this movement, it dominates the crowds as well as the order of presentation followed in guidebooks. Being printed publications, guidebooks inevitably have to employ a linear arrangement. They always start with Main Street USA (World Bazaar) and then move to Adventureland, Westernland, Fantasyland, and finally Tomorrowland. This order is the same in the guides to all the Disney parks.

The "horde effect" of visitors' movement is readily visible in the morning—when Adventureland is packed with early visitors while Tomorrowland is still relatively empty—and in the afternoon, when the shopping mall of the World Bazaar becomes immensely crowded. This pattern of movement characterizes first visitors more than repeaters. The latter often head directly to their favorite attraction. In addition, the accumulation of crowds in the World Bazaar in the afternoon is also due to the fact that most visitors do their shopping toward the end of their

visit. My observations regarding the pattern of movement were confirmed in an interview with Shibata Chizuko, a senior member of OLC's
Marketing Division, who said:

> It's true that our guidebooks have this order of presentation. However, it
> is not intended to actually prescribe the pattern of guests' movement
> around the park. The existence of such a pattern, that's something psy-
> chological. People always go clockwise. Early guests always go to their left,
> where they find Adventureland. This is what our experts say. By the way,
> the phenomenon is not unique to TDL. You can see it happening in sub-
> way stations, too.

Incidentally, all the official guided tours in which I participated followed
the clockwise course. Haden-Guest (1972: 226) also noted that Disneyland's "radial plan (plus its single entrance) exemplify a subtle control
mechanism. . . . Namely, that we enter and move clockwise."

In terms of the clockwise pattern of movement, Meet the World is
for most visitors the last attraction at the end of the radial course. Shibata acknowledged this observation, but was quick to add that "we don't
look at it as the end." Shibata's own opinion is that Meet the World was
placed in Tomorrowland because it is a "show on history with a look to
the future." Symbolically speaking, however, Meet the World is also "the
last attraction." Its interior capacity (about 150 seats) is relatively small,
compared to big Tomorrowland. It was usually half-filled on the various
occasions I visited it. "Revolve on a carousel through time and relive
Japan's fascinating encounters with other cultures," states the blurb for
Meet the World in TDL's guidebooks. One enters the show through a
round anteroom. A digital clock above the door counts the minutes remaining until the end of the show currently running inside. The arched
ceiling features a map of the world, with digital clocks showing the time
in various cities, such as New York, Beijing, and Moscow. Sightseeing
films taken at these metropolises are shown on television screens placed
in the walls. The visitor is therefore surrounded by a truly cosmopolitan
ambiance. The guides' uniforms, in contrast, are distinctively Japanese.
All of them wear a kimono-like costume for women. This is the only
place in TDL in which the uniforms resemble traditional Japanese
clothing. Looking around this anteroom, one senses that something is

missing. It takes a few minutes to realize what it is. There is nothing Disney here. No Mickey, no Goofy, no Pixie Dust.[4] We are inside TDL, in a show specific to it, but we are at the same time outside the Magic Kingdom. Meet the World is a show about and for the Japanese.

The show itself takes less than 30 minutes and consists of a film, with three mechanical figures as narrators: a crane and a brother and sister. It begins as the two children are sitting on a beach viewing the sea. The sister asks her brother:

> "How did it all come about?"
> "It took thousands of years to form the Japanese islands," he replies.
> "How do you know?"
> "I learned it at school."

(In quoting the spiel, I use the official TDL English translation, available over telephones in the last row. The regular spiel of Meet the World is in Japanese. In those cases in which the Japanese spiel diverts from the English version, I will note that.) Following this exchange, a mechanical white crane (a Japanese symbol for longevity) appears and recounts the history of Japan through its relations with "the world" (namely, China, Portugal, Holland, and the United States). The narrative begins with the following exchange between the two children and the crane.

> Sister: "Where did this bird come from?"
> Crane: "That's far from important. Where did you come from?"
> Brother: "Yokohama."

In the meantime, the screen behind the three is continually changing. First, it shows the volcanic formation of the Japanese islands. Next, it shows the island's prehistoric inhabitants.

> Sister: "Where did all these people come from?"
> Crane: "Thousands of years ago, they banded together to survive. Most of them were fishermen."
> Sister: "Is this the beginning of your tricks?"
> Crane: "No, of the world."

The Japanese archipelago was first inhabited between 100,000 and 200,000 years ago. The shallow seas separating Japan from the Asian mainland were still incompletely formed, and waves of people could cross from the eastern shores of the Asian continent, from what is now Korea. This implies that the "first Japanese" might have well come from Korea (see DeVos & Lee 1980)—a fact often erased from Japanese history textbooks, since Koreans are negatively regarded as "outsiders" (Yoshino 1992; S. Tanaka 1993). Meet the World also omits Korea from its historical narrative, an observation to which I return below.

The film ignores Japan's Paleolithic ancestors, in favor of the traditional Japanese myth of origin, which regards the founding ancestors as the offspring of the gods, who created the islands and came down to inhabit them (see Cox 1964; the original myth is recorded in the *Kojiki*, the historical chronicle of Japan completed in 712). This myth of Japanese exceptionalism is echoed in the crane's comment that the beginning of Japanese civilization is "the beginning of the world." One can also trace it in the crane's summary of the cultural evolution of the Japanese: "Thousands of years ago, they banded together to survive. Most of them were fishermen." This assertion belongs to the traditional view that explains the fundamental social patterns of the Japanese as emanating from their ancestors' early social organization in villages. However, the first systematic development of wet-field rice agriculture is usually dated to after 300 B.C.E. (in the Yayoi period). The earlier fishermen of the Jomon period (ca. 10,000–300 B.C.E.) were mostly nomads who had probably banded together.

Following this historical exposition, the show goes on to describe the first of Japan's cultural encounters. To the strains of "We Meet the World with Love," the screen changes to reveal a group of Japanese people in what seems to be a court gathering.

> Crane: "Ah, this is Japan's first constitution. Please come closer, I'll show you. This is Prince Shōtoku."

Shōtoku is then shown greeting the Emperor of China. The crane explains:

> "It's an expedition to China. Tang Dynasty. More than a thousand years ago. Shōtoku Taishi is the official ambassador of Japan."
> Ambassador: "It took us a lot of years to come here."

A voice (the ambassador? the emperor?) then says: "These gifts are for you, they are given with our greatest respect."

Brother: "What kind of gifts?"
Crane: "I thought you'd never ask."

A picture of the Great Buddha (*Daibutsu*) of Nara fades into a calligraphic depiction of *kanji* (Chinese ideographs).

Crane: "Watch very closely, how we are cultivating Chinese *kanji* into our garden."

"Hiragana!" cry the children's voices as the letters of the syllabic writing system appears.

Sister: "All these things came from China?"
Crane: "Culture does not just come, it is refined through many years."

In Meet the World, the first encounter with the Other is with China. China has indeed exerted a prominent influence on Japanese culture. Buddhism came to Japan in the sixth century (the traditional date is 552) from the Korean kingdom of Paekche, but it was Chinese writing (*kanji*) that made the imported religion accessible to the nobility and also exposed them to the thought of the Chinese classics and writings of Confucius and Mencius. Japan's first constitution was promulgated in 604 by Prince Shōtoku (regent 593–622). This seventeen-article constitution—composed *after* his return from China—was influenced by Chinese models of central government. The two syllabaries (hiragana and katakana) are stylized and abbreviated forms of certain Chinese characters, created in the Heian period, around the ninth century. China's influence on Japan has long been a problem for theorists of Japanese uniqueness (*Nihonjinron*). The crane's comments about the "cultivation of Chinese kanji into Japan's garden" and how "culture is not just received, but refined through many years" testify to that problem and a possible way out of it. China's gifts, it implies, were imported and developed by the Japanese. They were seeds that, having been transplanted, grew to form a unique Japanese culture.

The next cultural encounter is with European merchants.

Crane: "He is called a Portuguese. He comes from afar. He and his men
are traders. He offers . . . " (a shooting sound interrupts, and the at-
tacked/attacking Portuguese shout "Per favor, senior")
Crane: "In 1550 guns were not known in Japan. The Japanese are eager for
change. Travelers are arriving. Science, Christianity, the Western hemi-
sphere. Finally, our leaders find the influence too destructive."
Brother: "Because of priests?"
Crane: "Not just them . . . financial, governmental pressure. Dutch traders
continue to come and through them we continue to learn. It is a time of
great artistic development for almost three centuries."

Two Japanese cartoon characters, Yaji-san and Kita-san (the popular
names of Yajirobe and Kitahachi, characters developed by Jippensha
Ikku, a famous comedy writer in the Tokugawa period; see Brannen
1992: 233), appear to be having fun on screen. They rapidly open and
close *fusuma* (sliding partitions) on which artistic treasures are displayed.

Crane: "Don't pay attention to those two. Don't watch them, but the
screens. They will tell you interesting things."

This part covers approximately the period from 1542 to 1853. The
Portuguese castaways who reached Japan in 1542 carried arquebuses,
which "are said to have caused the greatest excitement to the Japanese,
who met them in friendly manner" (Sansom 1973: 105). The Japanese
welcomed the strangers, who were soon followed by missionaries and
traders. At the beginning of the seventeenth century, when the Tokugawa family reigned supreme in Japan, not only the Portuguese and
the Spaniards but also the Dutch and the English competed for trade
privileges. The Tokugawa shōgun were determined to permit no activity
that might interfere with their primacy. Suspecting the complicity of the
Catholic church in alleged Spanish plots to invade Japan, the shōgunate
forced Japan into a period of isolation from other cultures (1636–1853).
According to Sansom (1973: 169), "it was only a reluctant recognition of
weakness (compared to the Western guns and ships) that caused Japan
to withdraw into almost complete seclusion." The only ports left open
were the Dutch (and Chinese) trading bases on the islet of Dejima in
Nagasaki harbor, and the limited trade with Korea through the *daimyō*

of the island of Tsushima (between Japan and Korea). Edo (old Tokyo) flourished with the "interesting things" shown on the *fusuma*, on which *ukiyo-e* prints illustrate the world of actors, sumo stars, geisha, and courtesans. The external "world," however, was not about to allow Japan to continue in isolation. At this point the screen becomes black and a silhouette of a steamboat gradually appears, with two soldiers on its deck.

> Crane: "The black ships! It's time for Japan to meet the world."
> First soldier [probably Commander Henry V. Adams, second-in-command]: "Shall we shoot the gun, sir?"
> Second soldier [probably Commodore Perry]: "No, we didn't come all this way to frighten, but to trade."

Japanese samurai are seen gathering on the shore. One of them says:

> "I shall notify Edo."
> Crane: "It doesn't matter how brave a samurai is, still he cannot beat time."

The ship disappears. We see a gathering of court (*bakufu*) leaders in Edo.

> Crane: "For Japan, fortunately, this is a time of great leaders. These are the sort of people that wanted to open Japan so that the ocean is no longer a barrier. We never became a colony. It was difficult, but we succeeded in keeping our independence. But before we could be respected, we had to become civilized. Japan developed a centralized government. But was this civilization? People need food and shelter. This is development [*bunmei*— civilization—in the Japanese spiel]."

In 1853, the U.S. East India Squadron, consisting of four steamships under Commodore Matthew C. Perry's command, arrived in Uraga Harbor, following many unsuccessful attempts by Britain, Russia, and the United States to make a treaty with Japan. During his first visit, Perry delivered a letter from U.S. president Millard Fillmore. It stated that "although America has friendly intentions, it would insist upon carrying out its policy of securing good treatment for distressed American seamen and some facilities for navigation and trade" (Sansom 1973: 277). There was no open threat, but only a promise that Perry would return with a larger force the following spring. On March 31, 1854, the treaty was concluded (for detailed accounts of the Perry expedition, see Statler 1964; Minear 1974: 65–72). Japan was brought to an agreement by a demonstration of power. Ever since, the word *kurofune* (black ship) has become an image for forced Americanization and the coerced opening of Japan to foreign influence (Butler & Kishida 1992).

Other treaties with foreign powers quickly followed the U.S.-Japan treaty, and the growing internal pressures for reform resulted, in 1868, in the dissolution of the shogunate and the Meiji Restoration. This was, to use the crane's comment, "a time of great leaders . . . that wanted to open Japan so that the ocean is no longer a barrier." In a few decades, Japan effectively restructured itself as a polity. One of the major drives of this effort was, indeed, meeting the rest of the world as an equal. The official policy was to hire foreign experts and advisors that would help Japan "catch up" with the West and join the path of progress. The crane's awkward mention of having to become civilized in order to be respected should be read in this context. Interestingly, the Japanese spiel uses the word *bunmei* to refer to this process of becoming civilized through modernization and development. Tessa Morris-Suzuki (1995: 762) notes that the modern meaning of *bunmei* became widely used in general discourse only after the Meiji Restoration:

> The famous phrase *bunmei kaika* ("civilization and enlightenment") was coined by Japan's westernizers to describe their entire project. As the zeal for westernization changed into a growing Japanese nationalism, so did the emphasis move from *bunmei* to *bunka*—from the horizontal similarities among particular societies (especially in terms of technology and economy, "base" and "superstructure") to a vertical division which separates humanity into cultures.

The second occasion on which Meet the World deals with Japan's relationships with the West is World War II. The last part of the show opens with an explosion, followed by 30 seconds of darkness.

Brother: "It's awfully dark."
Crane: "Yes, it was dark . . . but it's all over now."
Brother: "Are you the spirit of Japan?"
Crane: "No, I'm not —You are! The people are the spirit."
Sister: "Where are the people?"
Crane: "Look! There are the people, studying, working, building. People are like dreams; if they are basically good, they can grow and become

stronger. When those dreams develop well, other countries can also appreciate them. It's only fair to share."

The show then ends with the theme song, "We meet the world with love / *Ai no fune de* [in our love boat] / We meet the world with love." The optimistic, wishful history concludes with a happy ending; Japan has become a beautiful swan; the black ship has been turned into the love boat.

Meet the World attempts to merge two historiographic narratives. One is the popular narrative of Japan as an "island nation," isolated and unique. The other is the pragmatic account, equally popular, of Japan's skills in borrowing and adaptation. (A third master narrative, which is Marxist or conflictual in nature and has been very influential among Japanese scholars at least for the past fifty or so years, is completely missing.) Proceeding from the optimistic beliefs about the benefits to be had from "meeting the world," the show emphasizes time and again how these cultural encounters produced seeds that were cultivated "into our garden" and precious gifts that were imported, consumed, and later modified by the Japanese. Internationalizing while keeping Japan's unique culture—this goal is justified within an evolutionary logic of historical determinism. Japan might have started as "the world," but it must open itself to progress; "It doesn't matter how brave a samurai is, still he cannot beat time." An underlying theme is that Japanese cultural identity is never separate, that it can perceive itself only by using other cultures as mirrors (see also Ohnuki-Tierny 1990; Tobin 1992; in Japanese, see Kato Shuichi 1974). The same has also been generally said regarding the Japanese self (see, e.g., Doi 1973 or Bachnik 1986).

In a sense, Meet the World replicates in miniature the larger narrative of TDL as a whole, since TDL itself is a living proof of the success of, and the benefits inherent in, cultural importation. Such an interpretation is construed by the onstage. A more focused reading, however, would reveal aporias and omissions in the text. The most significant absence is Korea. Brannen (1992: 228) argues that "Korea is excluded because it is the Asian country most similar to Japan and therefore the one most difficult to differentiate from." Another example of the elision of Korea is the fact that the monument for Koreans who died in Hiroshima (one-fourth of the 100,000 people killed) was not permitted to be constructed inside the Peace Park (Brannen 1992: 233). To be sure, there are other occasions that were edited out of Meet the World: World War II, for example. However, the omission of the war can be explained in terms of ridding the spiel of inconsistencies, since the war cannot serve as a positive example of meeting the world. The omission of Korea is more difficult to explain.

One of my informants, an American imagineer working in TDL, had to say about Meet the World:

> Well, the spiel is full of mistakes, and nobody bothered to correct it. . . . Forget it. I don't want to talk about Meet the World. It's the only attraction that's free.[5] It's about Japan meeting the world. They have Perry coming in, threatening them with the gun, and it all suddenly becomes black. Believe me, it's an embarrassment for everyone. You can judge for yourself. As a matter of fact, that show was originally designed for EPCOT (the Experimental Community of the Future in WDW). If you ever go to EPCOT, go to the Japan pavilion, and you can see behind it a huge, enormous empty building where Meet the World was supposed to be shown. But they shipped it here instead. They modified it here, of course. It's a very strange show, they don't charge for it, and practically everybody would like to see it abolished.

If the imagineer is correct in saying that Meet the World was intended for EPCOT, then it might be that (at least part of) the spiel was written by and for Americans. Perhaps this is the source of the English version of the spiel; no English version of a spiel can be found in any other TDL attraction. (I tried to corroborate the imagineer's claim, but a formal reply to my query was not forthcoming and informal comments were ambiguous.) If this is true, then we must change—reverse—our analytical point of departure. This is a good example of the reversal effect I mentioned before. The omission of Korea could therefore be viewed as merely a "technical" error. In American (foreign) eyes, Korea has exerted only minor influence on Japan, because it has been subjected to the same major influences of China. As DeVos and Lee (1980: 15) point out, "Chinese were always given greater deference than Koreans, since they were thought to be the originators while the Koreans were carrying a borrowed culture." Buddhism first came to Japan from Korea, which received it from China. Koreans kept Japan's trade alive during the Tokugawa period, along with the Chinese. Finally, in trying to account for the omission of Korea, we should consider the formulaic constraints of the spiel. Meet the World deals with history in a very simplistic and concise manner. In the harsh light of the show, China's shadow is big enough to cover Korea.

The historical narrative of Meet the World, however, is too reminiscent of other Japanese accounts of Japan's history to be simply explained away as an implant from EPCOT. The typicality of the ideas presented in Meet the World is illustrated by a concise historical narrative recently presented in another popular medium, the *Virtual Times* (the internet edition of the *Japan Times*).

> In the past, the Japanese have eagerly learned foreign languages and cultures (particularly from China) so long as there was no real threat of foreign dominance. When they saw a threat in the form of rebellious Christians, they closed their doors and eliminated all foreign influences for about 250 years. Then Commodore Perry forced them to open up with his mighty black ship some 150 years ago. The conservative forces reconciled in a policy of adopting Western technologies while keeping Japanese spirit and values. Japan initiated a transition from a feudalistic state to a modern democratic state soon after the Meiji Restoration, about 130 years ago, gradually adopting Western legal and political systems. The process didn't get very far before it came to a halt under the war. When the war ended, Japan had to rebuild its society and economy and the US became the primary model. (Ueda 1994: 27–28)

The *Times*'s narrative repeats the omission of Korea and the emphasis on "adopting Western technologies while keeping Japanese spirit and values." The logic and optimism of Meet the World are replicated. This is the story as the Japanese would like to see it told, especially to foreigners; it is part of the Japanese self-presentation in public places (the preceding quotation is taken from the "international edition" of the *Japan Times*). If Meet the World is a text of cultural imperialism, then it seems to be Japan's cultural imperialism, rather than America's.

CHAPTER 2

The Exotic and the Familiar

Brannen (1992: 219) argues that "Disneyland is recontextualized in Tokyo . . . in two forms: making the exotic familiar and keeping the exotic
exotic." The "exotic" stands for the original American fantasy, the "familiar" denotes "Japan." This dichotomy, however, becomes blurred in
TDL, since both the "exotic" and the "familiar" are onstage effects and
belong to the order of the imaginary, the "hyperreal" as Baudrillard
would have it. They can therefore be reversed at any time. Depending on
one's perspective, the exotic is also a contrived Japanese fantasy, and the
familiar is sometimes Disney as we know it in America. For heuristic
reasons I organize this discussion around the presentation of these two
imaginaries—"America" and "Japan"—as onstage effects.

"America" on Stage

The previous sections analyzed the Japanization of TDL's attractions.
In the media and through its public relations, however, TDL markets
itself as a 100 percent copy of the American original. TDL is marketed
mainly through advertising and public relations. Its carefully contrived
self-presentation in public can metaphorically be seen as an extension of
TDL's onstage. Constructing an "image" for TDL is evidently under-
pinned by a "backstage" of marketing strategies.

Toshiharu Akiba, a spokesperson for TDL, told Mary Brannen (1992: 216) that "OLC really tried to avoid creating a Japanese version of Disneyland. We wanted the Japanese visitors to feel they were taking a foreign vacation by coming here, and to us Disneyland represents the best America has to offer." In its publications, TDL frequently uses translations of Walt Disney's sayings, the same sayings quoted in similar books on DL and WDW. The following Walt Disney quote, for example, is found in guidebooks, leaflets, and manuals: "I think what I want Disneyland to be most of all is a happy place—a place where adults and children can experience together some of the wonders of life, of adventure, and feel better because of it."

The manual "Tokyo Disneyland's Show," for example, reflects on this quote by adding that "visitors to TDL, who are referred to as 'guests,' can experience firsthand the magic of Disney. . . . In keeping with Walt Disney's philosophy, TDL is constantly improving and will never be completed." TDL is officially subtitled "The Kingdom of Dreams and Magic," which sounds very much like a play on "The Magic Kingdom." All these conscious references to Walt Disney, his vision, and his worlds obviously have a clear marketing rationale: showing off the brand name. Japanese consumers are *burando-shikō* (brand-name conscious; Tobin 1992: 19). The Japanese obsession with brand is not only consumerist, but also linguistic. Many trade names of imported Western products have become generic labels in Japan, for example *ray ban* for sunglasses (Stanlaw 1992: 66; Arakawa 1977). *Nantonaku, kurisutaru* (Somehow, crystal), a book by Tanaka Yasuo that was tremendously popular in the 1980s, is in fact a catalogue of brand-name goods (see Field 1989). (See below for the obsession with "Disney" as a brand name in the context of World Bazaar.)

Disneyland is marketed not only as a brand name but also as an image. TV commercials and ads for TDL always feature blonde, Caucasian models. This is true even when the commercial is designed in Japan for a show unique to TDL. A recent example was the advertising for the show Pecos Goofy Goes West, which featured three distinctly Caucasian models wearing sexy cowboy outfits, as well as Pecos Goofy himself. The same Pecos Goofy campaign, however, featured additional ads with no allusion to "America"; rather, these ads emphasized the proximity between Westernland (where Pecos Goofy performs) and Tokyo. One of these ads, hung in Yotsuya and other Tokyo train stations, simply stated: "Next [stop]: Westernland" (*Tsugi wa, Wesutanrando*).

The illusion that once you enter TDL, you enter America is maintained onstage. Cheerful American (Disney) music plays continuously along the walkways, American voices (as well as Japanese) can be heard over the public address system, and American-style food predominates in the 37 restaurants. Among the many employees at TDL are a host of real, live Americans, who, "along with the food and signboards, make the Japanese visitors feel they have truly spent a day in a magical kingdom—the United States" (Koren 1990: 159).[1] Hamburgers, American-style pizza, and popcorn have consistently been the top three dishes in TDL (TDL 1995: 9). For the Japanese visitor who steps into TDL, agrees Fusaho (1988: 59), "everything seems to say: 'This isn't Japan, Ladies and Gentleman; this is America!'" In order to keep "Japan" away from the park, OLC has imposed several restrictions. These restrictions are of particular interest since they attempt to prescribe the symbolic borders of TDL by drawing a line between "America" and "Japan." These two imaginary Siamese twins of TDL, however, are inescapably entangled, and the attempt at disconnection is associated with myths, prejudices, and preconceptions.

First, picnic lunches and beverages may not be brought into TDL. This rule, which applies as well to DL and WDW, is obviously connected with the fact that the park sells its own food. However, many Japanese writers see this as unique to TDL, where "a typically Japanese display of families and groups spreading mats over the ground, sit[ting] down, and unwrap[ing] their riceballs . . . would instantly dispel the 'this is America' atmosphere" (Fusaho 1988: 60). However, the restriction against *bentō* (lunchboxes) does not stop the Japanese from bringing mats into the park. About 30 minutes before each of the daily parades begins, the adjacent grounds and sidewalks become filled with mats on which families and groups are quietly waiting; many snack on the quintessential Japanese food for such occasions—riceballs (*onigiri*)—which they have carried into the park. It is, indeed, a very typical Japanese display. Incidentally, complaints by many visitors—especially the elderly—concerning the all-American menu inside the park led OLC to open a Japanese restaurant, called *Hokusai*, in the World Bazaar.

Second, there are no vending machines inside the park. This holds true for DL and WDW as well and probably serves to maximize revenues. As in the case of *bentō*, this restriction is reinterpreted in the context of TDL. Park officials, tour guides, and cast members have all told me that vending machines stand for "Japan," and this is the reason they are left outside. To be sure, the vending machine (*hanbaiki*) is now a quintessential symbol of the Japanese street. The Japanese vending machine market is one of the biggest in the world (Fields 1983: 25). Some of the latest models even speak in Japanese. However, as recently as the late 1970s the vending machine was a sign of Americanization, and drinking from the bottle (in the street!) was denigrated as *rappa nomi*, or drinking bugle style. In 1968, when a new television commercial featured a clean-cut, young Japanese star (Kayama Yūzō) drinking Coke from a bottle, American style, it was "seriously suggested that this went against conventional manners and was therefore not acceptable" (Fields 1983: 25). Today, however, the *hanbaiki* has been completely domesticated in Japan. "The vending machine story, that's just like Seven-Eleven," said an American who works in TDL as a face-cutter.[2] "The first Seven-Eleven started in Miami, but all the Japanese who work here think it's made in Japan. They bought the idea, then they bought the company, and now it's theirs." Finally, another explanation for the missing *hanbaiki* is provided by Tadokoro Makoto (1990: 100), who argues that "vending machines are kept out of the park for two reasons: (1) there is no *communication* [emphasis in the original] involved in buying from a vending machine, according to OLC managers; (2) it reduces the amount of garbage." Finally, TDL does not sell tobacco and alcoholic drinks. The absence of these two goes back, as cast members are quick to tell, to Walt himself, who did not regard them as part of "family entertainment."

The onstage image of TDL as "America" has gradually changed over the years. As one of the imagineers told me,

> Originally, TDL was like going to America without leaving Japan. That's true. But it's been changing. Now visitors go to the park for the park. As a result, we changed some of the onstage to make it more familiar. If you see the menus, once they had large English words for the food items, and below that there were smaller *katakana*. This is changing. The relationship is changing. Now the English is slowly coming down and replaced by

larger katakana. The American experience is not that important anymore. TDL is no longer an American experience.

The diminishing popularity of "America" as a consumerist image among Japan's young generation has been cited by other scholars (Skov & Moeran 1995). Some of my young discussants said that America was *dasai* (uncool or old-fashioned), and the *naui* (from "now," meaning trendy) thing to do was to eat *itameshi* (Italian food) and travel to Europe. Another reason behind this fading American experience was WDP's realization that TDL has an appeal of its own. I was told by a Disney marketing manager that WDP

> was trying to analyze the Disney brand name in Japan, how Japanese see Mickey. Well, basically they see Mickey in a different way. Those who responded to the questionnaire. . . . Were talking about the guy with the rubber head who is introducing all the other characters. They were talking about the costume. That guy, not even the animated cartoon, but the guy onstage, going hahahaha and speaking Japanese. That is the guy that they love. That's the person they are coming to meet in TDL. The guy in the tuxedo, the performer, the entertainer, the anchor man of TDL. This means that the park's Mickey is more effective, stronger than the original animated Mickey. This is very different from the States. It's phenomenal.

Having illustrated the "Japan" behind TDL's "America" facade, I next examine TDL's facades of "Japan" within the overall "America" onstage. The main attractions in this ride are the World Bazaar and the New Year's holidays.

"Japan" on Stage

World Bazaar is TDL's version of Main Street, USA. In DL and WDW, Main Street USA is "a fairy-tale version of a US town at the end of the 19th century . . . the home of nostalgia for a pre-urban Anglo-America" (Fjellman 1992: 170). As Richard Francaviglia (1981: 155) puts it, "the Main Street of the small town . . . is a repository of American longings." The imagineered version of Main Street, USA is, of course, a far cry from real main streets circa 1880–1910, which were often messy, unpaved, and muddy or dusty, depending on the weather. The romanticized imagineering of Main Street, USA belongs to Disney's American narrative, and I therefore do not discuss it here (see Fjellman 1992: 169–75; Francaviglia 1981).

DL's Main Street, USA has a red-brick Victorian train station, a "real" carriage drawn by a real horse, a city hall, a firehouse (with a small late-nineteenth-century firehouse exhibit) and a barbershop (in the Emporium building, where one can actually get a shave and a haircut). All these are lacking in TDL's World Bazaar, which is basically a glass-covered mall. Main Street, USA is a symbol of nostalgia that is totally missing from World Bazaar. Bruce Feiler (1991: 267), an American teacher in Japan, escorting his group of pupils during their annual school excursion to TDL, pinpoints this difference in his description:

> In the US, Disneyland aims to divert its guests from the present to a fond, misty memory of some make-believe golden age in America's past. But in Japan, the main street never had soda fountains with large bay windows or bakeries with gingerbread trim. What for Americans represents the romance of the past, for Japanese symbolizes a charmed vision of the future. Instead of a sense of loss, there is a sense of longing.

Equipped with more than twenty different shops selling Disney merchandise, "World" Bazaar serves the "gift-giving needs of the Japanese" (Brannen 1992: 223). Indeed, the shops of the World Bazaar have been rated as having the highest sales efficiency in Japan, calculated on a square-meter basis. The average visitor to the park spent ¥8,490 yen (about U.S.$80) in fiscal year 1990, out of which ¥3,290 (about $30) was spent at shops in the World Bazaar (Warren 1993: 36). The American sense of *furusato* (old hometown) has thus given way to the Japanese zeal for *omiyage* (souvenirs). There is no "world" in the World Bazaar, unless "world" refers to Disney's World. In that sense it is as ethnocentric as its Victorian-style facades. Incidentally, the World Bazaar does have the red carriage, but it is a horseless carriage. "Sorry, we couldn't keep the horse; it was too messy," I was told by Shibata Chizuko of OLC, "but for us, this street is still good old America. The Victorian style, this is turn-of-the-century America."

To reiterate Brannen's point, the World Bazaar serves the "gift-giving needs of the Japanese." As Mauss (1954: 1) noted, the bonds of social life are woven through the exchange of gifts, exchange that is voluntary in theory but in fact given and repaid under obligation. In addition to the twice-yearly seasonal gift tradition (*oseibo* [New Year's] and *ochūgen* [midsummer]), there is the *omiyage*, defined by Nitta Fumiteru (1992: 209) as "local specialties purchased as gifts for families and friends at home." Souvenirs are usually something one buys for oneself. *Omiyage* are return gifts to those closely associated with the traveler. Historically, this custom was part of the *senbetsu* (sending-off money) system. Hidetoshi Kato (cited in Nitta 1992: 210) argues that historically "the receipt of *senbetsu* established an obligatory relationship. Travellers, who were usually pilgrims, usually brought some small things bought at the shrine. These small items were known as '*miyage*,' which literally means 'shrine box.'"

Today, although the tradition of *senbetsu* has almost died out, Japanese tourists buy *omiyage* for family members, friends, neighbors, and colleagues (Keown 1989). Pupils on their *shūgaku ryokō* (school excursion) to Nikkō, Kamakura, Kyoto, or TDL, use the *okozukai* (spending money) their parents give them to pay for their *omiyage* (for *shūgaku ryokō* to TDL, see Part III). Finally, the *omiyage* must have a legitimating "trade mark" of the place where it was bought, proving that it was purchased on site. Almost all of Japan's travel sites have a rubber stamp available for *kinen sutampu* (commemorative stamp). In the same manner, all TDL's souvenirs have TOKYO DISNEYLAND marked on them.

Another blatant show of "Japan" on stage is performed during the *shōgatsu* (New Year's celebrations). *Shōgatsu*, widely considered the most important event in the Japanese calendar, usually takes up the first week of January. "There is," as Clayton Naff (1994: 237) notes, "a deep tranquility in the Japanese New Year. Work stops for three days. Traffic thins. A hush falls over the entire nation, except, of course, in the vicinity of Tokyo Disneyland." The Japanese New Year is a series of rituals and observances, not just a one-shot frivolity as in the West. Furthermore, *shōgatsu* is primarily a religious event, centered around traditional pilgrimages, food, decorations, and games. Some of the traditions that best characterize *shōgatsu* are *hatsu-mōde* (the year's first worship at shrines and temples), *matsu-kazari* (special decorations consisting of bamboo branches with pine branches, straw, and paper), *ozoni* (special *mochi*—glutinous rice cakes—cooked in soup) and *nenga-jō* (the obligatory New

Fig. 1 *Shōgatsu* (New Year's) celebrations at TDL

Year's postcard). TDL has them all. During *shōgatsu* it is transformed
into a hyperreal shrine. The hoards of believers coming for *hatsu-mōde*
are greeted by Mickey and Minnie in traditional kimono and by
splendid sets of *matsu-kazari* located in World Bazaar (see Fig. 1).
Those who want can mail *nenga-jō* postcards stamped with a special
Mickey Mouse *kinen* stamp, or enjoy *ozoni* in the World Bazaar's
Japanese restaurant, *Hokusai*.

Shōgatsu means great business for TDL. January 1–5 are Starlight
Days on which special-value (namely, reduced-price) Starlight Passports are available and valid for admission to the park from 5:00 P.M.
These passports (admission tickets) cater to a more mature audience
coming for the romance of the nighttime fireworks and parades. TDL
throws a special "countdown party" on New Year's Eve, during which
the park is open until 4:00 A.M. Clayton Naff (1994: 28), then a corre-
spondent for United Press International, described the 1990 New
Year's Eve *hatsu-mōde* to TDL:

> As I watched NHK (the National Broadcasting Service) for its annual
> midnight roundup of temple visits . . . it wasn't the Buddhist temples

that caught my attention; it was that shrine to American fantasia, Tokyo Disneyland. More than 50,000 Japanese in their teens and twenties had shouldered into Disneyland that night, NHK reported, and thousands more waited in a three-mile-long traffic jam outside the gates. . . . Here was spectacular evidence that Mickey, Minnie, and Goofy had supplanted the native gods in the pantheon of Japanese youth. (Naff 1994: 28)

The notion of Disney's heroes as gods in TDL's *America no matsuri* (American festival) has also been suggested by Japanese scholars (particularly Awata & Takanarita 1984: pt. IV). This part has illustrated how the dichotomies of "America" and "Japan," the "exotic" and the "familiar," are continuously blurred and reversed in TDL, where these onstage effects belong to the order of the hyperreal. At this point our ride moves backstage.

PART II

BACKSTAGE

CHAPTER 3

WORKING FOR TDL

You can dream, design and build the most wonderful place in the world, but it requires people to make the dream a reality.
—Walt Disney, cited in TDL Manuals: "Tips on Magic,"
"Casting for You," "The Disney Tradition"

TDL is a big organization. As of April 1, 1995, it had 12,390 cast members; 2,540 of these were regular employees, and 9,850 part-time employees (TDL 1995: 2). Every day, over 600 entertainers appear in its stage shows, musical performances, and parades. Employees are divided into two groups: part-time workers and regular employees (*shain*). Student part-timers are generally called *arubaito* in Japan; *pāto* is the standard term for working housewives. These two groups are termed *junshain* in more formal company jargon throughout Japan. OLC managers usually say that these two groups exist in two different worlds. This division of the workforce exists both in WDW and DL, as well as in local Japanese organizations. Below I first discuss the part-timers, and then the regular workers. My presentation focuses on hiring, training, and socialization to work. Promotion and seniority, which are more relevant to the world of regular employees, are discussed in the section devoted to them. Hiring, orientation, and training are at the heart of Disney's "organizational culture." Disney's standard procedures, codified in the manuals, have

already been much studied for DL and WDW (Schickel 1968; Haden-
Guest 1972; Van Mannen 1989, 1991; Smith & Eisenberg 1987; Spinelli
1992). This provides a relatively solid basis of information for comparing
TDL with the "original" models.

On a more macro-theoretical level, company-specific practices such
as hiring, training, and promotion are behind the so-called balkanization
of labor markets (Kerr 1977) leading to the creation of "internal labor
markets" (Doeringer and Piore 1985). TDL's labor market is internal,
that is, people outside the company have little or no access to it. OLC
controls the entry to this market, the career courses of those working in
it, and the economic incentives to which they respond. This situation is,
of course, not unique to TDL or to Disney; most workers work in internal markets, whether in union or nonunion firms (Abraham and Medoff
1984; Hashimoto and Raisian 1985). The dual market structure of part-
and full-time work is a prominent example of the control exerted by
companies on their internal labor market. The difference between part-
and full-time workers is particularly blatant in Japan, where the "three
pillars" of the Japanese system—seniority system, lifetime employment,
and company union membership—are limited to regular workers. Part-
timers, therefore, are the first to feel the effects of an economic downturn: in the oil shock of 1973, for example, they were the proverbial "first
fired" (Nakamura 1981: 171; cited in Kondo 1990: 275). In general, however, the part-time labor market has increased remarkably in Japan since
the end of World War II, particularly with the increased entry of unmarried, as well as married, women into the paid labor force, usually as
part-time workers, and usually in the retail and service sectors (Lo 1990;
Kondo 1990). For the employer, part-time labor offers savings in wages,
a solution to labor shortages (of permanent workers), and flexibility in
responding to fluctuations in the pace of work and in demand for a
product or service. For the worker, the opportunity to work on a part-
time basis usually accommodates the need to earn supplemental income
while honoring a primary loyalty elsewhere (family, school). Employers,
in turn, generally point to these attitudes as a justification for keeping
part-time workers in low-paying jobs with little hope for promotion. (I
will return to this category of workers in my discussion of office ladies as
a distinct market segment of Disney customers.)

The everyday life of the 12,390 cast members is beyond the scope of this (or any) study. The daily work of a *junshain* depends, for example, on his or her specific job in a specific division and a specific attraction, shop, or restaurant. With some 30 job categories, 39 restaurants, 39 rides, and 59 shops (TDL 1995), the selection is simply too varied. My focus on general practices such as hiring and training allows me to provide the ethnography with a descriptive framework. Following the presentation of hiring, training, and socialization practices at TDL, I compare my findings with the organizational culture of DL and WDW, and then with that of Kōrakuen, a conventional Japanese amusement park. I conclude with a discussion and an ideological critique of organizational constructs such as "manual society," the "smile factory," and Taylorism.

Part-time Employees

Although all part-time workers are paid by the hour, they can be divided into several subcategories. "Regular" (as opposed to seasonal) part-timers are hired on a six-month renewable contract. There are various contracts for regular part-timers, depending on the number of days and hours worked. These workers are called "casual regular" or "permanent temporary" in WDW terminology (Kuenz 1995: 118). Next, and lower in rank, are the seasonal part-timers, called CTs (casual temporaries) at WDW (Kraus & Curtis 1986: 151). These are hired for the busy periods, particularly the summer, on a non-renewable contract basis. As of October 1993, Disney's job-application packet listed the starting wage for most entry-level jobs as $5.95 an hour (Kuenz 1995: 136). In TDL, the wage is about 1,000 yen (about $10) an hour, a little higher than the average wage for part-time workers in Japan. The actual wage depends on the job as well as on the shift. (See below for a list of jobs and their wages.)

Disney part-timers can work on stage or backstage and are assigned to a specific division and placed in a specific attraction, restaurant, or shop. (See the following section for OLC's organizational structure.) All part-timers, however, must proceed from a job interview to "basic training" in the Tokyo Disneyland University, which is followed by a division training as well as on-the-job training (OJT). The whole process is summarized in an eight-step scheme that appears in TDL's training guide under the English title "Fantasy Come True" (the original scheme cannot be replicated here for copyright reasons): (1) employment ad, (2) telephone call, (3) job interview, (4) hiring notification, (5) Tokyo Disneyland orientation, (6) welcome and division training, (7) OJT, and (8) I'm a cast member. In the following I describe this path, beginning with the employment ad.

OLC conducts massive hiring of part-timers around February, before the beginning of the Japanese fiscal year. Hiring for the summer months is done around May. There are two additional hiring periods in winter and fall. Before the hiring begins, help wanted ads from TDL's "Casting Center" are put in busy subway lines (such as the Marunouchi line) and in trendy magazines. One such ad appeared on January 29, 1996, in the semimonthly magazine *an-an*, a young women's (age 18–25) magazine with a circulation of 650,000 (Kinsella 1995: 253), whose intention is "linking ready-made cute fashions with the youth market" (Ueno 1987: 136; cited in Skov & Moeran 1995: 60). The ad's opening line declares, in pink letters, that "every day is meeting and discovery." Below this title, various cast members in Disney costumes stand among large cubes whose surfaces are inscribed "Sun," "Mon," "Wed," and so on. The message is that every day in TDL you can meet different people and enjoy different experiences. (In reality, workers have very little contact with anyone in the park outside those with whom they work, and transfer of workers among divisions is strictly forbidden.) In the ad, all workers are portrayed as part of the "TDL family." The blurb to the right of the picture optimistically says, "In this coming spring, who are you going to meet and what will you discover? It's time to hire the new cast members of TDL, and it's your turn." Below the picture, another title (in red letters) asserts: "Tokyo Disneyland begins hiring new cast members." The Disney word "cast" appears in *katakana* (pronounced *kasuto*). Floating above it are smaller *katakana* that read *arubaito*. Borrowed from the German word for "work" (*arbeit*), *arubaito* has been completely domesticated in Japanese. It means "part-time work" and therefore appears as an interpretive aid to the foreign Disney word *kasuto*. When I asked a former TDL cast member about his reaction to the word "cast," he told me, "Actually, I didn't know what it meant, but I could understand it because the ad had drawings of all the jobs, and the context was clear enough." In smaller print below the ad's red title, the job openings are described: "type 1" (five work days per week, including Saturdays and Sundays during spring vacation—May 16 to April 1—and Golden Week) and "type 2" (seven work days per week; another type, for week-end work only, designed for students, was not mentioned here). It is specified that contracts are for six months and that males or females from 18 to 40 years old are eligible. OLC will also pay up to 50,000 yen a month for transportation (between the worker's home and the park). In the bottom left corner appears a table of wages according to jobs and type of shift (TDL divides the day into two shifts: 9:00 A.M.–7:00 P.M., or 7:00 P.M.–9:00 A.M.). Jobs in attractions, merchandise, food service, and costumes divisions pay 900 yen per hour; security, 930; parking, 950; cooking, cleaning, and merchandising in the park hotels (called Disney Fantasy), 1,000; dishwashing and driving, 1,050. A registered nurse can earn 1,300 yen an hour. For work between 7:00 and 9:00 A.M. or 7:00 and 10:00 P.M., the wage increases by 200 yen per hour; and for work between 10:00 P.M. and 7:00 A.M. by 225 yen. TDL's employment ad, like its self-advertising in general, conveys a sense of singularity. I will illustrate this by comparing TDL's ad to a similar employment ad published by Kōrakuen in the same year (see Fig. 2).

Whereas TDL published a full-page color ad in a trendy magazine, Kōrakuen limited itself to a small black-and-white ad in a daily newspaper. TDL's ad boasts cast members wearing costumes of the familiar Disney characters. Kōrakuen has a manga-like, simple drawing of kids having fun in the park. In Kōrakuen's ad there are no creative teasers, only a title announcing that "new staff" is wanted. "New staff" is written in katakana (as nyūsutaffu), which illustrates the overall Americanization of the Japanese service industry (see below). Kōrakuen has two shifts, early (9:00 A.M.—5:00 P.M.) and late (1:00 P.M.—9:00 P.M.), and pays between 850 and 1,000 yen per hour according to shift and job category. The wages paid in TDL and Kōrakuen are therefore much the same.

The next step for prospective TDL workers is the job interview (mensetsu). OLC completely separates job interviews for part-timers from those for regulars. The former are conducted in Makuhari Messe in order to accommodate the enormous numbers of applicants, who for the most part are college students and housewives (no high school pupils are

Fig. 2 Kōrakuen employment ad

allowed). Makuhari Messe changes its name (in TDL lingo) during these days to TDL Casting Satellite (*Tōkyōdizuniirando kasutingu sateraito*). In an interview with me in 1996, Yasuko, a college student who worked for TDL during 1995, provided the following description of her *mensetsu*:

> "Last February I saw the ad in the train. . . . I called them up and asked for details. Then, I showed up for the interview. I had no idea what kind of a job I wanted to do. I went there with my girlfriend. We arrived at Makuhari Messe around 11:00. I had to wait for about six hours. Lots of people came. They said they'd interview me at 11: 15, but I still had to wait. What's worse, there was no way to go shopping, nothing, just waiting. They gave us some forms to fill out while we were waiting. Yes, and they showed us stupid Disney cartoons, it was no fun. Those forms were résumé questionnaires. It was stupid, because they also asked us to bring a

résumé with us to the interview. This paper asked me everything. Address, numbers, names of parents, what kind of job I want, and which hours. How long does it take to TDL from my place. They prefer people living in Chiba, of course. There was another girl there, who said it was her second interview. She was not accepted because her home was too far away: three hours ride one way.

"Then it was finally my turn. This guy was asking me, how come you want Disneyland? He asked me, why do you want to work here? I said, because I like it. I can't remember exactly. He said, how come you want to work for Attractions? Well, I said I like the kids and I want to take care of them. Another girl who was interviewed next to me knew everything about Disneyland, it was scary, she knew all the attractions by name, I cannot remember all the names. Then I asked him how many people came and how many they would take. He told me that I could expect to have a position and he was smiling and I was smiling and he said, 'That is a Disney smile!' (*Sore de dizunii sumairu desu ne*). . . . I remember that."

"Does Disney pay more?"

"They pay normally. An OL gets about 1,000 (yen per hour). But it doesn't matter, what matters is that you work for Disney. Everybody wants to work there."

"Why?"

"Because Disneyland is special."

"Even if you just sell snacks?"

"Yeah, you still have to be proud of yourself because you do it for Disney. Anyway, the interview was over after about five minutes. We wrote our name and address on a sticker. They said that their replies would arrive after about ten days on a postcard. My postcard was positive.[1] I was so happy! I called them up, and they told me I had been accepted for the Food Division."

Yasuko's description captures some of the problems of the job interview. Although most applicants yearn for jobs in the Attractions Division, most of them will end up in the Food, Merchandising, or Custodial divisions. Many of those with whom I spoke told me that they had accepted the job with the idea of requesting a transfer to Attractions after a while. "I thought it would be easier to get to Attractions if I already had some work experience in TDL" and "I was sure they had some system allowing for job transfer" were common accounts. However, OLC prohibits such transfers. If a worker wants to change his or her job, s/he must first quit and then reapply for a new job interview. None of this is told to the applicants. This was confirmed by an OLC manager, who said: "These people have their preferences, we have ours."

The next stage is orientation, which is divided into two parts: TDL orientation (one day) and the divisional orientation (the number of days depends on the division). On the first day of orientation (called *nyūsha*, the day of entering the company), would-be cast members swarm to the *honsha*, the OLC's main office (see Map 2). The first day takes about eight hours. It includes a survey of Disney history (mainly a film about Walt Disney as a creative risk taker), an introduction to the Disney philosophy (mainly the SCSE code: safety, courtesy, show, efficiency), a film on Disneyland, a lecture on the Disney Look, and practice of the Disney Smile. According to Yasuko, "They gave each one of us a mirror, and we just smiled. They didn't say anything. Only, 'Everybody make a Disney smile.'" The orientation also includes quizzes, described in the following section. The indoctrination of Disney typologies does not work perfectly. Many part-timers told me that the Disney philosophy is "the three S's: safety, smile, souvenirs." The most important thing in the first day of orientation is probably the paperwork, which includes arrangements for payment of wages and transportation reimbursement, signing of the contract, and issuance of security (ID pass) papers. The ID pass is inserted into an ATR (an identification scanner with a clock) whenever the worker enters and leaves the park. At the end of the first day, recruits receive a blue card bearing the title "Tokyo Disneyland Orientation." The printed card, which has each recruit's full name in handwriting, reads: "How was the orientation? We bet you understood the unique system of Tokyo Disneyland. This orientation was brought to you by the General Service Department." The card is signed by the "Disney University, Tokyo Disneyland" with a logo of Mickey Mouse in a graduation gown holding a diploma in his white gloves.

The next day the "divisional orientation" begins in the Training Center, a two-story building inside the park, with an interior not unlike that of a classroom (see Map 2). The Food Division orientation is the

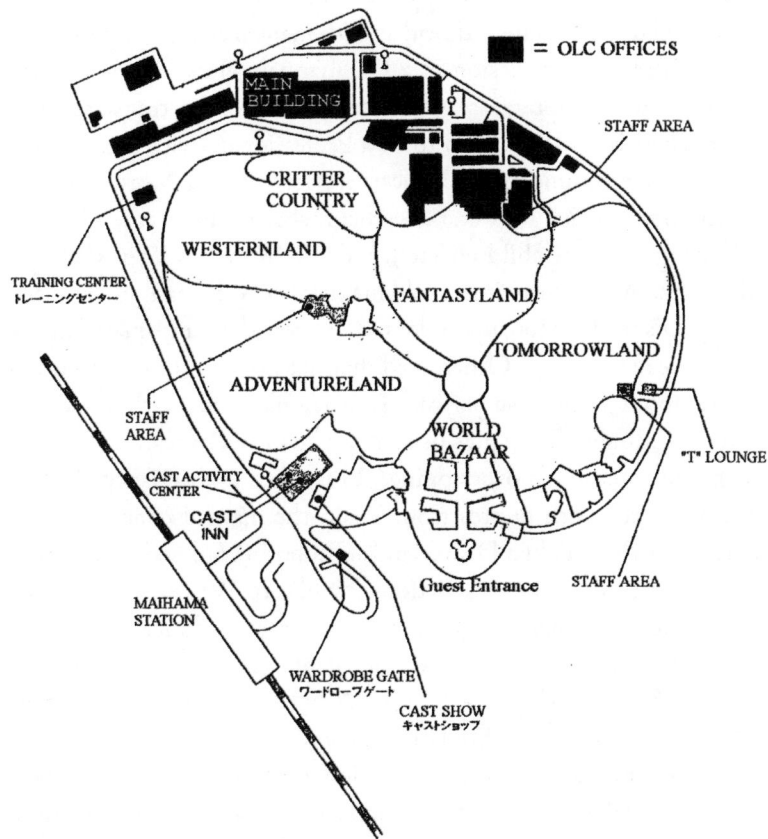

= OLC OFFICES

STAFF AREA

MAIN
BUILDING

CRITTER
COUNTRY

WESTERNLAND

TRAINING CENTER
トレーニングセンター

FANTASYLAND

TOMORROWLAND

ADVENTURELAND

STAFF
AREA

WORLD
BAZAAR

"T" LOUNGE

CAST ACTIVITY
CENTER

CAST
INN

MAIHAMA
STATION

Guest Entrance   STAFF AREA

WARDROBE GATE
ワードローブゲート

CAST SHOW
キャストショップ

Map 2   Backstage map of TDL and OLC buildings. Some of the names also
appear in Japanese, as illustrations of the domestication of DisneyTalk.

shortest: it does not require more than five–six hours. Orientation for
the Custodial and Merchandising divisions takes one to two days, and
Attractions require two to nine days (see also Tadokoro 1990: 78). Divisional orientation is done in a classroom and features oral teaching.
It is devoted to such basic matters as the location of one's workplace
and how to get there, the content of the job, special rules of the specific workplace, the system of wardrobes, costumes, lockers, and so on.
In addition, the OJT trainer is introduced, and relevant spiels are rehearsed. Also explicated are the rules of the Disney Look, a compli-

cated set of instructions on appearance management. The recruits are instructed to take home and read a TDL manual called "Tips on Magic." This is a translated version of a DL manual, whose table of contents includes such chapters as "Our Service" (with the translated motto 'Every guest is a VIP'), "How to Be a Professional" (with tips on onstage behavior, communication), "Guest Service," "For a More Wonderful Experience" (which tells cast members what to do in case of fire, lost belongings, missing children, etc.), and also "Facilities (*Shisetsu*) for Cast Members." Many part-timers told me that "nobody reads it, because our Leads (DisneyTalk for supervisors) . . . never ask us any questions about it, and we're too busy." Others said that "it's not exactly about work, but rather about *Dizunii no yarikata* (Disney-like behavior), so we don't bother reading it. They give us so many manuals to read, and so much of the information is overlapping." Illustrated with Disney characters and decorated with quotes from Walt, the manual concludes with a section entitled "Tokyo Disneyland's Taboos" ("Tōkyōdizuniirando no tabū"), which describes restrictions (similar to WDW's and DL's "taboos") such as incorrect behavior with visitors, defiance of the Disney Look, use of narcotics or intoxicants, gambling, dishonesty, and so on (see also Kraus & Curtis 1986: 134). According to the manual, "any of these things can get you fired on the spot."

Following the divisional orientation, new employees begin a period of OJT. Considered a hallmark of Japanese personnel training (Inohara 1990), OJT is the major form of "in-house education" in almost every Japanese company (Nakamura et al. 1994). The principle is that experienced employees teach the younger ones while actually working. In TDL, as in other companies, the OJT trainer is a *senpai-shain* (*shain* is short for *seishain*: a regular employee, and *senpai* literally means "the one who comes before," namely, a senior).[2] However, OLC also uses the DisneyWord "lead" (written in katakana as *rido*). "Lead" is the regular employee in charge of operations in every attraction, shop, or restaurant. The number of days required for OJT depends on the division. In the Food Division, OJT takes only three days. Recruits are required to wear their costume and name tag. The tag is printed with the last name in roman letters (in contrast, name tags at DL and WDW give the employee's first name). In OJT, the new recruit is already working in his or her intended job, a position decided by the Personnel Department. During OJT the hires receive a manual specific to their workplace. These manuals are less decorated and more to the point. Many cast members told me that they found these manuals to be the most helpful. In the Plaza Pavilion Restaurant manual, for example, the "spieler" (the cast member standing outside and introducing the restaurant; called *jōhō*, "information," in Japanese) is given the following instructions:

> Stand straight. You are the representative of Plaza Pavilion. Make a big smile. The smile is necessary. When you speak up, pretend that you are meeting somebody you love or haven't seen for a long time. Pay attention to eye contact. You should see the eyes of the guests you are addressing. Say the introduction of the restaurant clearly ("Hi. This is Plaza Pavilion Restaurant. This is a buffet-type restaurant. We have cold drinks, hot drinks, desserts. We have spaghetti, grilled beef.") Be friendly. Say: *Konnichi wa.* Be friendly to children. Say: *Kyō wa genki?* (Feeling good today?) If they are taking a picture, offer to help. Say: "Would you like me to take your picture?"

This routine is repeated for a shift of fifteen minutes. Upon completion of OJT, the hire is now ready to begin his or her career as a cast member.

Hiring and Training in TDL, Disney, and Kōrakuen

This section examines TDL's hiring and training procedures as yet another aspect of the Japanization of Disney. How were Disney management procedures—despite their standardization and ubiquity—modified in Japan; in what respects do TDL practices copy Disney, and in what ways are they similar to the Japanese workplace? The previous section describes the standard, global procedure; this section focuses on differences within the larger scheme.

The WDW Casting Center greets new hires with fifteen Disney characters that stand atop twelve pedestals (Heise 1994). Illustrations on the ceiling depict Peter Pan and Tinkerbell flying across the sky. There are no such decorations in TDL's Casting Satellite (Makuhari Messe) and not a trace of pixie dust in TDL's Training Center. The structure of the job interview is also different. Every applicant for an hourly job at WDW is given a preliminary eight-to-ten minute interview (Blocklyn

1988). This preliminary interview is meant to make sure that the applicant understands the requirements of the job, such as hours, shifts, the Disney look, and the Disney way. An explanatory video has recently been substituted for the same purpose (Heise 1994). Mike McGuffey, a WDW casting supervisor, says that "the unusually strong corporate culture at Disney means that a career at the resort is not for everyone" (cited in Blocklyn 1988: 30). The introductory process therefore "saves face" (Heise 1994: 18).

This preliminary interview has no counterpart at TDL. OLC managers told me that Japanese part-timers are already accustomed to working during holidays and vacations as well as adhering to strict grooming standards; apparently there is no need to prepare them for this. The "strong culture" of Disney is perhaps not that out-of-the-ordinary in Japanese terms.

Grooming is an example of this. The universal Disney Look is based on an appearance-management manual for men and women that presents the requirements for Disney employees worldwide. (Photographs from the manual cannot, unfortunately, be replicated as they are intended for "internal use" only.) The Disney Look specifies that women's and men's hair is to be natural and clean, without dying or bleaching. Neither a mustache nor a beard is allowed. If a woman's hair is too long (below the shoulder line), she must pin it up. No hair ribbons are allowed. Women are allowed only "natural" makeup. For both men and women, nails must not be "longer than the finger as seen from the palm side." Nail polish is not allowed. Costumes must always be worn with a name tag. Socks, shoes, and shoelaces must be black. Women's shoe heels must not be higher than 5 cm or lower than 2.5 cm (ca. 1–2 inches). Accessories are never allowed for men; women may wear simple, plain earrings that are not longer than 2 cm. Watches are not allowed because "they carry germs." Wristwatches may be carried in the pocket. However, *shain* (regular workers) are allowed to wear a wristwatch.

This list might look somewhat uncompromising to Americans, but it held no surprises for the TDL employees I spoke with. Appearance management, or *midashinami*, is an integral part of the Japanese socialization and work environment. Kōrakuen has a *midashinami* section in its manuals similar to that in the TDL manual, although not as colorful and

graphically enhanced. The text instructs the reader to "wear your uniform correctly and keep yourself neat on the way to work. . . . As the
proverb says: 'Fine feathers make a fine bird.'" The Kōrakuen manual
stipulates that men's hair is to be kept clean and short. It must not cover
the ears or the shirt collar. *Pāma* (permanent wave) hair "like that worn
by the *yakuza*" is not allowed. Women's hair must be kept short: "arrange
your hair so it doesn't cover your eyes when you bow." Men's and
women's fingernails must be kept short, although women may use a
transparent or light-pink nail polish. Socks can be black, brown, navy,
gray, or white, as long as they are the same color as the shoes and pants.
Women may wear flesh-tone stockings and white shoes in summer.
Although this list seems slightly less rigid than the Disney Look, it is
meant for regular office workers rather than cast members. Similar instructions appear in any Japanese office manual describing the *shokuba no
manā to rūru*, manners and rules of the office (see, for example, the similarly titled popular videotape by the Japanese Management Center
[JMAM 1992] or the popular OL manual published by Yuki shobō in
1990).

Manuals of appearance management are not limited to the workplace in Japan. They appear as early as elementary school. Each school
may establish its own regulations. Many schools provide their pupils
with manuals called *seito techō* (students' pocketbook), containing such
items as the school song, a short history of the school, rules of behavior,
and *midashinami*. A typical appearance-management section includes the
following instructions (see White 1993: 223–26 for similar regulations).
No artificial changes like a permanent wave and dying or bleaching hair
are allowed. Hair must be uniformly cut, and a boy's hair should not
touch the eyebrows, the ears, or the top of the collar. Some schools require those whose hair is naturally curly to inform the school of that fact
and carry a proper certificate attesting to that fact issued by the school.
All schools prohibit makeup: foundation, lipstick, eye shadow, mascara,
eye tape, false eyelashes, and perfume. Some prohibit the use of accessories; others allow a hair ribbon provided that it is black, dark blue, or
brown, and its width is less than 2.5 cm. Pupils must come to school
wearing their uniforms. Socks and shoes must be black. Nails must be
short and without nail polish. When I asked TDL part-timers whose

midashinami were more strict (*motto kibishii*): TDL's, that of other work-places, or their school's, the general reply was that "TDL is not particularly strict." As far as Japanese manuals go, the Disney Look is not the exception, but the rule. The view that the Japanese are generally more willing to accept a strong organizational culture like Disney's is confirmed by the news of labor problems at Disneyland Paris. The standard Disney training and management procedures, which worked so well in Japan, apparently antagonized many French part-timers.[3]

Further differences between practices at TDL and those found elsewhere in the Disney organization are apparent in the job interview. At WDW, those applicants who can accept the conditions of employment are given a 45-minute interview (Blocklyn 1988: 30). A high premium is placed on the applicant's personality. The interviewer often relies on his or her "gut reaction" to an applicant. Hiring decisions are usually made on the spot. Although interviewing at WDW takes much longer, it shares TDL's "hiring on first sight" policy. This seems to be the common hiring strategy of the service industry, which is the largest job market for part-timers (with the highest turnover rate). In the worlds of Disney, however, hiring takes a special emphasis. According to a WDW director of employee relations, "we are looking for types of people rather than skills. We do not think of 'hiring for the job' but rather of 'casting for a role'" (cited in Haden-Guest 1972: 230). An important part of the desired profile, at DL, WDW, and TDL, is appearance. Haden-Guest (1972: 230) observed that "employees are chosen to Disney specifications, which is to say that they are young, outgoing and personable ('personable' means good-looking)."

Van Maanen (in Van Maanen & Kunda 1989: 58–59) similarly claims that "each successful applicant must conform to certain highly particularistic standards of appearance. Complexion, height and weight, straightness and color of teeth, or disfigurement of any sort are all grounds for flunking the Disneyland body test." This same criteria are evidently in place at TDL, where cast members are surprisingly tall, well-shaped, and acne-free. In the past, "race, sex, nationality, age and accent operated openly as a basis for staffing in DL. . . . Such matters are no longer open, although to a large degree they still operate" (Van Maanen & Kunda 1989: 59). A similar attitude was reported to me by a TDL cast interviewer:

I never thought about this question of race or nationality, because the kids who come here are all Japanese. . . . But I'm sure that a Korean, even if he has a Japanese citizenship and lives in the area, would not be a likely candidate for hiring. No doubt he will have the same problem in many other workplaces, especially in frontline service. But for us this is particularly important. Since we hire such a relatively homogenous population, all Japanese, Tokyo accent, etc., another Asian type will stand out and interfere with the show.

Takashi Shimamura, senior hiring supervisor at Kōrakuen's Arubaito Sentā (part-time work center), gave me a similar account of his work in an interview in 1996.

> Takashi: The first impression is the most important.
> Raz: What is first impression?
> T: Appearance. They have to be good-looking, of course. Personality. And smile. In addition, the atmosphere. Friendliness.
> R: But how do you know if a person is "really" friendly or just faking it?
> T: According to his reactions.
> R: Do you have a script for testing this?
> T: Yes, but it is not important. I just ask the person general questions. In my final decision, I take into account also his university, and his family background.
> R: Do you have specific "friendliness questions"?
> T: Yes. For example, what did you do last weekend? I want to hear about his leisure activities. I ask him, what did you do on Sunday?
> R: What would be a good answer?
> T: It doesn't matter. I'm waiting to hear how he expresses himself, if it's an interesting story, told in a friendly manner.
> R: Did you get any special psychological training for this job?
> T: No training. Just OJT (laughing).

This exchange conveys a similar message to that reported by OLC interviewers as well as by Duncan Dickson, director of casting in WDW: "We're looking for personality, not cognitive ability. Only applicants seeking a job that involves handling cash take a simple math test. We can train for skills" (cited in Henkoff 1994: 108).

There are also differences in the preliminary training of the new hire. Orientation at WDW's Disney University consists of two (rather than

one) day-long "traditions" courses followed by one to fourteen days of
OJT (Blocklyn 1988: 32; three days to three weeks according to Heise
1994). The first day of the traditions courses, often referred to as "Traditions 1," gives the cast member an overview of the history, achievements,
and philosophy of WDW. This is followed by a tour of the Disney
property. The second day of classes includes an introduction to Disney
policies and procedures, a summary of the benefits available to the cast,
and an orientation to the cast member's new work area. TDL's orientation is different, with less emphasis on traditions and more on the divisional orientation. There is, however, another interesting difference.
During the Traditions 1 and 2 classes, the new WDW cast members are
asked to work on a quiz answering questions about the company's history and future goals.

> After receiving their instructions, the instructor leaves the room. As they
> begin working, someone realizes that an answer is on the wall, they let
> someone else at their table know the answer. Then someone at the next ta-
> ble hears it and shares the answer. They soon realize that they are not in
> competition with each other, but they are actually working all together.
> Teamwork is the key. (Heise 1994: 19)

The teamwork quiz is missing from TDL's orientation. No TDL cast
member whom I interviewed could recall it, and in fact every one of them
thought it was a strange idea. A manager in OLC Personnel Department
(Jinji-sei-ka) confirmed that OLC had scrapped that quiz. "You see," he
explained, "we Japanese don't need such a quiz. For us it's childish. We
are already used to teamwork. We have been used to teamwork ever
since elementary school, no, kindergarten." (See Part III of this book for
a more detailed discussion of teamwork socialization in the context of
the group activities [han-katsudō] of school pupils during their school
excursion to TDL.)

To be sure, TDL's orientation has its own share of childish quizzes.
The style and vocabulary of one such quiz, handed out during orientation as part of the manual "Tips on Magic," are typically American. The
first question of that quiz is: "1. We TDL cast members provide _____
to all the guests." Answers are: "a. Service (sābisu); b. Happiness (hapinesu); c. Disney goods (dizuniiguzzu)." The correct answer, I was told by

a former cast member, is "happiness" (I incorrectly guessed "service"). Note that all three answers in the Japanese text are American words written in *katakana*. The next question reads: "2. Tokyo Disneyland is like a _____ under the big blue sky." The answers are: "a. amusement park (*yūenchi*); b. leisure land (*rejārando*); c. stage (*sutēji*)." The correct answer is "stage." According to Miyo, a cast member, "nobody circles *yūenchi*, because it's obvious that an original Japanese word is not the correct answer. It must be something in *katakana*." The remaining questions are purely technical, such as 'which words does SCSE stand for' and questions on information found in the "Tips on Magic" manual.

To sum up, TDL's *nyūshabi* (first-day orientation / the day of entering the company) is a slimmer version of the two-day WDW traditions courses. OLC managers removed what they thought was "unnecessary training" for Japanese personnel, such as the teamwork quiz and what one described to me as "too much fussing about what the Americans call 'getting an emotional buy-in to the Disney culture.'" The same "we Japanese don't need it" approach was apparently also behind the classroom look of TDL's Training Center (in contrast to WDW's extensive use of pixie dust, DisneyTalk for stylish decor featuring Disney icons). Instead, OLC introduces divisional orientation on the second day. In WDW, "divisional orientation begins [on the third day] through the field Human Resource Development offices" (Heise 1994: 19). Incidentally, in DL, WDW, and TDL, casting interviewers (job interviewers) and orientation instructors (traditions assistants) are cast members selected, trained, and pulled out of work for one or two days a month for that purpose. The reason behind it, which apparently works well in all Disney's worlds, is that "these are the people who know what it is like to work in 90 degree heat and 90 percent humidity. . . . [In the job interview] they can identify people like themselves to work for the Company . . . and can tell them what it is really like out there" (Heise 1994: 19).

How does the training at TDL compare with that at Kōrakuen? Tokyo Dome (ToDo, for short) Corporation was founded in 1936 as Kōrakuen Company, Ltd., for the purpose of constructing and operating Japan's first baseball stadium (ToDo 1995: 1). In the early 1950s, Kōrakuen amusement park—Japan's first urban amusement park—was built near the stadium. The company is one of Japan's pioneers in the field of leisure and a typical representative of that tradition (Yoshimitsu 1970). In 1988 the baseball stadium was rebuilt and rechristened Tokyo Dome, Japan's first all-weather stadium. Known as the "Big EGG" (for "big entertainment and golden games"), Tokyo Dome hosts events ranging from concerts and exhibitions to baseball and other sporting games. In 1995 Tokyo Dome had 1,200 regular employees and about 5,000 part-timers. Big EGG has about ten million visitors per year. Kōrakuen stages live shows on Japanese popular themes, including the Goreinjā (Japan's Power Rangers) and the popular manga characters for girls, Seramūn (Sailor Moon).

In Kōrakuen (following the usage of its employees, I use the old name of the Tokyo Dome Corporation), hiring of part-timers is done in the Arubaito Sentā located at the bottom-right corner of "Big EGG City" near the parking lots (see Map 3). As in TDL, job applicants prefer to work in attractions. According to Otsubo Ryuta, formerly a trainer in Kōrakuen, "Sometimes we give some incentives for working in food or merchandising, depending on the season." As in TDL, ToDo prohibits interdivision job transfers, a policy that is not revealed to applicants. Applicants are contacted by telephone about two weeks after the interview. Not unlike TDL's first-day orientation at the Disney University, Kōrakuen recruits pass through about two hours of "entrance training" at the Arubaito Sentā. The orientation conducted in the Arubaito Sentā, as well as the following OJT, is controlled by the division in which they will work. The Arubaito Sentā is equipped with various orientation videos, notably "Dream World," an introduction for part-timers produced in 1990; and "Smile on You" (1989), the part-timers' orientation to the amusement park, sales, and restaurants. There are also three shorter videos on behavior (1992, 1993). These videos are shown to employees at the request of the division. Otsubo Ryuta wrote the manuals for part-timers and directed these videos. According to Otsubo,

> ToDo inculcates the same service culture as TDL although we don't have their process. We have manuals, we have *midashinami*, we have spiels. TDL say they train for "communication," but they just train to spiel. We have the same spiel for greeting (*aisatsu*). TDL has a so-called Disney University. Our Arubaito Sentā is obviously not a "university," just a place where hiring is done. But you know of course that the Disney University is not

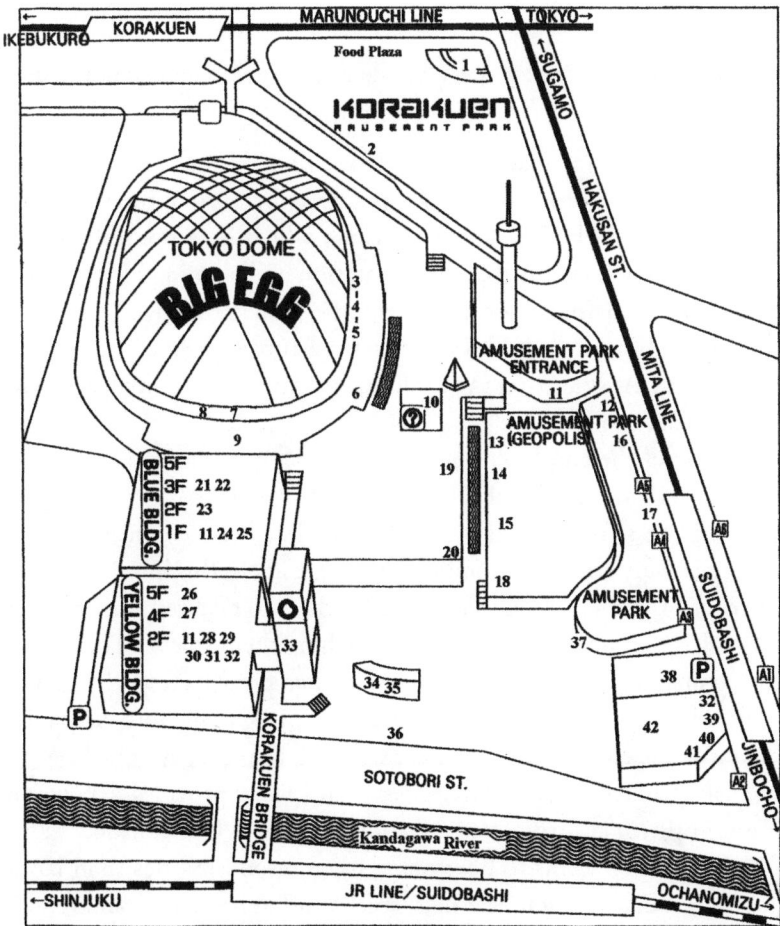

Map 3 Big EGG City guide map

1. Open-air theater (for live shows)
2. Dream Factory (character goods)
3. TO:DO (baseball goods specialty shop)
4. Baseball Hall of Fame
5. Humpty's Garden (hamburgers)
6. Tokyo Dome ticket booth
7. Hanamichi (Japanese shabu-shabu restaurant)
8. Mr. Pao (Chinese noodles)
9. Japanese restaurant (noodle, rice dishes, and yakitori)
10. Tokyo Dome advance ticket sales booth
11. Electronic game arcade
12. Little Mermaid (bakery)
13. Tokyo Treasure Island (variety goods)
14. Personal Point (animation characters)
15. Baseball Café (American restaurant)
16. Winners (diner)
17. Kōrakuen Sports Club
18. Category-1 (Japanese League official shop)
19. Prism (flowers and variety store)
20. Festa café (coffeehouse)
21. Sauna
22. Barbershop
23. Hanten (Chinese restaurant)
24. Fan Spot (baseball goods)
25. Vicky's (diner)
26. Bowling alley
27. Roller skating rink
28. Yamashita bookstore
29. Aoi (Japanese noodle restaurant)
30. Hot Dog Inn
31. Humpty's (hamburgers)
32. Cash dispenser
33. Paddock (food court)
34. Lottery booth
35. Curry House
36. Keyaki Garden (beer garden)
37. Kōrakuen Swimming School
38. Golf driving range
39. Mister Donuts
40. Travel agency
41. Kentucky Fried Chicken
42. Kōrakuen Arubaito Sentā (part-time employment and training center)

an actual place, but a process. We don't make such a fuss about this process.

Many ToDo managers have told me that the idea of a "Kōrakuen University" did come up, but was put away because of interdivisional disagreements. The Personnel Division, which is responsible for the Arubaito Sentā, claims that all orientation and training must be controlled by the divisions, because it requires "local knowledge." According to Takashi Shimamura, who works in the Arubaito Sentā, "the divisions may use the Arubaito Sentā's facilities and bring their employees to see the videos, of course."

Most of the employees in the ToDo Service System Department (Sābisu-sei-ka) agreed that TDL is more strict (kibishii), but argued that this strictness is superficial: "In TDL the line between backstage and onstage is very strict. In Kōrakuen we speak about this line, but it's not so strict." Instead, "we empower our workers to take responsibility for difficult situations, rather than just teaching them spiels." To sum up, the comparison between TDL and Kōrakuen presents underlying similarities as well as blatant differences. TDL has a far more elaborated organizational discourse, which was imported from Disney. The language of casting, onstage-backstage, guests, and leads provides a powerful framework for a strong organizational culture. In addition, TDL's Casting Center seems to have many more responsibilities than Kōrakuen's Arubaito Sentā. Manuals, spiels, and appearance management characterize both companies, although TDL invests more money in and pays more attention to these matters. To be sure, these elements characterize the Japanese service sector in general (Sano 1995). Almost all companies have nearly identical lists of standard phrases ("spiels" or kimarimonku), including formal greetings, bowing protocols, and apologies, that their employees must perform flawlessly. All companies give their non-regular employees some training on the history of the company, its current operations, and, most important, its manners and customer-service expectations. For example, even the part-time employees of Morinaga's Love restaurant chain receive 15 to 24 hours of training before they begin interfacing with customers in their roles as cashiers, cooks, and custodians (Sano 1995: 44). Unlike TDL, Kōrakuen, however, does not have a clear recipe for blending everything together and feeding it to the employees. Perhaps as a partial result, Kōrakuen has experienced discipline and service problems (see Chapter 4).

Regular Employees

Although the hiring, orientation, and training of part-timers largely follow the Disney prototype, these procedures are completely different for regular employees. In the words of OLC managers, "the world of part-timers is the world of America; the world of regular employees is the world of Japan." Although this statement is generally true, it is not the whole truth; there are instances in which this relation is reversed. I begin with the rule, and then proceed to its exceptions.

OLC hires its regular employees (*shain*) in April, in accordance with the Japanese hiring system. Graduation ceremonies are conducted in late March and April, and new graduates begin working in April. A key factor in hiring is the university from which the applicant has graduated. There is a "generally recognized hierarchy of high schools and universities" (*Japanese Corporate Decision Making* 1982: 10). According to Satō Akira, head of OLC Personnel Department (Jinjisei *kachō*), "OLC looks for graduates of four-year colleges like Sophia and Waseda, as well as state-run universities." Sophia and Waseda are not top-ranked universities like Keiō or Tōdai (Tokyo University), for example. They are considered "second-rank schools," and the implication of the OLC manager's remarks is that his company cannot compete with bigger firms for the best graduates.

Interviews for regular employment are conducted by the OLC in its *honkan* (main building) rather than in Makuhari Messe or the Casting Center (see Fig. 3). According to Satō, until recently Mitsui and Keisei sent their own *shain* to work in OLC. "Now we do all our hiring in-house," he said. "Mitsui stopped sending *shain* two years ago, and Keisei three–four years ago. You see, we're a young company." There is a major difference between job interviewing for regular employment in the United States and in Japan. In America, the applicant's background and professional experience are taken into account; in addition, recruiting is usually for a particular job opening. In Japan, the only background that

Fig. 3 OLC's *honkan* (main building)

matters is one's university; one's major is usually irrelevant. Previous professional experience is also irrelevant in *shinsotsu saiyō* (hiring new graduates), which is "the normal interpretation of the term 'hiring' in Japan" (Karthaüs-Tanaka 1995: 39). Applicants are not recruited for a particular job but into the company. To borrow the terminology used by Mitsui, post-graduates are "hired as 'raw material' to be trained and molded to suit the needs of the company" (Tung 1984: 30). These are expressions of an organizational culture apparently stronger than Disney's wildest dreams.

In the first years of OLC, American human resource managers sent by Disney to help the young company "stand on its feet" also participated in the process of hiring regular employees. Douglas Lipp, one of these trainers who later quit Disney, recently published a book describing his inside views entitled *The Truth About Tokyo Disneyland's Great Success* (Lipp 1994). The book was translated into Japanese from Lipp's English manuscript. Some of the breaches in cultural communication caused by the Japanese way of *shinsotsu saiyō* are described in the following account taken from Lipp's book (1994: 130–31). It begins by quoting fragments from a job interview in which the interviewer is an American trainer.

> "What did you study in your university?"
> "Economics."
> "What would you like to do in our company?"
> "Anything will be fine."
> "Isn't there any field which you are especially good at? What is the benefit for us hiring you?"
> "I don't know about it very well, but I've been thinking that I would like to do a job like this."
> "Then, 5 years from now, what would you like to be doing?"
> "Well, I am ready to do anything that the company wants me to do."
> (We then asked him what was his interest in Disney).
> "I've loved Disney since my childhood. Also, it is a big company in the US and famous in Japan, too."

Lipp continues:

> After every interview the American staff would have an evaluation meeting. We agreed that the person was not suitable. He did not have his own will, he was lacking self-promotion. "To begin with" we told OLC people, "he doesn't have any motivation to work for Tokyo Disneyland."
>
> One of my (American) colleagues was particularly disappointed about the passive approach of the applicant. In his opinion, this applicant was too unconcerned about his job. The American side therefore agreed that the person seemed to be unsuitable. Then, however, the Japanese personnel manager in charge said: "No. He is excellent. I think he will be able to adjust himself very well to the company. Definitely we should hire him. His school background is not bad, and we have received a recommendation from a professor at his university." We [the Americans] were simply astonished.

For the new *shain* hires, orientation (referred to in Japanese organizational parlance as "off-the-job training") takes 40 days. According to Satō Akira, "This is the Japanese way. They are taught company manners, history, office rules, and so on. Not just Disney stuff, but a lot of Japanese know-how. They learn how to be adult members of society (*shakaijin*)." Such assertions are common in Japan, where "the company as family" is a long-standing and all-embracing metaphor. According to Sano Yoko (1995: 43), "When a new employee joins a firm in Japan, s/he steps out of childhood and into adulthood. . . . Leaving their biological families to join their corporate family." Thomas Rohlen (1974: 37) describes how new hires at a bank are greeted by the president as *shakaijin*, meaning that "they now have heavy responsibilities to serve the society and thus to repay it and their parents for the nurture and sacrifice of raising them from infancy." The new "family" has a new organizational language and office manners. OLC's newly hired *shain* are *keiyaku-shain*, hired on one-year-contract basis (*keiyaku* means contract). In 1989, there were 600 *keiyaku-shain* compared to 2,200 *shain* in OLC's workforce (Komuya 1989: 152). *Keiyaku-shain* receive a low monthly salary of about 140,000 yen (approximately $1,400). According to Takahashi Shimamura, a *junshain* who works a lot of hours will easily earn more than a *keiyaku-shain*. After one year, those *keiyaku-shain* who have performed well take a test and are then eligible for permanent employment. The test has "very easy questions," mainly on business manners. After passing the test, the *shain*'s salary increases to about 250,000 yen (approximately $2,500). The new *shain* have to work backstage and onstage for three years before they can be promoted. As *keiyaku-shain*, they have to master all the regular Disney manuals (which are also given to part-time cast members) in addition to the Disney Trainer Manual and OLC manuals.

A typical OLC manual is called "The Office and You" ("Ofisu to anata"). Although the familiar logo of the Disney University appears on the bottom-left corner of its cover, the manual contains no other cheerful Disney illustrations. The only exception is a picture of Jiminy Cricket looking at the table of contents. The presence of this well-known "voice of conscience" is also a reminder of the normalizing discourse inscribed in the manual. It is much longer (about 40 pages) than the *junshain* manuals, and much of its contents do not appear in the guides for part-timers. Among the chapters are "Office Rules," "Manners of the Company Person," "How to Talk and Listen," "How to Answer the Phone," and "How to Serve Tea." The last two chapters are evidently aimed at OLs. If the manuals intended for Disney cast members seem full of indoctrination, this manual easily surpasses them. The section about *kōshō*, or proper conversation in the office, for example, discusses the rules for using honorific suffixes (*san, sama*) and rank titles (*kachō, buchō*). Interestingly, the manual shows some American influence. "If you are at the office with your colleagues," it says, "just call their names, without *san* or even title. This is Walt Disney's way" (p. 6). However, "when answering the phone, talking to strangers, or in public, always refer to your colleagues with *san* and rank title" (p. 6). There are further sections on how to bow, open and close the door, sit down, give (and receive) a business card, talk to people, introduce and be introduced, and so on. The section on bowing is representative of the rest of the manual.

> How to Bow
> They say that it takes three seconds to decide if you can trust the person in front of you. So it makes things better if on meeting people you know how to bow.
>   1. Get close to the other person. Stand up straight. Bow no matter what *aisatsu* (greeting) you use.
>   2. The angle should be about 45 degrees.
>   3. Bow lower than the other person(s). Rise from bowing only after they have done so.
>   4. Your hands should remain flanked to your body in a natural way. When bowing, the top of your fingers should reach the height of your knee.
>   5. Look at the floor ahead of you.
>   6. Rising is done in a slower speed than descending.

Japanese office life is filled with such traditional protocols, or *yarikata* (literally, "the way to do things").[4] Some of the traditional protocols contain interesting cultural idiosyncrasies. The protocol on "how to open a door," for example, advises employees to "knock three times (twice is for beggars—*monogoi*)" (p. 7). This rule was known to all the OLs with whom I spoke, although none knew how to explain it. Takigawa Yoshito, formerly a trainer in Nippon Steel, told me that it is based on a traditional saying: "If you knock once, the person inside doesn't notice you; if you knock three times, he will be annoyed. Therefore beggars knock twice." Another section in the manual is titled "A Study About Words" ("Kotoba ni tsuite no kenkyū"). After a table of pronunciation for practicing clear diction, the section discusses the grammatical rules

for polite speech (*keigo*). Like the rest of the manual's contents, this subject is a mandatory one for all company employees in Japan. *Keigo* is a
linguistic code of social relations. Different suffixes and verbs are used to
express different social relations—from the intimate to the respectful.
The manual describes the three basic categories of *keigo*—how to speak
"to your friend," "to a person you respect," and "on special occasions." For
example, *denwa o kakeru* (to telephone), used when speaking to a friend
becomes *odenwa o kakemasu* when addressing a person you respect and
odenwa o okake itashimasu when addressing a superior. Many trainers I
interviewed regarded *keigo* as one of the hallmarks of company socialization. According to one OLC trainer, "*Keigo* is one of the things that a
shakaijin [company person / member of society] has to master. To be a
shakaijin means to understand the status system. A correct usage of *keigo*
is the ultimate proof that one has such understanding." One job dominated by *keigo* is that of a telephone operator. Certain companies—
ToDo among them—have consequently issued specific *keigo* manuals for
telephone operators. OLC's manual has a large section with detailed
protocols for answering the phone, complete with "spiels" for explaining,
for example, several ways to reach the OLC offices from Tokyo.

The manual concludes with a section on serving tea and sweets.
"This duty," according to many OLs with whom I spoke, "is one of the
most important things we do around the office." Served together, the
combination of tea (*ocha*) and sweets (*okashi*) is traditionally referred to
as *chaka*. "It was a long time ago that the Japanese began to serve *chaka* to
their guests," the section (p. 30) begins.

> And in the last 15 years or so, companies have adopted this tradition. Our
> visitors come from a distant place. Let's refresh them by serving *chaka*. You
> should serve it even if your boss doesn't tell you to. How to serve:
> 1. Serve the guest first
> 2. Serve the higher-ranking guest first
> 3. If you don't know who has the higher rank, first serve the person
> who sits farthest from the door.

Rule 3 is based on the traditional Japanese system of sitting by rank.
According to this system (described on p. 14 of the manual), the best seat
(i.e., that reserved for the highest-ranking guest) is the remotest from the

door. The other chairs are marked according to their order of proximity to the door(s).

4. When you finish serving the guests, serve the company employees.

5. Clean up after they leave (especially ashtrays).

6. If you serve coffee, get a coaster and put it under the cup when you serve it. The spoon should be on the right side. The cup's handle should be on the left.

7. When you put the cups on the table, first put them down and then move them 5 mm closer to the guests, as if implying "please drink." If the cup has a picture, make sure the guest can see it.

8. If you spill something, do not panic. Say "excuse me" in a calm voice. Change the cup.

9. Bow slightly when you are finished serving.

To sum up, the essence of OLC's *shain* socialization is Japanese. It follows the Japanese recruiting style, the lifetime employment ideal, the rituals of business etiquette, and the "company as community" policy. It has a rigid hierarchical structure, in which age and length of service explicitly determine promotion. This follows the Japanese *nenkō*, seniority system (Oda 1983). OLC also has on-the-job training for a variety of jobs as well as job rotation. In terms of management-union relationships, however, OLC does not follow the Japanese style.

Regular employees of big Japanese companies usually depend on their workplace union (*kigyōbetsu rōdō kumiai*, or just *kumiai* for short; otherwise called "enterprise-based union" or, somewhat pejoratively, "company union"), rather than a trade union, for in-house bargaining with top management. This is common reality in Japan, where 90 percent of the Japanese labor unions are enterprise-based unions (Karthaüs-Tanaka 1995: 82). As Harvey Leibenstein (1987: 211) points out, "since there is no special attachment by employees to a specific job (because of job rotation), trade unions associated with jobs would seem unsuitable to Japan."[5]

Part-timers are usually not entitled to membership in the workplace union. This is the privilege of regular employees. Leaders of the workplace union usually have two offices in their dual capacity as managers as well as union leaders. It is not rare to find a union president who, on his way up the promotion ladder, finally becomes company president. OLC has its own union called OFS—Oriental (Land) Friendship Society. However, nobody seems to take it seriously. When I asked OLC managers if OFS is their union, they said, "No, it's a little bit different." According to Tadokoro (1990: 125), "OFS is a puppet union." Kōrakuen managers say their colleagues in OLC "already get enough money, so they don't need to bargain." Perhaps, as Tadokoro (1990: 126) hopes, "OFS is a new type of labor union for the future."

What the union bargains for are wages and bonuses. Japanese employees generally receive their income in two parts: the normal wage and semiannual bonuses. Bonuses frequently amount to about 30 percent of the normal wage (Leibenstein 1987: 212). The bonus system is one of the "exotic" features of the Japanese labor markets that have long fascinated outsiders. It may also have important macro-economic implications. For example, Japan's remarkable ability to stabilize unemployment at low, steady rates is partially due to the "automatic pay flexibility that comes with revenue sharing" (Freeman 1989: 249). Normally, unions negotiate for the bonuses as well as for the regular salary. One of the most famous occasions for this is the annual April negotiations called shuntō (shun means spring, tō is war). The "spring offensive" (and to a lesser extent the November negotiations over the yearend bonus) is a serious event in company life (W. Gould 1984: 155). In Kōrakuen, for example, shuntō is a month-long ritual that includes a pre-negotiation phase, surreptitious research on other companies' bonus policy, the involvement of negotiators and go-betweens, bargaining, and finally contract signing. When asked to be more precise about the activities of OFS, an OLC manager told me that "it's not really a union because OFS is really very close to the top management. We do shuntō, but the bargaining is minimal. I think this is because we're a very young company."

At this point it should be tempting to compare OFS with Walt Disney's radical anti-unionist policy. Walt used the "family metaphor" to contest unionization. According to David Boje (1995: 1013), "Walt fired people according to his mood and paid low wages . . . but he sold himself as father to the 'boys'—his term for the male animators, storymen, and gag writers—and 'girls,' his term for the women doing the inking and repetitive drawing work." Mark Eliot (1993: xii, 265) describes how Walt Disney shattered the 1941 strike at the studio by telling stories about communist strike leaders to the House Un-American Activities Committee, and later systematically fired everyone who engaged in unionization (Boje 1995: 1006). Legend has it that the clowns who sing the song "We're Gonna Hit the Big Boss for a Raise" in *Dumbo* (1941) were "malicious caricatures of striking Disney Studio cartoonists" (Allen & Denning 1993: 89). Disney, like other studios, later resisted the union movement by forming company unions (the Disney Studio Federation) that were less politically active and less demanding of wage increases.

The Oriental Friendship Society is in a sense a direct offspring of the Disney Studio Federation. When I told OLC managers about this, they shook their heads in disbelief; the only Disney history they know is the "Disney version," from which such negative accounts have been excised. In the case of OLC, however, top management did not have to discipline its OFS by firing union activists. Incidentally, the automatic disqualification of part-timers and seasonal workers for union membership is common both in TDL and in WDW. In WDW, costumed characters are not allowed to join the actors' union because, according to Disney, they do not have speaking parts (Kuenz 1995: 238 [note]).

I next turn to the reception of the Disney Way among TDL workers, focusing on the part-timers who, while being intensively disciplined, are exempted from many of the privileges of regular employment.

CHAPTER 4

ORGANIZATIONAL CULTURE AND ORGANIZATIONAL CRITIQUE

The Disney Training Program is highly regarded among both Americans and Japanese. Disney repeatedly appears as one of the top five American service companies in many American surveys and industry magazines (Carey 1995; Castoro 1995; Peters & Waterman 1982). The thriving genre of publications on the "secrets of TDL" attests to a similar Japanese view. In Japan Disney is considered the model for service in the same way that McDonald's is the model for the fast-food industry. In a fascinating contrast to these management studies, sociologists have eagerly been discussing Disney as an indoctrination machine. This chapter elaborates on the dark side of Disney's personnel management as it reappears, complied with and contested, in TDL. I concentrate on the cultural meaning of the manual in the context of contemporary Japan and on emotion management in TDL.

Service Culture and the "Manual Society"

Sociological accounts of work in DL and WDW have focused on its social engineering. This concern reflects the sociological interest, developed in the 1980s, in the concept of organizational culture. The concept was first developed in ethnographic and symbolic-interactionist accounts of the workplace (Kanter 1977; Hochschild 1983; for a review, see Fine 1984; a more recent addition to this genre is Kunda 1994). It was then elaborated through the comparative study of organizations; for example, Japanese versus American (Ouchi & Wilkins 1985; Frost et al. 1985). A decade later, it featured in the titles of textbooks on organizational behavior (e.g., Martin 1992). It was John Van Maanen who, in a series of four innovative papers, made Disneyland into a case-study of organizational culture (Van Maanen 1989, 1991, 1992; Van Maanen & Kunda 1989). The significance of organizational culture at Disneyland was phrased by Van Maanen (in Van Maanen & Kunda 1989: 68) through a paradox: "Disneyland does not pay well, supervision is arbitrary and skin close, its working conditions are chaotic, its jobs require minimal amounts of intelligence or judgement, and it asks of its employees a kind of loyalty that is almost fanatical. Yet it attracts a particularly able workforce . . . (whose) adherence and support for the 'Disney Way' is remarkable."

Let us consider this paradox in the context of TDL. As mentioned above, TDL wages are normal for the service industry. Supervision is close and may be arbitrary. The *shain* in the nearby office may step into the kitchen or the shop at any time. Working conditions are tough, but not chaotic. Part-timers decide on the days they will work, and although hourly shifts are changed by the *shain*, there is some room for negotiation. The jobs require minimal intelligence or judgment—like many other jobs in the service sector. It is true, however, that TDL demands an almost fanatical loyalty from its employees. Cast members' "communication" with visitors is totally prescribed by the manual, and it is forbidden to talk about any OLC matter with an outsider. Yet it is also true that adherence to and support of the Disney Way are remarkable among TDL employees. For Van Maanen (1989), the explanation lies in the strong organizational culture, of which peer pressure and supervision play an important role. Socialization, emotion management, and inspection obviously prevail as much at TDL as they do at WDW and DL. This was demonstrated in the previous chapter. The TDL cast members whom I interviewed, however, felt no paradox in their situation. The typical explanation was "If I look around me, what are the alternatives?

I would be earning the same money working for a restaurant, a shop, or another park. Here, I work at Disneyland."

A common alternative, for example, would be working for McDonald's. Disney and McDonald's indeed have a lot in common: the Disney and Hamburger universities are acclaimed as training centers; both are renowned for the excellence of their service; and they share a deep concern with order and cleanliness, a target audience of middle-class families, and worldwide success. Indeed, some writers have drawn parallels between the Disney theme parks and McDonald's restaurants (King 1983; Bryman 1995: 122–25). Both organizations also lent their name to (relatively similar) sociological processes: Disneyfication and McDonaldization (Ritzer 1993). An OLC *keiyaku-shain* who had been hired by OLC's Food Division after working for four years part-time at McDonald's told me: "The hourly wages are about the same. McDonald's has tougher training, but the work is more boring. In Disney, it's more important to show that you are enjoying yourself. And you feel differently, not like selling hamburgers. You feel better because you're working in Disneyland."

I will argue that organizational culture should be considered, in the case of TDL, in the light of two broader "cultures": Japan's service culture and the popular culture of Disney in Japan. This chapter focuses on Japan's service culture; the culture of Disney in Japan is examined in Part III of this book.

MANUAL SOCIETY AND JAPANESE INDUSTRIAL RELATIONS

The Japanese workforce—regular employees and part-timers—certainly has an image of "willing workers" (Sengoku 1985). This image is usually backed up by statistics regarding the relative absence of strikes and their most visible marker—loss of working days (see Table 1). According to Kumazawa Makoto (1996: 6–7), "industrial harmony" (as marked by infrequent strikes) in Japan is often (and most convincingly) accounted for by Japanese-style management. Kumazawa argues that even though after 1975 Japan's economic growth rate fell sharply, the number of strikes kept dropping decisively. Although it is also true that Japanese

TABLE I

Working Days Lost Per Worker Due to Labor Disputes:
An International Comparison, 1967–91

1967–76	1978–87	1988–91
Italy 14.5	Italy 21.87	Italy —
Canada 7.4	Canada 5.21	Canada 1.31
Australia 5.7	UK 4.73	Australia 0.89
US 4.8	Australia 3.92	Sweden 0.50
UK 4.3	Sweden 1.53	UK 0.45
France 2.1	US 1.27	France 0.15
Japan 1.3	France 0.83	US 0.14
Sweden 0.4	West Germany 0.46	Netherlands 0.07
West Germany 0.3	Netherlands 0.18	Germany 0.02
Netherlands 0.3	Japan 0.14	Japan 0.01

NOTE: The figures were calculated by taking the total number of working days lost due to labor disputes in each of the periods concerned and dividing each of these totals by the total number of laborers employed in the final year of that period. SOURCE: International Labor Organization, *ILO Yearbook of Labor Statistics* (Geneva: ILO, 1977, 1988, and 1992). Taken from Kumazawa 1996: 5. Copyright © by WestviewPress. Reprinted by permission of WestviewPress.

law prohibits strikes by government workers and employees in public corporations, still it was unions in the private sector that took the lead in abandoning strikes as a weapon. Given all this, Kumazawa concludes, one must endorse the institutional explanation that attributes infrequent strikes to the predominance of "enterprise-based" (workplace) unions. This can be regarded as the conventional paradigm of Japan's industrial relations. Unions in Japan are indeed enterprise-based, and the value systems of management and union are hence extremely similar.

Since the 1970s, with Japan's "modernization" accomplished or recognized, this paradigm of Japanese-style management has also been nourished by a wave of writings on "'Japan, Inc.' and other portrayals of overly coordinated or orchestrated 'economic animals'" (Sugimoto and

Mouer 1981: 6). The image of Japan as "number one" (Vogel 1979), as an unprecedented economic success, has since flooded libraries with books aiming to reveal the social structure behind the "enigma of Japanese power" (van Wolferen 1989), the "samurai society" (Masatsugu 1982) behind the worker bees. "Japan as a classless society" was another powerful image that supported the notion of Japan, Inc. George DeVos (1973) maintained that class conflict has never appealed to the Japanese. The *Economist* (Mar. 3, 1973) went so far as to describe Japan as being "the most unMarxist society." The popularity in the United States of this view of Japanese society was part of the "model" image of "Japan" (Schodt 1994). Un-Marxist Japan proved the superiority of capitalism and the faults of the communist model.

As Kumazawa rightfully argues, the institutional explanation omits the particular consciousness of the human subjects who form the system of enterprise-based unions. One needs to look at the ways in which Japan, Inc. has recently been viewed and contested by its seemingly passive agents. In Japanese eyes, industrial relations are constructed along two different lines. First, industrial relations are split between public and private, image and reality, *tatemae* and *honne*. On the one hand is an acknowledgment of the economic significance of Japanese-style management and of an autonomous "worker society" that is culturally distinct from the individualistic pursuits of Western capitalism. On the other hand, there is a growing aversion in Japan today toward bureaucracy, corporatism, and the "straight-jacket society." The once-lauded workaholism of salarymen (*sarariiman*) is contrasted with the establishment in 1990 of a National Defense Council for the victims of death from overwork, *karōshi*. This double-bind notion is well illustrated in the book *Japan, Inc.* Although superficially taken by Western observers as devoted to the Japanese "economic miracle," Ishinomori's (1986) popular *manga* actually emphasizes Japan's economic problems and vulnerability and reflects a deep suspicion of politicians and bureaucrats.

The second split in the Japan, Inc. image is between regular workers and part-timers. The number of part-time workers has grown faster than that of full-time workers, and the majority of part-timers are women, particularly married women. According to the popular image, full-time workers are hardworking university graduates with the values of the "old generation," and part-timers are unconcerned housewives and irresponsible students with the lack of values characteristic of the "new generation," "the generation that awaits directions" (Sengoku 1985). This split is backed up by real facts. Regular workers usually have lifetime employment and can count on the seniority system (*nenkō*) and rely on the union. Part-timers cannot. Regulars are fully socialized into company life; part-timers are "cheap labor" trained to do a routine, semiskilled job. According to the common assertion, only *seishain*, not *junshain*, become *shakaijin* (society people; adults) by virtue of joining the company.[1] This last difference is illustrated by TDL's manuals for *seishain* and *junshain*.

In the previous chapter, I described at length the prevalence of cultural protocols such as greetings, formal expressions, appearance management, and teamwork in the manuals. Additional mechanisms of normative control are provided by groupism and a general educational emphasis on discipline, or *shitsuke* (see Feiler 1991: 39; Singleton 1989; DeVos 1973; Rohlen 1983; Passin 1965). All this cultural conditioning seems to allow for a greater degree of organizational authority and therefore might suggest a supplementary explanation for the success of the Disney Way at TDL. However, in most Japanese companies there is much more emphasis on those protocols at the *seishain* level. The popular JMAM (1992) video series is intended for *seishain* and not *junshain*. The voluminous OL manuals belong to the category of *seishain* manuals. Kōrakuen manuals are designed for *seishain*; *junshain*, in contrast, watch a twenty-minute video, "Smile on You," during their orientation. TDL manuals for *junshain*, which were evidently copied from Disney manuals, are an exception in Japan. In this respect, the strong organizational culture of TDL's *junshain* is a result of the Disney Way. It stands in contrast to the relatively weak organizational culture of part-timers in the Japanese service sector. This is a crucial difference, since the service sector has the highest rate of employment as well as the highest rate of turnover among part-timers. Many Japanese commentators have hailed the Disney manuals for part-timers as the "secret of TDL's success" (Komuya 1989; Tadokoro 1990). Eberts and Eberts (1995: 185) cite a Japanese executive as saying:

Japan has very little more to learn about management from the US. There is one exception, though. We have been impressed with Disneyland. Do you know that when Disneyland was opened in Tokyo, they had a book this large which explained everybody's job completely? The book also explained policies and procedures for the park. Everything ran smoothly when it opened, with no problems and no uncertainties in job assignments.

Similar remarks about Disney's model management are cited by Peter Drucker (1992: 182–83). According to Fusaho Awata (1988: 60), "There are manuals—manuals detailing the ways the cast should stand and sit, wave and whistle—which are undoubtedly at the heart of the Disney management system. . . . Since younger Japanese cannot reasonably be expected to follow the traditional pattern and sacrifice themselves for duty's sake, the manual system ensures cheerful service from all employees."

The admiration of the manual is a new cultural phenomenon. Many Japanese managers, both at OLC and Kōrakuen, who spent much of their careers as trainers told me that manuals are a foreign concept in Japan. This seems like a paradox, since manuals are based on protocols, and protocols are a dominant part of the Japanese organizational and service culture. However, it is American society which is often "referred to by Japanese businessmen and engineers as being a *manyuaru* [manual] society" (Schodt 1994: 170). In reply to my queries, Kōrakuen and OLC trainers said that there was no paradox here. Their common explanation was that two major differences distinguished traditional Japanese protocols from American service manuals. First, Japanese "manuals" traditionally neglected service. Second, traditional Japanese "service culture" lacked manuals. "House rules," the traditional Japanese forerunners of the manual, have a history of more than 400 years. Mitsui's house rules, which were written in the sixteenth century, lack any reference to "service." Traditional service, the argument continues, developed in intimate, one-on-one situations such as a stay in a *ryokan* (inn), an encounter with a *geisha,* or a daily walk to the neighborhood *sentō* (public bath), *chaya* (teahouse), or *nomiya* (drinking place) (see Takahashi 1994). "Service" professionals were apprenticed and trained over many years and were consequently committed to and took pride in their work. Strictly speaking, the manual is the opposite of the Japanese traditional apprenticeship system of *minarai*, or learning by watching the master. All this changed in the context of mass-consumed, anonymously delivered modern service. The Western concept of "service" is rendered in katakana as *sābisu*, connoting its foreign and sometimes strange nature. Part-timers in the service sector find themselves at a certain place for a certain amount of time. Fluctuations in sales make no difference in their pay. There is no promotion or bonus to be gained. This is hardly a work environment that encourages the traditional Japanese commitment and "sacrifice for one's company, section chief or superiors, or the sacrifice of present for future" (Sengoku 1985: 5–6). It is the kind of environment that requires manuals, according to trainers. Manuals are also made necessary by the job-rotation system in large service companies. Because of job rotation, experienced *shūnin* (inspectors) are frequently replaced with inexperienced ones.

Not all manuals are good, and direct importation of American manuals to Japan has often proved problematic. For example, when the original manuals for Kentucky Fried Chicken (KFC) were used during initial test operations in the Osaka area, two of three stores never registered sales above calculated breakeven points and were subsequently closed (Tsurumi 1975: 5). KFC-Japan had to introduce radical changes in the manuals, including its style of promotion (to target upscale young couples with children), price competitiveness (prices had to be adjusted to compete with a typical Japanese-style takeout pork dish), store size (reduced by half), and store function (eat-on-premises to be promoted). However, the current Japanese admiration of manuals is all-embracing. This esteem is part and parcel of the recent rise of the service sector in Japan and the concurrent popularity of borrowed American terms such as "customer satisfaction" (CS). In organizational terms, the admiration of Japanese managers for the American service manual is a part of a strategy to reduce uncertainty in the face of enormous numbers of transient part-timers. Employees change, but the manual remains the same. Sociologically speaking, the manual is a disciplinary tool in a generational conflict. As Sengoku Tamotsu (1985: 3) puts it, "Our Japanese youth today is a generation that does little more than await directions."

Kano Yasuhisa (1986: 115) argues that "the *shinjinrui* generation belong to the manual society." *Shinjinrui,* which now stands for all those born since 1960, has negative nuances in Japanese. Nakano Osamu (1988: 14), for example, claims that "in considering the personality traits of the *shinjinrui,* the first characteristic we note is that they are 'moratorium people'— that is, they do not want to grow up."

These observations are written by the *sarariiman* generation—the *kyūjinrui,* postwar baby boomers who are today's section managers and trainers of the *shinjinrui.* For them, the manual is a symbol of the younger generation, who "do not want to grow up." The reluctance of the *shinjinrui* to attain full-fledged adulthood is indeed confirmed by the fact that they are "part-timers"; as long as they do not become *shain,* they are exempted from being *shakaijin,* adult members of society (see Okonogi 1978). The argument here is that both the manual and the part-timers are infantile. This kind of argument is legitimized within the middle-age discourse of authority in Western countries as well. In contrast to these general notions of the *shinjinrui* as a manual society, many of my informants were critical of TDL's manual culture and the rigidity it entailed (see the following section). By far the most critical comment I heard was made by an ex–cast member (Food Division) who said: "Do you know why they don't have *hanbaiki* [vending machines] at TDL? They don't need it. We are the *hanbaiki.* Customers push, and we throw out a spiel." I argue therefore that the link between manuals and the *shinjinrui* is an ideological facade. The discourse of the *shinjinrui* is part of the authority structure of the middle-age company men, the *kyūjinrui.*

There are other readings of the manual. Culturally speaking, the manual is perceived by many in Japan as "sign of the times," a symbol of commodification and mass consumer culture, as well as a reminder of the anachronism of "old Japan." According to Otsubo Ryuta (personal interview), service manuals first became popular in Japan following the birth of McDonald's-Japan in 1972. A parallel observation is made by Kano (1986: 108): "TDL made American service techniques popular in Japan. Before TDL, these techniques were accepted mainly by the food service industry." The Japanese part-time service sector is currently in an early stage of maturation in terms of its assimilation of the manual and the American principles of customer satisfaction. I illustrate this claim here through a brief description of Kōrakuen's Behavior Campaign. I then examine the reception of manual culture by TDL cast members.

THE WARM HEART: KŌRAKUEN'S BEHAVIOR CAMPAIGN

On November 16, 1992, Kōrakuen's Service Division launched its Behavior Campaign. A special memorandum, issued the same day, described the campaign's objective (to establish a service code) and the schedule for the campaign. Every three months another theme (*tēma*) would be emphasized, starting with the "smile" and moving to greetings (*aisatsu*), appearance (*midashinami*), behavior (*taido*), manner of speech (*kotobazukai*), cleanliness, safety, customer complaints, and so on. Three videos were produced for the campaign, and various newsletters, posters, stickers, and telephone cards were prepared. The posters for 1994, in my opinion, were especially impressive. One of them had a large golden title, occupying about half the poster, that read: "Declaration of Customer Principles" (*kasutoma-nizumi sengen*). Below the title, over a white illustration of the Tokyo Dome, a diagonal question begs the reader in yellow: "Are you customanist?" (*kasutomanisuto ka?*). Below that, a *sarariiman* posing like the Uncle-Sam-Wants-You ad points his finger at us. The Behavior '93 poster was more modest. A vertical sentence printed in black over a background of red hearts states: "To begin with, a warm heart" (*hajimari wa, uōmi hāto*). The extensive use of katakana Americanisms ("warm heart," "behavior campaign," "customer") illustrates how the new service culture is being reproduced and marketed in Japanese organizations. *Uōmi hāto* (warm heart) is the *sunao na kokoro* ("naive heart," the traditional ideal of cultivating selfhood through work) of the 1990s. Like Taylorism in the 1920s and quality circles in the 1950s, "CS" and "service manuals" are the American imports that characterize Japan of the 1990s.

The results of the Behavior Campaign, however, were not encouraging. According to Otsubo, a final report submitted to the top management was filed away and forgotten. Otsubo, as well as the head (*buchō*) of the Service Division, subsequently left the campaign as a result of job rotation. Otsubo blames what he calls the mentality of Kōrakuen's top management: "Our company works top-down. Top management decides what to do. Unfortunately, our top management has an image of Kōrakuen as a real estate company, rather than as a service company. They dream of becoming Mitsui Real Estate." Some Kōrakuen workers, the subject of the Behavior Campaign, were also critical. While relaxing with a cup of coffee in one of the Arubaito Sentā's break areas, one of my escorts, a regular employee, pointed at the campaign's posters on the walls and said: "I wonder why they called it a campaign. Don't you think that's strange? A campaign is a one-time event, but this thing was repeated for, I don't remember exactly, two or more years. So what's the meaning of calling it a campaign? It's like trying to instill verve in something which is actually an empty ritual."

Another proof of the inadequacy of the Behavior Campaign came after its early termination in 1994. Sales of goods decreased 10 percent that year, although the number of visitors increased (Tokyo Dome Company 1995). Yamada, then a young clerk (tantō) in Sales Division (Eigyō-bu), was appointed to study the problem.

> I was told that we are not expected to increase sales, because of the recession. Our goal was to keep sales at the same level, as much as possible. We couldn't introduce new goods in our baseball specialty shop, because the Tokyo Giants (our sponsoring baseball team) controlled all the merchandise. Our strategy was to improve management on the one hand and service on the other. We knew there was a problem with service, because shop personnel did not say irasshaimase or arigatō gozaimashita—at least they didn't say it when a large number of customers came in after a baseball game in Tokyo Dome.

Yamada videotaped the shop personnel at work, placing the camera behind the registers. On crowded nights, the video showed the four cashiers talking among themselves while many customers waited in line. When the cashiers handed the merchandise to the customer, they did not say thank you. Yamada: "I didn't work in the shop, and the staff didn't know me. Maybe they thought I was just videotaping the customers." Both shain and part-timers presented the same behavior during overcrowded times. According to Yamada, they later explained to him that "so many customers were coming anyhow, we didn't think we had to worry about aisatsu." Yamada embarked on a "behavior campaign" of his own. He invited a consulting company, his boss, and the shop's *shain* to the *kenshū*, Kōrakuen's instruction center, and showed the video. Later, the consulting company conducted an off-the-job training seminar for the *shain*. The shop managers (ranked as *shunin*), however, refused to attend the seminar. Meanwhile, part-timers received off-the-job after-hours training. It consisted of voice training, the practice of *aisatsu*, role-playing, and explanations of goods using a script. Yamada's story encapsulates Kōrakuen's drawbacks compared to TDL: the absence of a strong, central training center, lack of inspection procedures, and inadequate manuals. In one of our conversations, I asked Yamada why cast members working in TDL's World Bazaar do not lose their grip when the pace picks up after 5:00 P.M. His reply was: "You're right. They have a word for it in the manual; it's called *shitsuke*. Discipline." So, I insisted, why not train for *shitsuke* in Kōrakuen? "Are you crazy?" he said. "*Shitsuke* is a word for children. They use it in elementary school. We cannot put it in our manuals; the employees will think we are treating them like children."

Despite the strong (in Japanese terms) organizational culture of TDL's part-timers, and although TDL employees generally present a remarkable level of *shitsuke*, there are many instances in which the system is subverted. By focusing on these, we can get a better sense of the employee's point-of-view. This is the subject of the following section.

The Smile Factory

Smiles are the foundation of beauty.

—Edgar Rice Burroughs, *Tarzan of the Apes*

Some observers of the backstage of DL and WDW emerge with a blatantly critical view of the Magic Kingdom. Haden-Guest (1972: 231) sardonically remarks that "the Disney Way is impressed on junior personnel with an efficiency rare outside some of the more highly disciplined religious movements. . . . 'We hope you'll enjoy thinking our way!' runs one of the Disney University campus directives. Or, presumably, else." The Disney University is similarly disdained by Richard Schickel (1968: 318) for "training employees in the modern American art forms of the frozen smile and the canned answer delivered with enough spon-taneity to make it seem unprogrammed." What are we to make of this? How does it match the apparent appreciation of the Disney smile and service by so many visitors, about 90 percent of whom are repeat visitors? Perhaps there is no discrepancy; what we may have here are alternative readings of the text. The Disney smile winks in our face.

Disney's worlds are a fertile ground for a sensitive and critical sociol-ogy of emotions. Indeed, the Disney view of human nature is basically emotional; according to TDL's Trainer's Guide, the correct answer to the question "What moves people?" is "20 percent reason, 80 percent emotion" (p. 9). Previous chapters deal with TDL training and work from the manual's point-of-view. This chapter aims for a critical consid-eration of the employee's point-of-view. A full description of life in TDL is impossible. The tour guide, the ride operator, the cashier, and the girl behind the food wagon all have their public and private life, on stage and backstage. Despite OLC's warnings—perhaps because of them—*jun-shain* (unlike *shain*) were eager to share their experiences. I have heard innumerable anecdotes about working in the Kingdom of Dreams and Magic, as TDL refers to itself in its manuals and guidebooks. Repre-senting the voices of employees inevitably requires brute editorial selec-tion. The point-of-departure behind this section is that life in TDL involves a great deal of emotion management. This perspective is in line both with a critique of organizational culture and with the common themes that emerged from the employees' stories.

The previous section began with Van Maanen's paradox of work at DL: Why, when the work is so low-paying, strict, and monotonous, do workers seem so happy? Strong organizational culture is the answer given in that section. There is, however, another perspective, more sub-jective in nature, that focuses on "looking happy" as emotion manage-ment within the employee. Cast members are told that Disneyland is a happy place—indeed, the happiest place on earth. It is part of their role in the show to be happy. They have to smile, but smile honestly; other-wise it is not a Disney smile. In Disney University manuals the following lines are ubiquitous: "At Disneyland we get tired, but never bored, and even if it's a rough day, we appear happy. You've got to have an honest smile. It's got to come from within. And to accomplish this you've got to develop a sense of humor and a genuine interest in people. If nothing else helps, remember that you get paid for smiling." The manuals do not explain how to smile honestly, however. That is part of the oral tradition of Disneyland, part of the stories told in orientation, the folklore propounded by the leads, and the daily lives of employees. How this honesty is worked out—how the authentic is staged and how it is contested by other (more "real"?) feelings—is the paradox underpinning this section.

In her influential book *The Managed Heart: Commercialization of Human Feeling*, Arlie Hochschild (1983) coined the term "emotion management" in the context of the service work of flight attendants working for Delta Airlines. She defined "emotion management" as a transmutation of three basic elements of emotional life: emotion work, feeling rules, and social exchange. These elements are part of everyday emotional life, but employees of service companies are taught to *manage* them in a special way. First, emotion work is "no longer a private act but a public act, bought on the one hand and sold on the other" (Hochschild 1983: 118). It is no longer the individual who decides on the right emotional display, but the company as represented by the trainer, the manual, and the management. Second, feeling rules—social scripts that tell us what to feel and how to express our feelings in various situations—are no longer an unwritten, personal, and often vague matter, contingent on the individual's upbringing and character. Feeling rules are now spelled out publicly—in the "Tips on Magic" and other Disney manuals, in training programs, and in the discourse of supervisors at all levels. Third, social exchange is forced into narrow channels. It is no longer an improvised, real-time, on-the-spot, face-to-face interaction, but a carefully prescribed, prescripted and stage-managed "show." In what follows I examine three types of work stories: morality stories referred to as "magic moments," complaint stories about what the company calls "communication," and horror stories. These stories illustrate how the transmutation of feeling into managed emotion is achieved in TDL, and at what price.

MAGIC MOMENTS

Emotion management begins on the first day of orientation, when instructors beseech recruits to wish every guest "have a nice day" (*tanoshimi kudasai*, in TDL's spiel). The service motto on the "Tips on Magic" manual is "We create happiness." "Happiness" (*hapinesu*) is also the correct answer to the orientation-quiz question "We TDL cast members provide _____ to all the guests." Even more direct emotional manipulation is involved in the prohibition, first uttered in orientation, not to talk with guests about what happens backstage. Miyo, a young cast member, told me: "Trainers say, people have dreams about Disneyland, you cannot break their dream, it would break their heart." And, there are the customary "magic moments" stories. In WDW, the most popular of these is "the popcorn story."

> Emerging from the theatre, a mother buys her young son a box of popcorn from an open-air stand. Seconds later, the lad, who looks to be about four, trips and falls. The popcorn spills, the boy bawls, the mother screams. A costumed Cast Member on his way to another attraction happens by. Barely breaking stride, he scoops up the empty cardboard box, takes it to the popcorn stand for a refill, presents it to the shattered child, and continues on his way. (WDW trainer Robert Sias, cited in Henkoff 1995: 115)

I have heard the same story told about ice-cream cones and balloons. Always a child is involved; there are no stories about refilling mom's spilt coffee. The magic is always spontaneous.

A number of interrelated lessons about emotions are instilled in these stories. The first implies that everything in the park should be controlled, every mishap quickly taken care of, because this is the meaning of "happiness." Cast members therefore learn that everything they do on stage is meaningful and should therefore be totally controlled. It is a show, but it must look real, including the production of spontaneity and the stage-management of emotion-conveying behavior such as smiling, welcoming, or thanking. Emotion-management training uses these stories in two important ways. First, by emphasizing such magic moments, trainers try to instill verve in jobs that are otherwise tightly regimented. Second, the magic moment implies an emotional reward to be gained from doing your job, as monotonous as it is. By producing "happiness," you make yourself happy. There is ample emotional conditioning at work here. The magic moment teaches the employee that s/he does not work for such mundane matters as getting paid, but for a greater cause—for the "happiness" of guests, maybe even for one's own "happiness." This is explicitly suggested in "The Tokyo Disneyland Show," a manual handed to cast members during orientation, which begins with the following recommendation (written inside a Mickey-shaped frame): "the key to happiness is communicating with guests. . . . We also hope you will be able to find your own happiness through working here" (signed by the OLC president).

Academic cynicism aside, these moments might be magical for the "four-year-old child" who dropped his or her popcorn. However, many cast members soon realize the magician's sleight of hand behind such stories and the commodification of emotion underlying their work environment. While discussing the "magic moments" stories, one cast member said:

> You know, they have a message service in the park, the one you usually hear Disney music coming through. It's not supposed to be used as a message service, though. The leads realize we know it exists, so they tell us, if a guest comes to you in panic because she hasn't seen her baby for an hour, don't mention the message system. They tell us, using the message system too often will destroy the atmosphere of dreams and magic. It's there only for emergencies, you know. In the bottom line, the "atmosphere" is more important than actually helping out people.

Other workers recalled the strict prohibition against speaking with family members who might be visiting the park: "Leads tell us: you're on duty, don't talk personally. Even if we want to make a phone call to home during breaks, we must do it through the area office telephone, and only emergency calls are allowed. It's like being in jail." Other cast members mentioned the accidents manual ("incidents" in DisneyTalk). This manual was copied directly from WDW. Following an accident, the closest employee (usually a part-timer) is to call a supervisor (management) and then first aid. "Why not the first aid first?" I was asked by several naive cast members. The manual then instructs the employees attending the victim to immediately write down any admissions uttered by him or her regarding self-carelessness (for a discussion of the similar DL and WDW manual, see Adler 1983; Toufexis 1985; Bryman 1995: 121).

Some of the magic moments stories were apparently too manipulative. Yamada, a custodial cast member at TDL, recounted the following story told during custodial orientation:

> They told us about a young custodian who used to give names to every toilet stool. This way he could work harder. We were laughing, because the trainer used silly names to illustrate this. Anyway, the story goes on. The young custodian was thinking of quitting his job, it was too hard for him. But then, OLC sent him for a training visit to Disneyland. We were going, "Sugoi!" [Cool!] It's good to know that we too might get to fly to California. Anyway, while in Disneyland this Japanese custodian meets with an American colleague, and he asks the American: "Excuse me, what do you do to get through the hard work?" So the American goes, "All these toilets here are my friends. I give them names." I remember thinking, it must be pretty rough out there if these are the best stories they could come up with to encourage us.

A similar "toilet story" is cited by Kano (1986: 102).

COMMUNICATION STORIES

More mundane work stories reveal a common denominator that is another hallmark of Disney language: communication. Many cast members experienced their "emotional dissonance" in the context of communication. According to Miyo,

> In front of where I work there's a toilet. Guests come and ask me "Where's the toilet?" and I point toward that direction. After a few minutes they come back and ask me in a low voice, "Isn't that a restaurant?" You see, the toilet has an English sign saying "rest rooms," and they think "rest" stands for *resuto* [a Japanese rendering for *restaurant*]. I've asked my leads so many times why they won't change the sign. They replied that it's good for communication.

Many cast members are conscious of the stage-management of communication. "We all know why OLC wants us to say *ohayō gozaimasu* instead of *irasshaimase*," said a shop clerk ("merchandising assistant"); "They can call it 'communication' if they like. . . . It's just another label, a page from the manual."

Although the communication spiel is part of the global DisneyTalk, reactions to it among cast members differ by locality. TDL cast members generally find it easier than U.S. cast members to distance themselves from the Disney language because it is, after all, a foreign language. *Communication* is conceived as yet another buzzword, a facade, something "imported from America," a trendy slogan that has no contents. For Japanese cast members, this holds true for DisneyTalk in general. Disney language, like all language, plays a crucial role in socialization and emotion management (see Eisenberg & Goodall 1993 for a discussion of the organizational role of Disney language). As Kuenz (1995: 112) argues, "Most [WDW cast members] have internalized the Disney terms; they *never* say uniform, but costume, just as they always say cast, onstage, and backstage." Smith and Eisenberg (1987) similarly report that in their interviews with DL employees, no one used taboo terms such as *customer*, *amusement park*, or *uniforms* when talking about their work. In TDL, in contrast, Disney language will always remain foreign to cast members. They learn it, use it, and play with it, but they leave it behind them when they go home. Many have told me that "using the Disney language when speaking with family or friends would simply require too much explaining."

The reaction to DisneyTalk reflects the overall use of English as a foreign language in Japan. The contemporary Japanese city dweller regards English primarily as a fun language of brand names, TV commercials, and the "new music" designed for the "new generation" of Japanese teenagers and young adults (Stanlow 1992). In *Nantonaku, kurisutaru* (Somehow, crystal), the 1981 best-seller that celebrated the fashion-driven, commodified urban Japanese society, author Tanaka Yasuo suggested that labeling an item with an English loanword made it special. He gives the example of *rein būtsu* (rain boots): "They are just *nagagutsu* [boots; literally, "long shoes"]. However, when they are called *rein būtsu*, even a rainy day makes us feel real up, and when there is a puddle we try to jump into it with a splash, on purpose" (Tanaka 1981: 151; cited in Stanlow 1992: 67).

In TDL, Disney's *communication* works like Tanaka's *rein būtsu*. It is used to make one "feel real up," while at the same time openly acknowledging the illusion. For the Japanese, Disney parlance ultimately consists of loanwords—not organizational metaphors to live by, but temporary facades to play with. Most cast members I talked with did not use the Disney words naturally, unlike Kuenz's (1995) informants or Van Maanen's (1991) ride operators. For example, attraction guides used the Japanese word *serifu* (theatrical text) instead of *spiel*, and merchandising assistants talked about *aisatsu* in this context. Nobody ever said *spieler*; instead they used the term *jōhō* (literally "information," the title of the cast member who spiels in front of a restaurant, for example). In a similar vein, most cast members referred to themselves as *junshain* and to their lead as *senpai-shain*.

DisneyTalk is a major protagonist in the story of communication at TDL. Overall, DisneyTalk at TDL reflects the use of English in Japan, which represents an intriguing case of domestication. Whereas the use of English after the war and perhaps up to the 1960s could be viewed as a symbol of Americanization, or of a strong American influence, during the past twenty years the use of English has developed many characteristics of its own. The Japanese-English vocabulary has "incorporated many elements which are not understandable for Americans or other people who speak English as a native language. The Japanese mass media producers have created their own standards for using English, promoting English as a symbol of modernity" (Haarmann 1989: 16).

The appropriation of English in Japan usually does not induce linguistic change within the host language. That is, the increasing use of English has not changed the structure of Japanese in terms of syntax and semantics. Because of orthography, English itself is being changed: the katakana used to write a foreign word, as Stanlow (1992: 70) describes it, "instantly domesticates it by forcing the borrowed term to conform to the Japanese phonological system." The language contact between Japanese and English therefore does not follow a pattern of pidginization or creolization, but rather a kind of "departmentalization" (or maybe "depātoizeishun"). English loanwords and catch phrases, in their (globally incomprehensible) Japanese pronunciation, enjoy a commercial appeal and recognition, but their meaning is completely clear "only to a minority" (Haarmann 1989: 145). English in Japan is arguably a copyrighted language, largely considered as artificial and superficial—the language of the department store, the *depāto*. Because of its cultural adaptation, today it would seem odd to speak of the use of English as a sign of Americanization. I stressed this point since it is equally relevant to TDL. Both the use of DisneyTalk in TDL and the use of English in Japan exemplify the way Japan has locally adapted global culture.

Communication, as any cast member will confirm, is not just in the manual. Customers' complaints can be a real nuisance and generate yet another form of emotional dissonance. This was indeed a prevalent subject in the interviews. Most of my respondents mentioned the strict prohibition against talking back to the customer ("It is something you get fired for right on the spot") and then proceeded to describe "how annoying some of the customers can be." Most of these complaint stories were told by employees of the Food Division. Indeed, most of my informants came from the Food Division. This is not surprising if we recall that many TDL restaurant workers originally wanted to be in attractions. Food work is the lowest-ranking occupation in the park. The same is true at DL, where the lowest rank belongs to "the sub-proletarian (below the Sweepers) or peasant status Food and Concession workers" (Van Maanen 1991: 61). Spinelli (1992: 260) gives a similar description of the hierarchy of employment status, which she terms as the "caste system": at the top of the pyramid are the tour guides, followed by those in operations (ride operators, ticket sellers, and custodians, in that order); below that are those who work in merchandising; at the bottom of the ladder are the food workers.

A common complaint story in the Foods Division regards the issue of tables. In some restaurants and "buffeterias," there is a rule that if all the tables inside are taken, guests cannot wait inside for a table. The guest must take a table outside. This rule is often contested on cold winter days. Restaurant part-timers are forbidden to talk to the customer in such a case. They have to get a *shain* to deal with it. In telling me various versions of this story, part-timers did not criticize the customers, but the company. According to Yasuko, "the guest is doing a perfectly normal thing, as far as he's concerned. My problem is with the company. Why can't I explain the situation? I could do it just as well as a *shain*, but according to the manual I would then be fired." The point here is not who deals with customers' demands, but the disillusionment about one's own role in the show. In fact, I heard few complaint stories about angry or annoying customers. In that respect, working with a Japanese audience usually appears to be (but is not always) easier than dealing with American visitors. TDL cast members are usually spared the "cumulative annoyance of having children and adults asking whether the water in the lagoon is real, or whether a character is 'really real'" (Van Maanen & Kunda 1989: 69). The general tendency of passive indulgence that (often, but not always) characterizes the Japanese customer is probably behind TDL's lack of unofficial "remedy practices" developed to teach deviant customers a lesson (for a vivid description of these practices, see Van Maanen & Kunda 1989: 67). TDL cast members, in contrast, let their creative energies out through small offenses like taking pictures near the showers and wardrobes with costumes on, eating from leftovers or while making the food in the backstage kitchen, or pocketing desserts and eating them in the bathroom. One cast member recalled:

> "If you were hungry during work, and there were leftovers, we would eat and drink them. It's not allowed to eat leftovers. You are not allowed to eat from the food that you are making. I always have eaten from it. Or, for example, I was in the last shift and called the runners to come and take new food and they returned and told us that it's not needed. So we ate it ourselves. Everybody did that."
>
> "And what if someone told the *shain*?"
>
> "We did it secretly. If shain was tough, it was a problem. You could get fired. But if he was a friend, he would come in and eat with us. One time I got caught eating leftovers by *shain* and he didn't say anything, just: 'Don't get sick.'"

Cast members smiled as they recounted these stories to me, and it did not quite seem to be the Disney smile. Or was it?

HORROR STORIES

Another popular type of cast member narratives, and perhaps the most creative of them, is the horror story. This intriguing genre is the dark opposite of the bright magic moments recounted by the company's trainers. Hirono, a cast member in the Foods Division, recalled: "There's this rumor: We have a rest room next to the Plaza Pavilion Restaurant. One day a lady was screaming 'help me,' her kid was stuck in the toilet. *Shain* went to see what happened and pulled out the kid. She was dead already because it was too late and nobody could help her. It's a tragic story."

Such unauthorized, unofficial, subterranean "urban myths" are a global phenomenon. They can be found in all of Disney's worlds, indeed everywhere for that matter (Goode and Ben-Yehuda 1994: 108–12; Best 1989). They are told as true, and are widely believed, but lack factual verification. According to Kuenz's (1995: 117) respondents, WDW has a much larger and more brutal share of horror stories: "No one (outside the company) has ever heard the story of the young mother whose rented paddle boat was sucked into the wake of the *Empress Lily* where, before the eyes of her gasping seven-year-old, the ship's paddle wheel chopped her quite in half."

This cross-cultural prevalence of horror stories, notwithstanding their possible factuality, is a subversive act. First, it subverts the company's prescribed myth of total control over its property, employees, and customers. Second, it subverts company rules "forbidding anyone even to raise the issue." Some of these horror stories, like Jungian nightmares, capture the essence of Disney culture, its totems and taboos. It is particularly intriguing when two or more stories, told independently in Japan and America, embody a similar narrative. One such pair of stories deals with what is inside the Mickey Mouse costume. "A family from Kyūshū once came to TDL. Two parents and three big children. The children were determined to see who's inside Mickey Mouse, and they tore off the costume's head. OLC sued them and they had to pay 10 million yen." The second story, entitled "the first Mickey Mouse," is a WDW horror story: "[The first Mickey Mouse] has a bad skin problem. He has cancer of the skin. He got it from wearing the mask of Mickey Mouse—the head gear. His mother sued for him—he'd never been married—and he has a job guaranteed with Disney for the rest of his life. He's in his late fifties at least. But he has to be behind the scenes because of his skin. Nobody wants to look at him" (Kuenz 1995: 116).

Although different, the two stories share a similar, obsessive concern with the mask—the head gear—of Mickey Mouse and the real face behind it. The question "Who (or what) lurks behind the mask?" is a traditional horror-story theme, but its meaning is arguably expanded here. The two stories illustrate that the answer to that question is never pleasant; seeing the forbidden face always involve a punishment or other dire consequences. To tear Mickey's head off and expose the cancer-ridden face behind it evidently reflects a desire to dispel the illusion of Disney. Company rules strictly forbid removal of the head gear in public; doing this under any circumstances means automatic dismissal. There are various horror stories about Disney characters vomiting inside the head or passing out because of the heat and being left on the float until the parade returns backstage (Kuenz 1995: 137). The Disney characters, although invisible inside their costumes, are subjected to the most stringent control. Not only they but all employees are repeatedly warned not to "break character." This warning is turned into a horror story even by management. According to Kuenz (1995: 137), "one management type recounted in a training session the story of taking his visiting niece into the tunnels to find Snow White. When they met her, she turned on them, cigarette and Diet Coke in hand, and told them 'Get the hell out of here. I'm on break.' The child was crushed, the spell broken."

All these different "mask stories" were told by different people in different times and places. For that reason alone, their surface similarities are amazing. The stories can be located sociologically in two larger contexts: the organizational and the cultural.

Arguably, working for Disney—the "iron cage of fun"—has produced the similar narrative of these stories. The narrative can be concisely defined as a "crime and punishment" formula. It begins with a specific transgression: the need to talk to or about the "real" person inside the costume. This feat is achieved only with much planning and trouble. The quest for the "real" person under the disguise reveals an obsession with the strict company line separating onstage (the mask, the costume) from backstage (the face, the person). The horror stories show how this company rule has been transmuted into and internalized as a feeling rule. To cross the line, to tear off the mask, is to "break character." Within the horror story, this obsession is temporarily thrown into relief and given a cathartic release; then it is quickly punished. At the end of the day, the mask returns to its place. Nobody wants or dares to look at the real face behind it. This is, in a nutshell, the story of Disney's emotional subjugation. Every horror story always already contains its own self-disciplinary moral.

Similar horror stories are probably told, with local variations, in every large service company. Flight attendants, for example, spoke of "anger fantasies" with a strong oral component, such as "befouling the passenger's food and watching him eat it" (Hochschild 1983: 114). The strict feeling rules, drawn by the Disney company between onstage and backstage, yield similar horror-and-moral stories in the United States and Japan. However, such stories should also be located in a second, broader cultural context. Anthropological research on Japanese culture and socialization suggests that the onstage/backstage line is more easily accommodated by Japanese cast members than by their American counterparts. The onstage/backstage distinction fits into the traditional and much-discussed Japanese duality of *tatemae/honne*. This paradigm, approximately the difference between public/private and appearance/reality, is not unique to Japan; rather, it is a universal "ideal type" of human psychology (see also Moeran 1989: 3). Mead's (1932) famous distinction between the "I" and the "me," two major constructs of Western social psychology, is an example of that universality. However, sociologists studying Japan have long argued that Japanese society has taken the I/me duality much further and much more for granted. Feeling rules that define and link *tatemae* (onstage) and *honne* (backstage) are more uniformly and closely scripted in Japan than in the United States, for example (Tobin et al. 1989). Given the prevalence of this cultural script in Japan, the implication is that Japanese cast members are likely to be less concerned than Americans about "being phony"—a central issue in both Hochschild's (1983) study of flight attendants and Kuenz's (1995) study on WDW cast members. As White (1993: 39) argues, "In the American context, appearance and reality are not a matched pair, but a contrasting set, representing not a balance but a flawed contradiction."[2]

Is this cultural conditioning, of appearance and reality as a matched pair, visible among Japanese cast members? The answer is, to say the least, complicated. Measuring resistance to emotional subjugation (if that is possible) is an intricate feat, particularly when "real feelings" are discussed in the artificial context of an interview. The range of cast members' reactions to my questions about this issue was varied, and it is difficult to generalize. Overall, however, TDL cast members expressed relatively little concern about "being phony." It was taken for granted as part of the job, part of the show, and part of social life in general. Furthermore, most TDL cast members expressed their frustration not with the Disney Way, but rather with their position in the Foods Division (and not attractions). "Role distance"—distancing one's "private" self from the social, or organizational, role one is assigned "onstage"—was therefore much less of a problem in the eyes of Japanese cast members. A receptionist working for OLC said that she used *keigo* (polite, onstage speech) unconsciously because it had become second nature. This illustrates how cultural conditioning can provide a better socialization for organizational roles. A cast member in Attractions said that she "enjoyed working for Disney.... Disney is so special. Even when I got tired of working at TDL, Disney was still special to me. Even if you're tired, and all worked out, and angry, once you see a stuffed Mickey, it makes you feel better. I'm not sure why."

Although one can never deduce someone else's "true" emotional reactions with certainty, I can assert with some confidence that no "redefinition of self," as Hochschild describes it, was necessary for the Japanese cast members I interviewed. Rather, what those working in the Foods Division wanted was a redefinition of their job. However, this was due not to emotional subjugation at work, but to the boredom, physical difficulty, and low status of the job. Those who considered the job too boring or without real chances of promotion simply quit. Cast members who expressed their resistance to TDL's emotional subjugation in explicit terms were in the minority. I already mentioned the ex–cast member who compared his role to that of a vending machine ("customers push ... we throw out a spiel"). Notwithstanding the possible authenticity of his remark, the speaker was not on favorable terms with TDL, having quit his job in the Foods Division. Other cast members did not refer explicitly to emotional subjugation, but recounted stories, such as those discussed above, that showed they were aware of the subjugation. The majority of cast members, as these stories illustrate, were aware of the emotional subjugation, but thought it was pointless to criticize it. Moreover, most of them did not regard it as hypocritical. As one cast member said, "The Disney Way is what Disneyland is all about. This is what visitors come for. This is what Disney is famous for. This is the show we're selling, and I think it's a good show." Pride in one's work and a deeper sense of teamwork were more associated with high-status jobs, particularly attractions. Those who worked in attractions spent more time together after work. They had Saturday-night parties and "drinking meetings" (*nomikai*), which gained them the title of *dizunii-shakai* (Disney Society) among workers in foods and merchandising. Such activities were regarded positively by management and served as an extension to on-the-job emotional subjugation. In principle, every restaurant, shop, or attraction could have its own party or get-together. There was some social pressure to attend such activities. As one cast member in Foods said, "It's great if you like this sort of thing. . . . At first I didn't mind. It cost money, but if you didn't go, it was like being unfriendly."

I heard of several middle-age managers in OLC who quit because, as one OLC manager put it, "they said that, being in their thirties, they cannot continue with the *burikko* [childish pretense, associated with Disney and hence with working at TDL]." These managers, however, usually moved to other service companies. As for the horror stories, they were not, I believe, a sign of resisting "phoniness" on the part of cast members. Horror stories were told and enjoyed, and small mischiefs were perpetrated, but overall they were more playful than emotionally loaded. A similar playful attitude was described in the context of DisneyTalk—the language of Disney socialization. All this differs from the reactions of American cast members, at least according to what the Japanese cast members revealed in the interviews—which could have been yet another form of *tatemae*.

THE MANAGED HEART REVISITED

The analysis of emotion management in TDL has further implications for a sociology of emotions that is sensitive to its global moment. A double juxtaposition is involved here: a comparison of TDL (Japan) with DL or WDW (America), as well as a comparison of the Disney Way with other service codes turned into feeling rules, as, for example, the behavior of American flight attendants. In the first type of comparison, local cultural variations emerge; the second type of comparison focuses on one culture, "service culture," as a global project. Although Hochschild's analytical categories (such as "feeling rules") proved to be relevant to TDL (thus highlighting the common, global features of service culture), this comparison also undermines some of Hochschild's analytical premises. Hochschild's sociology of emotions generalizes on the flight attendants' conceptualizations of, and reactions to, feeling rules and emotion management. It sometimes ignores the fact, however, that these conceptualizations and reactions are themselves part of a larger cultural system that goes beyond service culture, commercialization, and capitalism (in this sense I agree with some of Wouters's [1989] criticisms). When flight attendants (and Hochschild) worry about "true" and "false" selves in the culture-specific way in which they worry about them, it is not just because of the "commercialization of human life" and their work in the service sector; it is also because they are American. As White (1993: 97) puts it in the context of teenage socialization:

> The Japanese teen is, by the end of middle school, acutely aware of the distinction between private propensities and values (*honne*) on the one hand, and correct social performance (*tatemae*) on the other. . . . American teens, too, are aware of this, but *they see more often the distinction as disillusioning: their sensitivity to what they see as hypocritical is conditioned by a cultural norm which favors "being yourself" over an accommodation to others through self-discipline and sensitivity.* (Italics added)

This study focuses on one organization; it certainly does not purport to serve as a general basis for analyzing all other service settings. Its strength, I think, rests with the global perspective it provides. I like to think of TDL as providing a "case study" in between *the managed heart* of Hochschild's (1983) American flight attendants and the *crafting selves* of Kondo's (1990) Japanese artisans.[3] The local adaptation at TDL of the global Disney service culture highlights the cultural conditioning that exists before the job and after it. The common feeling rules that are part of the job, on the other hand, illustrate the global similarities of part-time work in the service industry.

Service culture, to be sure, has become something of a post-industrial black ship. A sociology of emotions will no doubt benefit from studying feeling rules in the service cultures of secretaries, waitresses, sales clerks, social workers, and teachers. These, and not merely software engineers, are the new jobs of post-industrial society, where fewer workers make things, and more workers deliver services. While doing so, they engage in what Hochschild (1989) correctly defined as *emotion work* and rightfully called attention to. Hochschild's seemingly decontextualized feeling rules should, however, be further grounded through cultural comparison.

My analysis will focus on one of the more intriguing of Hochschild's conceptual pairs: surface versus deep acting. Hochschild argues that, in coping with their work, flight attendants "are faced with the dilemma of how to feel identified with their role without becoming infused with it" (Shilling 1993: 119). One response is that of surface acting or "simple pretending" (Hochschild 1983: 33). However, can a flight attendant suppress her anger at a passenger who insults her? Delta Airlines teaches her to do so through "deep acting," a skill learned in Delta's Recurrent Training course. For example, in dealing with rude or aggressive passengers, flight attendants are trained to think of reasons to excuse the passengers' behavior and make themselves feel sorry or sympathetic rather than angry. To recapitulate, surface acting is acting "by the manual," acting with the body (prompt and proper outward gestures) but without "the feeling." It is *katachi* (form) without *kokoro* (feeling), to use Dorinne Kondo's (1990) concepts. Deep acting is both form and feeling. It is Stanislavsky's method acting. It is acting "as if this unruly passenger has a traumatic past" (Hochschild 1983: 120). Intriguingly, for Hochschild and the flight attendants, it is still "acting," whereas for Kondo and the Japanese artisans she studied it is (supposedly) the cultivation of selfhood through work.

Surface and deep acting may be a characteristic of flight attendants, who work in a unique service territory in which interactions are long-term (a fifteen-hour flight is not inconceivable) and performed in a narrow and overpopulated enclosure (the airplane). In TDL and many other service settings, the employee usually does not see the same customer again (at least not on the same day). The cast members I interviewed did not speak about "surface" versus "deep" acting in the same way that Hochschild's flight attendants did. Nor is this distinction (or a similar one) mentioned in the Disney manuals. To be sure, the manuals had a lot to say about the cast members' role in the show, and employees took it for granted that they were supposed to be acting. But it was one-dimensional acting. It was service acting. Indeed, as cast members (and most other service attendants) know too well, the "acting" and "cast" image are not *real*. They are things the company has sold them, a rhetorical facade made to keep them "up."

I suggest that what we can call "ephemeral service"—part-time, short-term, short-lived, mass-produced, and anonymously delivered service—involves another conceptualization of acting, different from either surface or deep acting. The mode of service acting that is inculcated and practiced in TDL can be defined as *symbolic typing*. I suggest that this concept is also relevant to other forms of ephemeral service. Symbolic types are reified paradigms of behavior embodied by participants through a fixed set of performative practices. Their existence is not limited to and did not start in service culture. On the contrary, these are age-old cultural constructs. The harlequin and the rogue, for example, are well-known symbolic types in the Western theater. This legacy is particularly relevant to the symbolic typing of cast members inside Disney's costumed characters. The concept of "symbolic types" was originally suggested by Richard Grathoff (1970) as a replacement for the conventional concept of roles, which was seen as too limited by its functionalistic definition. It was further elaborated by Don Handelman (1986, 1992), who defined symbolic typing as coming into existence when, and only when, a person ceases to modify his or her behavior in response to the reactions of others. Symbolic types, then, are unique kinds of roles that do not depend on social give-and-take. Roles are continuously modified, produced, and reproduced through interpersonal give-and-take, always constituted through perspectives that combine "self" and "other." Symbolic types, in contrast, are stable, permanent performative patterns of behavior that, through their inner consistency, self-referentiality, and independence of social context, serve to create a reality of their own.

Whereas everyday roles are subject to the social flux and uncertainty that energize human interaction, service acting is meant to regulate and control that flux. Many service jobs involve fixed performative patterns.

The procedures of symbolic typing are laid out in service manuals. The spiel, the set menu, the Disney smile, all enable and dictate ritualized performance. This is why cast members are warned never to talk back to an angry customer. Instead, they must alert a supervisor. When reality evades the manual, part-timers are no longer fit to deal with it (unless they are "empowered" by the company to do so under predefined circumstances). Symbolic typing is performed within an atemporal realm. This is "service time"—a cyclical time where linear progression is replaced by routinized cycles and shifts.[4] This is why part-timers in TDL are not allowed to wear wristwatches, whose presence might detract from the standardized appearance. This is also a symbolic reminder of the cyclical tyranny of time in Disneyland—time as frozen within a myth (Frontierland, Fantasyland); within a bureaucracy (the company's clocks, shifts, and timecards); and within behavior (the symbolic typing of service culture).

Service culture, enacted through symbolic typing, is a *patronizing* performance. It habituates and conditions us, the customers (patrons). It colonizes our mind through indulgence. As patrons, we must cooperate with the spiel, follow it, and choose from it (try asking for something not on the menu, even a combination of items not prescribed as such). Social interaction becomes a big Nintendo game, with lots of prizes to win if you push the right buttons and route your character correctly in the predesigned maze. Otherwise, order is lost, and we are back into the flux. Symbolic typing, as inculcated by the service manual, abolishes one of the basic constructs of symbolic interaction: the "looking glass self," a term coined by Charles Cooley (1964: 183) to describe how our awareness of our own experience is shaped by what others around us think, say, and do about it. Significant others are the "looking glass" wherein we see our reflection. In contrast, symbolic typing—and hence service culture—is locked in a *mirror* stage. Service attendants are attentive to our facial expressions and to a basic vocabulary of linguistic expressions, but this awareness must be only skin-deep. In symbolic typing, there are no more "looking glass selves," only "mirroring bodies"—Arthur Frank's (1991) conceptualization of the body in consumerism (see also O'Neill 1985: 23; Falk 1993). This is perhaps the deep *consummation* of service culture and its oracle, the service manual. It is a Taylorist world whose influence on the post-modern Self is not entirely ephemeral.

I conclude this discussion of emotion management and symbolic typing with a tribute to the rank-and-file of communication at TDL and other service settings: the telephone operator. This last example also serves to demonstrate the workings of an important Japanese cultural script upon which *tatemae* is constructed beginning early in the socialization process, namely, polite speech, or *keigo*. Both OLC and Kōrakuen have a manual for telephone operators. This manual has two parts. One is the English manual, which is in fact a book of spiels for answering common queries in English. The second part deals, in a much more elaborate manner, with the Japanese rules of telephone talk (*denwa no kimarimonku*). This is the corporate concept of communication in its most crystallized and efficient form. Telephone communication is loaded with *keigo*, the polite speech described in the discussion of *shain* manuals in the previous chapter. A telephone operator must use *keigo* because her status is *prima facie* lower in relation to the other person on the line. Her work therefore epitomizes the gendered and formalized aspects of service communication. A telephone operator or any OL who makes a telephone call for her boss must always acknowledge the higher status of her respondent through her choice of verb suffixes and grammatical forms as well as the use of a high-pitched "service voice," the *koneko-chan* (kitty) voice. This complicated status language is learned through socialization. Many new OLs listen to the telephone in silence while an experienced telephone operator answers and demonstrates the spiel. The following excerpt, taken from the TDL's biweekly communication newsletter *Line* (15, no. 5, May 15, 1996, p. 8) presents some of the emotion management involved in telephone operating. In an article entitled "Hello, This is Oriental Land," in the section "From Cast to Cast," Saitō Yoshiko of the General Service Division (Jeneraru sābisu bu) recounts the official story of three OLC telephone operators.

> We, the three operators—they say our voices, at least, are beautiful—are working with big smiles every day.
> When making telephone calls to big hospitals or hotels, have you ever had a doubt if the operator was an android because the way she answered you was too mechanical?
> In a way, telephone operators don't need emotions to do their job. But

we, the operators of The Kingdom of Dreams and Magic, do our job with human kindness and warmth. . . .

Sometimes, of course, too much humanity can cause accidents. One day I remember hearing a new fellow operator receiving a call by saying "Osewa ni natte imasu!"[5] [Thank you for giving me this service.] Instead of preaching, I gave her a big hand, saying "That's a good one!" I think I heard the man laughing over the line. . . . When you receive phonecalls, try to smile, too. Your smile will no doubt go through the telephone wire and reach the other person.

Reading this excerpt, one is overwhelmed by the quotas of the TDL smile factory. "Smiles" are produced even through the telephone line. I interviewed one of the many OLC operators, Akiko, and asked if she was not bothered by always having to be lower in status. The reply was diplomatic, *tatemae*, as could be expected. "It would have been easier without *keigo*, but not using it is dangerous for you." She added that she preferred to speak in English over the phone because English did not require *keigo*. "But when I speak in Japanese, I use *keigo* unconsciously. It has become second nature."

Language thus emerges as crucially important. The language that enables Japanese cast members to shift "with exquisite ease" between formal onstage and intimate backstage is also the language that allows them to playfully assimilate DisneyTalk without "really" buying into it. Language, the instrument of consent, is also a means of resistance. Although perhaps stressing the obvious, my point here is that language should be viewed—in studying organizational identities as well as everything else—as a frame of mind rather than merely a vehicle for communication.

The Taylorist System

"Do you know Taylor? Do you know Dr. Deming? Disney is better with people. Our courses are better. We are the quality control and customer satisfaction model for the 1990s."

—An OLC trainer, bragging in the presence of
a trainer from Kōrakuen

In this section I describe yet another perspective that offers insight into the management system of TDL. My argument is that the Disney management of part-timers is directly informed by Taylor's principles of scientific management. The Japanese view of TDL as a model for management can therefore be compared with previous adaptations, in Japan, of Taylorist production-management and quality-control methods. I begin by introducing the historical influence of Taylorism, both in Walt Disney Productions and in Japan and then discuss the meaning of Taylorism in the various facades of TDL—managerial, productive, and cultural.

Early in the twentieth century many animation studios "taylorized" cartoons. Like others in this industry, Walt Disney became an enthusiast of scientific management (Boje 1995: 1012). In the late 1920s, the Disney studio was redesigned according to Taylorist principles. According to Crafton (1982: 259; see also Holliss & Sibley 1988), this included

> (a) division of management from labor, (b) use of untrained women and children as cheap labor force in art departments (performing specialized inking tasks) under the watchful eyes of inspectors, (c) a pyramid of functionally managed departments with gang bosses, speed bosses, repair bosses and inspectors, and finally (d) the suppression of all individuality via predetermined schedules, formulas, and interchangeable tasks.

Walt Disney would eventually use the same rational principles to manufacture his theme parks. A major element of the Disney parks is control: control over the immediate, "imagineered" environment, control over visitors' movements and imagination, control over the appearance and behavior of employees. Control is used to achieve predictability and efficiency, the two pillars of scientific management. The following is a well-known anecdote (according to Bright 1987; cited in Bryman 1995: 118).

> Walt went on a Jungle Cruise at Disneyland and timed it at four-and-a-half minutes. He discovered that the ride should have been seven minutes, which prompted him to fulminate about the deficiency to Dick Nunis, who at the time managed Adventureland. Walt complained that the ride was too fast. . . . For three weeks Nunis retrained the boat operators until the rides were timed to perfection.

As the previous chapter illustrated, efficiency, predictability, division of management and labor, and specification of job responsibilities are instilled down to the smallest detail in the Disney manuals.

Several historians of Japanese management have recently suggested that Taylorism was an important factor in the development of Japanese organizations. Taylorism stands for the concepts and techniques developed by Frederick Winslow Taylor (1856–1915) and his followers, subsumed under the rubric of "scientific management" (see Merkle 1980). Taylorite thought was introduced to Japan around 1913 with the publication of several Japanese renditions of Taylor's (1911) *Principles of Scientific Management*. Its influence can be traced in the Japanese "efficiency movement" of the 1920s, the Depression-era "industrial rationalization," the postwar drive for "productivity" and later, total quality management (Tsutsui 1995; Warner 1994).

In certain respects, however, the Japanese management system appears not to follow what is generally perceived as the Taylorist stereotype. The "three pillars" of the Japanese system (OECD 1977)— the seniority system, lifetime employment, and enterprise unionism— seem uniquely Japanese and are more easily associated with industrial relations and human-resource management than with the legacy of Taylorist efficiency techniques and time-motion studies. This paradox has been approached from several directions. William Tsutsui (1995) largely evades it by focusing on production and shop management (including QC circles) in Japanese industry. Malcolm Warner (1994), in contrast, distinguishes between "early" and "late" Taylorism, the second being closer to industrial psychology and focusing on work performance, authority, workflow, and payment systems as techniques for controlling labor (see Spender 1989, 1991; Kelly 1982). These techniques, the argument goes, were later implemented by Japanese employers who set out, in the interwar period following an upsurge of strikes, to build organizational cultures that involved high levels of worker commitment. Industrial stability was thus secured through "seducing" workers with the "enterprise as community" structure that included the three pillars (see also Gordon 1985; Kawanishi 1992; Kinzley 1991).

There is another direction for approaching Taylorism, at TDL in particular and in the Japanese service sector in general. A major principle of scientific management is the division between management and labor. The worker surrenders control over how the work is to be done. The "manual society" is the product and perpetuator of this condition, which, as Harry Braverman (1974) argues, has been a general trend in the twentieth century. The "mind" of the work process moves up the company hierarchy, creating workers who are skilled in implementing standard procedures but are otherwise deskilled. Within the boundaries of the job, more and more subtasks are specified. This Taylorification of the job is arguably prevalent everywhere in the part-timers market. The service industry, however, is unique for making Tayloristic demands on emotional work, too. Hochschild (1983), in describing the work of American flight attendants, uses almost the same protocol mentioned above in regard to the Disney smile: "Did the flight attendant hand out magazines? How many times? How were the magazines handed out? With a smile? With a *sincere* smile? . . . In the course of offering these skills, trainers contribute to a system of deskilling."

The Taylorification of work, both physically and emotionally, is of upmost importance at TDL. The world of part-timers, where the Taylorist system predominates, lacks the counter-Taylorist corporate familialism, built on the three pillars of the Japanese management system, which is reserved for *seishain*. The life of part-timers at TDL is by and large controlled by the principles of scientific management. This is to a large extent true of all part-timers in the service sector. Although this sector is the fastest-growing in Japan today, it has thus far been relatively neglected by researchers.

Taylorism provides the conceptual and practical system for part-time work at TDL. All four components of Taylor's "job analysis" can be found at work here (see Howard & Crompton 1980 and Sterle & Duncan 1973 for a discussion of how to implement Taylorism in recreation and leisure management).

1. Analysis of the basic components of every task as a means of discovering the one best way to perform that task. This is the focus of Disney training as well as the cast members' shift schedule. Every job at TDL (or any Disney World for that matter) is carefully defined and

broken down into a checklist that has to be memorized: Did you smile? Was it an honest smile? Did you say thank you? Shift changes are punctually defined. A cast member in a TDL buffeteria, for example, may work one hour as a "runner" (checking the buffet and bringing more food from the kitchen as needed), then change costume and do fifteen minutes outside as a "spieler" (introducing the place to guests), and finally work an hour as a "busman" (cleaning up the tables after guests leave and carrying the dirty dishes to the kitchen). The work schedule and procedures (how many plates to carry at one time, which table to start with) are tightly defined, almost like the timing of the various attractions. This is the Disney version of Taylor's time and motion studies.

2. Standards. The park is obsessed with time standards based on the most efficient way of doing the job. Attractions are timed in seconds and half-seconds. Lines are timed, and retimed, in minutes. There is also an obsession with standardizing the requirements for materials, machines, tools, working conditions, and the staff to fill the job. Wage charts for various hours and shifts are meticulously defined and standardized.

3. Planning of work. Job standards, argued Taylor, allow management to plan the work rationally for an entire company. Moreover, the initial planning does not depend on individual workers but on job standards. It can therefore be written down and codified in a manual. Taylor was one of the first organizational innovators to glorify the manual as the epitome of standardization, efficiency, and rationality in the workplace. It should be clear by now that TDL has wholeheartedly implemented this recommendation.

4. Maintenance of standards. Taylor called for a system of inspection and control to assure adherence to standards. This system is daily at work in the park, in the form of visible supervisors, the leads, as well as invisible inspectors, or "shoppers" (a Disney term for supervisors disguised as customers).

Finally, Taylor and Disney shared quite a similar concern for the "human dimension of work." Some organizational theorists/practitioners (the distinction is often blurred) have argued that although Taylor concentrated on the physical aspects of the job, he "did not neglect the human element, as is so often suggested, but stressed the individual and not the group side of man. . . . Taylor's synthesis came through his call for a 'mental revolution' that sought to fuse the interests of labor and management into a mutually rewarding whole" (Wren 1972: 146). In other words, Taylor's call was a self-fulfilling prophecy of the strong organizational culture, and his mental revolution can be seen to underlie the Disney Way imparted to the "Disney Family."

TDL's success has made it into a model for management. The management guru Peter Drucker (1992: 182; cited in Eberts & Eberts 1995: 185) reports the following conversation with a leading industrialist in Japan. "We all knew that it would take Disney three years to work the bugs out of this huge undertaking (i.e., TDL)," the industrialist said. "Instead, TDL ran with zero defects the day it opened. Every single operation had been engineered all the way through and simulated on the computer and trained for, and it suddenly dawned on us that we could do this too." "Zero-defects management," as it is called today, means that "every job has been completely engineered so that every worker knows what to do" (Eberts & Eberts 1995: 185). In Taylor's words (cited in Howard & Crompton 1980: 188), "a worker, to achieve his maximum productivity, must be given a definite job to do in a definite manner, in a definite time." Disneyland is therefore replacing, for some Japanese, the Deming management method as the transplanted image of quality control. One major difference from the earlier approach is that the "zero-defects approach pursued by Japanese companies relies more on the individual worker, instead of management via industrial engineers, to find the most efficient way to perform a job" (Eberts & Eberts 1995: 186).

Putting the Heart Back in the Manual

Reliance on the individual worker spells a growing criticism of the manual. Whereas reliance on the individual is positively considered as being traditionally Japanese, the manual is perceived (sometimes negatively) as made in America. I have often heard this kind of ideological binarism both from OLC and from Kōrakuen trainers. "The manual," for each of these companies, is a powerful symbol of Americanization that raises strong emotions. For Satō Akira, head of OLC Personnel Department, the manual represents a challenge to his managerial authority. He therefore tends to belittle its importance.

Satō: "We got all these manuals from America, where they need it. Here in Japan we don't need the manual. We already have our standards. We are not very different as individuals. We are already a group. Therefore we don't *have to* have a manual."
Raz: "But all the books argue that manuals are the secret of TDL's success."
S: "Yes, well, these books were written just after we opened. Of course it's easier to have manuals when you just start. But once we got started, we didn't need the manual. *Shitsuke* does not come from the manual. It comes from the heart (*kokoro*). My personal opinion is that the manual is not such a big deal. I'm afraid that the people at the University Department will disagree."

The last remark reveals that Satō's denigration of the manual reflects an internal conflict in OLC. Given the emphasis in Japanese companies on education, training, and job rotation, the personnel department was traditionally the most powerful in a Japanese organization (Tung 1984: 50–51). In OLC, however, there is also a University Department (Unibāhiti-ka), which is responsible for the training of *junshain*. The two sections belong to the Personnel Division (Jinji-bu). "Personnel" and "university," *seishain* and *junshain*, *kokoro* (heart) and *manyuaru* (manual), and ultimately "Japan" and "America" are therefore also ideological facades in OLC's corporate power structure. A similar terminology can be found in Kōrakuen. In this case, however, the "enemy" is not internal but external: it is Kōrakuen versus TDL. Again, the primary blame is put on the manual. According to Otsubo Ryuta,

the Japanese started using manuals after McDonald's. McDonald's introduced the manual as a tool for training of part-timers. Before that, we didn't have this kind of manuals. This is not a part of traditional Japanese culture. Originally our service culture was one-on-one and from the heart. We had hospitality, not service. In McDonald's, they put "smile" on the price board: a smile "costs nothing." In TDL, they put smile in the manual. This is the American way. . . . If you ask me, Disneyland should be in the United States, where it belongs. Here it's just another black ship. My goal is to make Kōrakuen superior by putting *kokoro* into the manuals.

There is no doubt that TDL has stolen some of Kōrakuen's visitors. Kōrakuen's cumulative decreases in revenues following the recession (1991 and after) have made TDL's stable success all the more disturbing. Kōrakuen's latest attractions (the Geo-Police) are explicitly directed toward "young adults"—the "disenfranchised youth," as Michael Eisner calls them in the Walt Disney Company's 1994 annual report—rather than families with children. The Geo-Police shows, including "fantastic symphony" and "hyperball," are performed late at night, admit no one under 18, sell alcohol, and have distinctive sexual overtones; the aim is to provide an alternative to TDL's family entertainment.

Taylorism, Service Work, and the Dialectic of Form and Feeling

Kokoro, the word used by Otsubo to criticize the American manual, has unique connotations for the Japanese. *Kokoro* is defined in the dictionary as "heart, mind, mentality, feeling, sincerity, sympathy." It is a much-invoked concept in both ethnic theories and advertising to denote that which is uniquely Japanese. *Kokoro* could therefore be invoked by Otsubo as an opposite of the American manual. In a similar manner, Marilyn Ivy (1996: 42) describes how Dentsū, in its 1970s campaign to promote domestic tourism (entitled "Discover Japan"), used *kokoro* (and *tabi*) in an appeal to nostalgia for origins, and an "antithesis of Americanized rationalism and materialism." Brian Moeran (1989) has similarly discussed the ubiquity of *kokoro* in the language of Japanese advertising. *Kokoro* is not, however, necessarily opposed to rationalism and work procedures. On the contrary, a major pedagogic tradition in Japan stresses that one must first follow the rules of the prescribed format (*katachi*) before one can be creative. Indeed, a common Japanese teaching stresses that the heart (the feeling) can be found only within the rules (the form). However meticulous and repetitious the procedure may be, its mastery is often considered the only road to self-expression. One must be completely trained in the rules for writing individual strokes, for example, before one can excel in calligraphy; a student of tea ceremony must repeat stereotyped movements such as walking, folding a napkin, and wiping the tea utensils until they are performed with a "disciplined grace." This principle of *katachi* (form) applies to the traditional training systems of Zen and the martial arts as well as to the Taylorist systems of contemporary service culture, with one major exception. Whereas traditional arts were meant to cultivate skill through individual apprenticeship, modern-day service is about training the part-time masses. The routinized procedures of the manual deskill the worker and make him or her easily replaceable. In a sense, this is the basic difference between craft and labor. The discipline inherent in both, however, served as a cultural conditioning for the Japanese domestication of the manual in general and of the Disney Way in particular. After all, spiels and manuals can be imitated, practiced, and performed like *kata*, the patterned movements of the martial arts or the arts of "the way" (*dō*).

Kokoro and *katachi* illustrate the dialectic of selfhood, in Japan and elsewhere. Like *tatemae* and *honne* and many other paired oppositions, they are flip sides of the same global coin. Kondo (1990) elaborates on the dialectic of *katachi*-form and *kokoro*-feeling in her discussion of the ethics center (*rinri gakuen*) where company employees receive lessons about work and selfhood. A central theory of pedagogy in the center was "imposing on the *kokoro* a variety of strict disciplines. . . . The rationale behind the exercises being to enter through the form (*katachi de hairu*). Do this and the *kokoro* will eventually follow" (Kondo 1990: 106). In a similar manner, Otsubo wanted to "introduce *kokoro* into the manual." His statement was not a subversive act but an acknowledgment of the system's power, which he appreciated and used. In a sense, it could not have been otherwise, since Otsubo was a trainer.

Seen through the Japanese dialectic of form and feeling, service work presents a different *stage* for the cultivation of selfhood through work. Symbolic typing—the key feature of service work—is not all *katachi* (form). It might appear to replace *kokoro* (feeling) with the manual, but *kokoro* itself stands for a disciplinary discourse (the managed heart). *Kokoro*, in the organizational world of TDL, is always the *managed* heart. Symbolic typing, as a key feature of service work, reflects a certain collapsing of the dialectics of form and feeling. TDL managers, its manuals, and its cast members almost never spoke of the cultivation of selfhood through work. The cast members at TDL, like the workers at other service companies in Japan, are not sent to an ethics center. Rather than cultivating the "self" through work, part-timers are expected to assume, temporarily, a "self" prescribed for them in the manual. They are expected to play their role in the show, keep up appearances, and smile honestly. If nothing else helps, they are reminded that they get paid for smiling.

Getting paid is perhaps the key term here. At TDL, the dialectic of form and feeling has become a more simple relation of domination, of people management, of Taylorism. Cast members may buy into the company's ideology of "magic moments," but at the end of the day, they are there for the money—only partially loyal, without a union, and always ready to quit. Part-time service work thus represents a rehearsal for the "real thing"—namely, regular work. It is an acting job that is supposed to prepare one for the real role. And it displaces industrial relations with an earlier and more stringent form of people management, namely Taylorism, thus keeping this seemingly outdated practice from the dark ages of capitalism alive within post-industrial society.

In 1991—following a period of particularly rocky relations with the United States due to trade friction and the unpopular Gulf War—Nagao Ryūichi, a professor at the elite University of Tokyo, wrote:

> Present-day US methods of management are based on the Frederick Taylor and Henry Ford systems of Scientific Management in mass production, and are supported by a Pavlovian or Skinnerian view that most human behavior is conditioned and reflexive. . . . American-style management continues to constantly alienate the work force and is thus doomed to fight a losing battle with Japanese corporations that enjoy the concentrated energies of their legions of employees. (Cited in Schodt 1994: 149–50)

The Taylorist system and its hallmark, the manual, therefore also have a symbolic life beyond the organization, in the broader realm of U.S.-Japan relations. Used in this ideological context, TDL can be seen as a black ship, a modern *kurofune*, which, like McDonald's, has forced Japan to open its gates to the American gospel of the manual. Otsubo, like many other Japanese, is constructing an ominous facade of globalization inspired by American cultural imperialism, with TDL as its fifth column / shock troops. The devil resides in Disneyland, and it is not the

Black Ghost, but the manual. This imagery is evidently yet another facade constructed through TDL. It illustrates yet another way in which
TDL is contextualized (this time in a way that alienates it) in Japan.
Such broader meanings of TDL as a cultural idiom within the popular
discourse of "Japan" brings us to the third, and final, part of this study.

PART III

OFFSTAGE

CHAPTER 5

THE THEME PARK BOOM: REMAKING THE WORLD IN JAPAN

The opening of Tokyo Disneyland was, in retrospect, the greatest cultural event in Japan during the 80's.

—Notoji Masako (1993: 225)

Part III of this study focuses on the Japanese reception of TDL. It begins with a discussion of the "theme park boom" that followed the opening of TDL. I analyze the sprouting of many "foreign lands" in Japan during the 1980s and the 1990s in the cultural context of "post-tourism" and "internationalization." I then move to consider the reception of TDL and Disney merchandise from a life-span perspective, describing different forms of reception in the context of various age groups. The analysis demonstrates how childhood, youth, and middle age are differently involved in the consumption of TDL and Disney.

The Theme Park Boom

From the 1980s to the 1990s, the leisure market in Japan grew exponentially (Economic Planning Agency 1995). Sports, hobbies, pastimes, and tourism have all increased in range and volume (Harada 1994; Linhart 1988). This decade was also characterized by the thriving of municipal expositions (or simply "expos"). These expos combined a global (or, rather, "worldly," as Walter Benjamin would have put it) theme, an international ambiance of consumerism, and amusement facilities (large Ferris wheels, for example), and they were huge successes. One of the first expos, the Osaka International Exposition—known better as "Expo '70"—attracted some 64 million visitors (over 60 percent of the Japanese population) to the pavilions of the 77 participating countries (Umesao 1985: 302). The same companies that organized these expos (such as Senyo kogyō, Togo, and Sansei yusoki) later financed and propelled the theme park boom (Matsuura 1989, 1990). Roller coasters were another popular form of amusement that thrived in the 1980s and continued to "ride out the recession" (Matsuura 1994).

In 1983, two of Japan's first theme parks opened: TDL and Orandamura (Holland Village) in Sasebo, Nagasaki prefecture, later to be renamed Huis Ten Bosch. Ever since its opening, TDL has been the most popular theme park in Japan. In its first year, it drew 9.9 million visitors; in 1984 the number of visitors was a little over 10 million, and this has grown to around 16 million in each of the years since 1990. In comparison, about 10 million Japanese traveled abroad in 1990 (*Japan Almanac* 1993: 159). TDL, as a single destination for domestic tourism, thus competes with the whole overseas market. Generally speaking, its attendance figures are the highest in the world (see Table 2 for an international comparison).

In its first ten years, TDL saw some 125 million visitors pass through its gates—a number nearly equal to the entire population of Japan. Japan's other theme parks are no match for TDL; the number of visitors to TDL is about the same as the aggregate number of visitors to all the other theme parks (Leisure Industry Data 1993: 87). In the wake of TDL's enormous success, little countries have sprouted all over Japan. These include, in a chronological order, Gluck Kingdom in Tokachi City, Hokkaidō; Space World in Kyūshū; Canadian World in Ashibetsu City, Hokkaidō; Tobu World Square near Nikkō; Shima Spanish Village; Sea Paradise in Yokohama; and a Universal Studio Tour to be opened in Osaka. The term *theme park* (*tēma-pāku*) has recently become a central cultural idiom in advertisements, trendy magazines, scholarly

TABLE 2

International Comparison of Attendance at
Major Theme Parks, 1993

Park	Attendance (in millions)
Tokyo Disneyland	16.03
Magic Kingdom at WDW	12.00
Disneyland	11.40
EPCOT at WDW	10.00
EuroDisney	10.00
Jaya Ancol Dreamland (Indonesia)	9.50
Disney-MGM Studios at WDW	8.00
Universal Studios Florida	7.40
Blackpool (UK) Pleasure Beach	6.80
Lotte World (Seoul, Korea)	5.00
Universal Studios Hollywood	4.95
Toshimaen Amusement Park (Tokyo)	4.81
Huis Ten Bosch (Nagasaki)	4.00
Kōrakuen Amusement Park (Tokyo)	2.55

NOTE: The change in attendance at any park over the 1992
season is always less than 5 percent.
SOURCE: Compiled from *Leisure Industry Data* 1994.

books, and even high school textbooks such as Shubun shuppan's *New Senior Total English II*, published in 1995. In a recent book entitled *The Theming of America*, Mark Gottdiener (1997) argues that from Las Vegas to Disney World to local shopping malls, Americans have become obsessed with "themed environments." The similar "theming of Japan" is therefore, at least superficially, part of a global consumer culture.

Huis Ten Bosch (after the name of Queen Beatrix's royal palace), operated by Nagasaki Oranda Mura Company, is, after TDL, the second most popular theme park in Japan. In 1992, it had almost 4 million visitors. It is spread over 152 hectares (375 acres) of theme park, forests, pastures, and canals, and includes several museums, a farmhouse, a seafood market, boat rides, five hotels, guest houses, and rental villas (Warren 1993). The architecture is seventeenth- to nineteenth-century European, and there are carriages drawn by Friesian horses (the breed indigenous to the Netherlands); a castle (Kasteel Nijenrode) that "reflects the romantic culture of medieval knighthood" with a display of swords and armor; a museum of traditional Dutch culture and lifestyle; an exhibit hall devoted to diamond cut glass; a real windmill with working machinery; an East-India Company pavilion, in which animated films present episodes of early trade exchanges between Japan and the Netherlands; and, of course, a shopping center. These are only a few of the attractions (for more details, see the Huis Ten Bosch homepage at http://www.bekkoame.or.jp; printed descriptions of the park can be found in *Leisure Industry Data* 1993 [in Japanese] as well as Warren 1993: 38).

Another major theme park in Kyūshū is Space World, operated by Nippon Steel on a 33-hectare site (82 acres) that was formerly a steel mill. Among other attractions, it boasts a space shuttle, a Galaxy Theatre showing films of space taken from the shuttle, a museum of space science, and several futuristic rides. Space World was opened in 1990 after Nippon Steel decided to "fight the downturn in the steel industry by getting on the leisure bandwagon" (Warren 1993: 39). In addition, a Space Camp similar to the one in Alabama is operated in Space World under license from the US Space Foundation. Space Camp Japan offers two- and four-day programs for youngsters. The complex attracted 1.9 million people in 1992.

Opened in 1990, Canadian World in Ashibetsu City, Hokkaidō, is—like Space World—the result of industrial recession, in this case in the coal-mining industry. The park's theme is a "blend of 19th-century Canadian life and Anne of Green Gables" (Paskal 1994: 13). It also has Japan's largest lavender field. From Canadian World, it is only a short trip to Gluck Kingdom in Tokachi, Hokkaidō. Opened in 1989, it is a miniature of Märchen Strasse, a 600-km German tourist route that runs through many of the sites made famous by the Grimm Brothers' fairy tales, such as the real-life castle of Sleeping Beauty and the forest through which Little Red Riding Hood skipped. Gluck Kingdom re-created scale models of some of these spots and replicated Castle Buckenburg, including the massive ceiling painting.

Tobu World Square was opened in 1993 by Tobu Railway in Fujiwara-cho, Tochigi prefecture. It features 102 models of famous edifices of the world (1/25 of actual size), including the Statue of Liberty, Empire State Building, Leaning Tower of Pisa, St. Peter's Cathedral, and Katsura Detached Palace. Parque Espagna, or *Shima Supein mura* (Shima Spanish Village) was opened on 1994 on Ise Island in Mie prefecture. Owned by Kinki Nihon Tetsudō (Kintetsu), the park is built on 113 hectares (279 acres) and features a mixed architecture of a coliseum, models of ancient Roman sites, and a roller coaster, as well as costumed characters like Don Quixote and Sancho Panza.

Theme parks in Japan do not feature only foreign worlds. There is an ample market for the theme of old Japan as well. Examples include Edo Village in Nikkō, Meiji Village near Nagoya, and Ise Sengoku Jidai Village (with a Ninja Training House and a museum devoted to the era of civil wars). There is, interestingly, only one big theme park dedicated to the heroes of Japanese popular culture: Sanrio Pierrotland (pronounced *purorando*) in Tama City, Tokyo. Opened in 1990, this park is operated by Sanrio, which develops and sells "cute" character goods, the most famous of which is Hello Kitty (see also Kinsella 1995: 226). There is also the smaller Anpanman Land (Anpanman is a popular cartoon character, a stuffed bun with super powers) opened in 1994 by Senyo kogyō in Expoland located in Senri Exposition Park, Suita City, Osaka prefecture. Kōrakuen has recently introduced live shows featuring the Power Rangers as well as shows with Sailor Moon, the animated characters. Table 3 presents comparative data on Japan's major theme parks.

There are other interesting theme parks under construction. The Makuhari Seaside Park adjacent to Makuhari Messe will offer replicas of the world's major port cities such as Venice, Alexandria, Bangkok, and Shanghai. Among the prospective rides are canal cruises on gondolas (Matsuura 1993: 49). The project is sponsored by thirteen companies, among them Senyo kogyō, Mitsui Shipbuilding, and Imajika. Another theme park, the Nishiki-no-hama Seashore of Kaizuka City, is being built in Osaka prefecture. Senyo kogyō is one of the main promoters,

TABLE 3
Major Theme Parks in Japan, 1990

Park	Annual sales (million ¥)	Employees		Visitors		
		full-time	part-time	adults	children	repeaters
				(as percent of total visitors)		
TDL	141,800	2,600	12,000	69	31	83
Huis Ten Bosch	—	2,750	1,000	87	13	—
Space World	—	320	1,000	75	25	40
Canadian World	880	63	100	89	11	20
Gluck Kingdom	2,860	100	150	75	25	35
Sanrio Purorando	—	250	300	70	30	30
Meiji Mura	1,122	110	—	75	25	50

SOURCE: *Leisure Industry Data* 1993: 89–90.

along with Nankai Electric Railways, Obayashi, Shimizu, Matsushita, and others. The park will duplicate volcanic islands of the South Seas. A simulation theater will replicate the "great voyages of Columbus" (Matsuura 1993: 50).

Most of Japan's new theme parks capitalize on the Japanese fascination with the West. Cleo Paskal (1994: 13) argues that "many of today's Japanese tourists don't want to be bothered by the horror, not to mention expense and trouble, of the real thing. They want a sanitized, Japanized version of the rest of the world, a virtual vacation. . . . TDL proved there was money to be made selling an idealized America."

TDL, in a sense, paved the way for Huis Ten Bosch—a demure homage to Japan's original Western barbarians—and later for the NASA-like Space World, the Russian Village in Niigata, Spain Village in Mie, Canadian World in Hokkaidō, Columbus in Osaka, and Venice in Chiba City. The cumulative impact of these re-creations of the foreign adds up to a special kind of cultural imperialism. This is particularly blatant in the miniature replicas of Tobu World Square. In another case, the Japanese firm Sanpo bought the stones of Rockhart Castle in Scotland (built in 1829 and ruined by time), transported them to Japan, and reassembled the castle in Marble Village, a theme park located in Takayama village, Gumma prefecture (Matsuura 1993: 50). This consumerist "cultural imperialism" spells a major reversal of traditional power relations: the "imperialist" here is the (Japanese) consumer rather than the (Western) producers. The cultural production/consumption of TDL has initiated and became part of this trend of Japanese imperialist consumption of the world.

Japan's Themed Lands in Sociological Perspective

The upsurge of foreign lands was facilitated by certain economic trends. These included governmental support projects, such as the 1987 law on resort zones and the provision of "100 million yen for every hometown project" (1988); the spread of the five-day workweek during the 1980s; and the bubble economy of the late 1980s. What interests me here, however, is the theme rather than the parks. The common cultural denominator of these leisure resorts is the remaking in Japan of a foreign part of

the world. This remaking focuses on the cute, superficial, and market-
able aspects of the foreign. There is ample sociological literature on
tourism, which has moved from staged authenticity to the transformation of self through tourism. The Japanese tourist visiting Japan's
themed lands arguably represents something different, however. This
disillusioned tourist no longer takes part in a "quest for authenticity"
(McCannell 1976a, b). Authenticity has long been replaced by the theme.
The Japanese example likewise precludes the popular sociological la-
menting of the commodification of native culture to suit tourist demands
(Bruner 1989, 1990; Cohen 1988; Volkman 1990). Native culture is merely
a theme, produced by the Japanese for their own consumption. Themed
traveling is also the current trend in overseas tourism. Sixty percent of
that market consists of package tours, of which theme tours are the most
popular (Kato Akinori 1994: 53–54). Themes for package tours include
honeymoon types, tours with a large portion of free time, sex tours, tours
to little-known regions, gourmet tours, urban tours, and countryside
tours. Themed rooms are also the latest hit in many of Japan's love hotels (Bornoff 1991). What are we to make of this fascination with themes?
Theorists have recently argued that today's tourist has a "playful sophistication" (Billig 1994: 159). This tourist, or rather "post-tourist," likes to
"explore backstage regions" (Featherstone 1991: 102; see also Urry 1988,
1990). Japan's theme parks exemplify this: they sell themselves as fictions,
thus consciously playing with appearances of reality.

Themes that originated in Disneyland were used to market TDL as
a place for "American culture" set apart from the everyday in Japan. This
was explicitly acknowledged by the Tokyo Bay Maihama Resort Community Council (formed in 1987), which decided to capitalize on TDL's
formula of success by "maintaining a unique atmosphere of America in
the whole area." *Tokyo Business Today* (October 1988: 46) reported on this
regional development decision under the enthusiastic title "The Disneyland Effect: California Dreaming in Urayasu." TDL's success is similarly
explained by some Japanese sociologists (notably Yoshimi Shun'ya) as
stemming from its reproduction of the experience of America, which was
"the spiritual foundation for Japanese society after the War" (cited in
Harada 1994: 283). The Japanese anthropologist Notoji Masako (1993:

227), in contrast, argues that for the younger generation, "Disneyland is not the holy land it is for Americans . . . but merely a gigantic amusement and consumption space with no extraneous properties." Incidentally, TDL as "merely" a gigantic amusement and consumption space may stand equally as well as a symbol for the stereotypical America, which (in comparison to Europe) "produces advanced technology" but is "poor in history and tradition, and lacks distinctive national characteristics" (Dentsū 1991). These opposite accounts may well coexist as different forms of reception, perhaps among different age groups.

Interpreted in the context of the theme parks boom, TDL's success can be seen as part of the Japanese fascination with popular images of the West—Holland, Venice, NASA, Disney, and so on. This is similar to the domestication of "things Western" in Japanese department stores (depāto), in which special areas are often themed for selling national specialties—a French cheese festival or a sale of British goods to commemorate Princess Diana's visit to Japan (Creighton 1991, 1992). The term domestication is used here to convey, to quote Joseph Tobin (1992: 4), "a process that is active (unlike westernization, modernization, or postmodernism), morally neutral (unlike imitation or parasitism), and demystifying (there is nothing inherently strange, exotic, or uniquely Japanese going on around here)." Others, however, would argue that there is a moral aspect to this process. Yoshimoto Mitsuhiro (1994: 198) regards TDL and the other theme parks as ironic images of "internationalization" (kokusaika)—the buzzword of the 1980s in Japan. He argues that kokusaika, like the theme parks, presents an accepted ("domesticated") fiction of the West while excluding it from genuine acceptance—the acceptance, for example, of foreigners and those Japanese who return to Japan after a sojourn abroad who are perceived as "contaminated" by the foreign.

CHAPTER 6

RECEPTIONS OF TDL-DISNEY

My purposes in this chapter are to repopulate the avenues of TDL and to describe the visitors to TDL not only while they are in the park but also before they go there and after they return home. I seek to expose the choices available to them as consumers of TDL-Disney and the constraints imposed upon them. To organize this audience research, I use a life-span perspective. Caution must be exercised in using this perspective, however. A self-declared "family entertainment," TDL-Disney cuts across age groups. Japanese constructions of Disney (as *kawaii*, cute, for example) also cut across age groups while having distinct age-specific expressions (for example, as explained below, Disney as *burikko* among OLs). In addition, age-specific influences of the Disney discourse, most notably socialization, presumably have an effect that lasts throughout the life span. Many middle-age Japanese, for example, say they want to take their children to TDL because twenty years ago they loved the popular *Mickey Mouse Club* television show. Finally, age categories (such as "adolescence," "office ladies," *shinjinrui*) are not taken here as given, fixed, and positivist entities but rather as social and consumerist constructions.

The life-span approach is used here as a heuristic framework. However, it can be justified on two additional grounds, both of which hinge on the larger context of consumerist society. First, the life-span approach is practiced for marketing in general and by Disney in particular. Entertainment marketing relies heavily on age gradations, some of them quite particular, such as "late parental stage," or "older single persons" (Howard and Crompton 1980: 346–47). This process of age gradation, termed "selecting and analyzing potential client groups," is involved in the construction of consumerist age groups, for example, such well-known Western constructions as the Pepsi Generation, Generation X, Yuppies, and DINCs (dual income, no children couples).

Second, the life-span approach has significant theoretical implications for the sociological study of consumerism, both in the West and in Japan. Sociologists have recently focused on the process by which consumer marketing leads to the construction of new categories in the life course as well as new age-specific images of identity. Consumerism, however, has also helped to de-differentiate previously defined categorizations of age and gender. The "unisex" style is a good example. Several sociologists, most notably Scott Lash (1990), have recently defined de-differentiation as a basic aspect of the post-modern condition. The cultural logic of consumer society—itself the product of late capitalism—is arguably an important aspect of post-modern life (Giddens 1991; Featherstone 1991; Jameson 1991). Moreover, a consumerist perspective on age groups and age boundaries reveals them to be inherently cultural constructs (Brandtstadter 1990) rather than universal sequences of stages, crises, and forms through which all "normal" selves develop (as they are considered, for example, by developmental psychologists).

The plethora of age groups in post-modern consumerist society can be viewed from two opposite ideological standpoints. The first sees the proliferation of such constructions as the result of a "project of modernity" reflecting the (capitalist) dream-come-true of progress, plentitude, and equal opportunity (Chaney 1993). This is the declared ideology of marketers, businessmen, and—most recently—multinational corporations and their managerial consultants (Ohmae 1991). This view was developed by sociologists who regard consumerism as a gateway for countercultures of popular protest and alternative lifestyles (Meyerowitz 1984; McGuigan 1992). Through consumption, subcultures of age, gender, class, style, and taste can become countercultures. Moreover, commodities can be symbolically "repossessed" in everyday life and endowed with oppositional meanings. In the consumption of music, for example, "heavy metal" is consumed by a market segment that opposes the more "conventional" pop music; whereas in the People's Republic of China, the same pop music—consumed by the younger generation—would be regarded as an oppositional Western import by the gatekeepers of socialism. The opposite view emphasizes the post-modern "consumerist paradise" as a means of social reification, normative control, and commodification (Featherstone 1991; Lee 1993). An example of this is the glorification of youth and the marginalization of old age in consumer society (Ewen and Ewen 1982). Consumer society obviously involves both de-differentiation and segregation, protest and subjugation, opportunities and control (A. King 1991). Below I illustrate how this duality operates in the specific case of OLs.

Consumerism and age groups are significantly linked in Japan. Vertical relations of authority, seniority systems, and honorific language have codified the age set of Japanese society. In Japan, age cohorts tend to be more coherent in terms of behavior (White 1995: 260), and life-stage activities—such as school completion, marriage, childbearing, workforce participation, and retirement—are particularly predictable. This age-governed system has been the backdrop against which media people and marketers "have generated and refined further age groupings and definitions of generations in terms of the consumer market. . . . Nowadays, consumer age-slots function as life stages through which Japanese men and women find themselves passing" (Skov & Moeran 1995: 56). Successful marketing campaigns have produced annual calendrical events (such as Valentine's Day, defined as an OLs' "chocolate orgy") as well as new age categories. Adolescence, for example, has only recently emerged as "a marked stage in the cultural conception of the Japanese life course" (White 1995: 255). Ivy (1993) notes that the Japanese media have created a "consumption definition of the middle class." Anderson and Wadkins (1992) similarly argue that the "new breed" (shinjin-rui) is also a consumerist creation. As in the West, the burgeoning of consumer culture in Japan has entailed the glorification of youth, capitalizing on the "Lolita complex" (roricon) of the Japanese male. Anne Allison (1996: xv) has dubbed the same phenomenon, which she traced in manga, as "the infantilization of female sex objects" (see also Schodt

1996: 37). According to Millie Creighton (1994: 94), "in Japan consumerism is less a way of 'finding oneself' and more a way of *linking selves* to others." One's magazine, for example, reflects and defines one's solidarity with an age group; a young woman in her late twenties reads *an-an*, moves to *More* when she gets slightly older, then switches to *Lee* after marriage (Skov & Moeran 1996: 66).

There is, finally, a third reason for the life-span approach. The question I have thus far refrained from addressing directly is how to explain TDL's success. In marketing terms, TDL's success depends on keeping its repeaters (around 85 percent of all visitors). In addition to adding a new "big attraction" every year or so to draw people to the park, TDL must work itself into everyday life. The question why a visit becomes part of everyday life for repeaters is complicated and more important than the simple observation that it does. TDL means different things to different groups and therefore gets used in a variety of ways. Each of the following sections provides a different perspective on these meanings of TDL. I now turn to my first, chronological point of departure, childhood.

Disneyland as Socialization: The Early Years

A variety of media keep Japanese children updated about Disney. For example, Disney enters many homes every Friday morning from 7:30 to 8:00 with the television program *Mickey Kids*. Hosted by Mickey Mouse and sponsored by TDL, the program is a quick sequence of TDL promotions, commercials for Disney merchandise, and glimpses of short excerpts from Disney cartoons. The program combines lots of Disney happiness with the Japanese adoration of sports and the *genki* spirit. It regularly opens up with characters in Disney costumes dancing with Japanese kids in TDL's central plaza, with Cinderella's Castle in the background, above a big title reading "Tokyo Disneyland." After some commercials, it returns to another regular insert—the Mickey *taisō* (gymnastics). A group of kindergarten children wearing Mouseketeer hats jump to the sounds of Disney music under Mami-chan's guidance. Such *taisō* and *undōkai*[1] are common in many kindergarten and elementary school yards in the morning. Although the Mouseketeer hats are not standard issue, many kindergarten teachers use Disney music (along with Japanese marching songs).

The exercises are followed by more commercials and then Mickey's Corner, where the costumed character talks to the viewers in person. When the Japanese calendar provides the opportunity, Mickey never fails to build his talk around local subjects, particularly *matsuri* (festivals). In a program aired on Setsubun (a popular celebration of the end of winter and the beginning of spring around February 3), Mickey explained the meaning of driving away the Oni (in its role—one of many—as the Buddhist demon) and then threw some beans while squeaking "Oni wa soto, fuku wa uchi" (Out with Oni, in with fortune). This is the traditional thing to say at Setsubun while driving away the demon by throwing beans at him—a cheerful ritual conducted in kindergartens and temples, for example—or scattering beans inside the home. The interlinking inserts just described are made in Japan, the speech is genuinely Japanese, and the *undōkai* and *matsuri* atmosphere is distinctly Japanese. Not surprisingly, many Japanese kids believe that Mickey is Japanese.

Mickey Kids is the Japanized offspring of the original Disney television shows, hosted by Walt, which were broadcast in Japan during the 1950s. Many of my middle-age respondents (now in their mid-forties) recalled these programs with nostalgia. Many recalled that *Walt Disney Presents* was broadcast every Sunday night at 8:00. Public television was introduced in Japan in 1953, and during the 1950s and the 1960s television shows from America, notably *Lassie, I Love Lucy, Sunset Boulevard*, and the Walt Disney shows, were popular (see also Ono 1983). All these shows were dubbed in Japanese. Their popularity decreased as Japanese-made shows became dominant. The socializing effect, however, was already internalized by many. A comment made in a personal interview in 1996 by Meguro Mika (currently a television playwright and a Disney fan 30 years ago) is typical: "Our generation probably received the biggest Disney influence because of the popular TV show. We later became parents when TDL was opened. So naturally, we wanted to take our children to TDL."

Early Disney socialization also included Disney animation. *The Opry House* was the first Mickey Mouse cartoon to be released in Japan, in

September 1929. It was love at first sight. Ono Kosei (1983: 7) notes that "Walt Disney cartoons charmed the Japanese. My father's generation was amused by the jovial adventures of a mouse full of fighting spirit who challenges an opponent much bigger than him out of concern for his girlfriend's safety.[2] From Disney's cartoon characters the Japanese came to grasp the image of America and its jovial, cheerful national traits." During the 1950s, Japanese children became fans of both the Disney television show and Disney feature animation films. First *Snow White and the Seven Dwarfs* (released in Japan in 1950) and then *Pinocchio* and *Bambi*, which the Disney studios had produced during the war but were banned at that time in Japan, as was everything American. Ono (1983: 7) recalls how "going to these movies became part of the schooling of those days. A whole theater would be reserved for the party of children. All the Disney movies had (for lack of dubbing technology at that time) Japanese subtitles. But it didn't bother us."

Disney animation and cartoons also had an important influence on the budding Japanese *manga* (comics) and *animē* (animation) industries. These two later underwent tremendous development and became major forms of popular culture unique to Japan. Animē and manga are obviously not restricted to one age group, although they are most blatantly consumed during primary, middle, and high school. In the context of what I am calling "early Disney socialization," Disney influenced the formation of animē and manga, and the bicultural fit between Disney and manga/animē (which have come to dominate Japanese popular culture) has indirectly promoted the reception of TDL in Japan. In a sense, TDL has capitalized on the local and wide-ranging familiarity of the Japanese market with the medium of cartoon characters and animated fantasy.

Manga and animē currently constitute a variable and complex cultural field that obviously deserves a more elaborate consideration (for English sources, see Schodt 1986, 1996; Schilling 1993; Tsurumi Shunsuke 1987; Kato Hidetoshi 1973; much more can be found in Japanese— see, for example, Satō Tadao 1973; Suyuma 1968; Tezuka 1979). Manga is, first and foremost, an original Japanese art whose roots can clearly be traced to traditional styles. One of these forebears is *emaki* (illustrated scrolls drawn with a brush, the practice dates from the tenth century).

The famous *Scroll of Frolicking Animals* (reputedly the work of Abbot Toba, A.D. 1053–1140) indeed "calls to mind Walt Disney's cartoons, a point made by an American student when Yashiro Yukio, an art historian, lectured at Harvard in the 1930s" (Tsurumi Shunsuke 1987: 31). Another uniquely Japanese form of narrative cartoon was *kami-shibai* (paper theater), which thrived between 1930 and 1955 (Kata 1979). *Kami-shibai*, illustrated outdoor storytelling using a sequence of hand-painted cardboard story boards, was unable to compete with film and television. Many of its practitioners consequently became leading *manga-ka* (cartoonists) (Schodt 1986: 62; Tsurumi Shunsuke 1987: 34). Today, manga, which enjoy an incredibly wide-ranging market and account for more than 40 percent of all books and magazines published in Japan, differ considerably from American comics. There are manga for all tastes, from the trashy to the edifying, and in all genres, from the serialized weekly to the high-school textbook. Manga is not "low culture" but, as is widely recognized, an educational and literary form. It has also developed a "unique visual code of close-ups, varied viewing angles, stop-frame techniques and visual 'sound effects'" (Duus 1988: xii). What interests me here, however, is how the mass production of manga following World War II was originally molded along the lines of patterns set by Disney and American comics/animation. My brief treatment of the subject begins with the influence of Disney on the formation of manga and animē, and then moves to its cultural and economic significance.

Ono (1983: 7) claims that Japanese cartoons introduced pie-cut eyes in imitation of the comic-strip Mickey Mouse and his companions. Even a samurai boy was drawn with such eyes. Other American cartoon characters were also influential. Pat Sullivan's *Felix the Cat*, for example, was graphically the father of Suiho Tagawa's famous cartoon *Norakuro* (see Fig. 4).[3] There was even a domesticated version of Mickey in Japan, an anthropomorphic mouse who helped a boy named Dankichi in a manga by Keizō Shimada called *Bōken Dankichi* (Dankichi the Adventurer) that appeared between 1933 and 1939. Disney movies were frantically welcomed during the 1950s and the 1960s, but since the 1970s, because of the maturation and popularity of Japanese animation, their reception has become calmer.

Fig. 4 Suiho Tagawa and Norakuro (photograph courtesy JunkoTakamizawa)

Perhaps the strongest evidence of the symmetry between Disney
and Japanese animation was the recent quarrel surrounding the release
of *The Lion King*, which many Japanese saw as a copy of Tezuka
Osamu's *Janguru taitei* (Jungle emperor). Tezuka, considered by many
the "god of manga" and the "Walt Disney of Japan," was initially influenced by the animation of Disney and Max Fleisher (Schodt 1986: 63).
Tezuka said he "has seen *Snow White* 50 times and *Bambi* 80 times"
(Ono 1983: 12). His first comic book, published in 1947, was called
Shintakarajima (New treasure island). It immediately became a smash
hit. Tezuka then created *Janguru taitei*, a serialized comic he later animated for television. The TV series was shown in the United States
during 1966 as *Kimba, the White Lion. Janguru taitei* made news again in
1994, with the release in Japan of Disney's *Lion King*. A petition of protest, alleging that the Disney film had been plagiarized from Tezuka's
earlier work and seeking credit for Tezuka, was signed by 488 Japanese
cartoonists (by September 1994, the number reached 1,126) and sent to
the Japanese distributor of Disney films.[4] The two films indeed share
several basic themes. Tezuka's English-version lion prince was called

Kimba (Simba in Disney's version); his lioness was called Laya (Nala, in Disney). The two films share the eye-scarred, black-maned villainous uncle backed by hyenas; the chattering bird friend; the wise baboon; the promotional shot of the jutting rock, the father lion in the clouds talking to his son, the stony wilderness habitat, and so on. Although these similarities speak for themselves, I do not intend to discuss the question of plagiarism here.[5] The *"Lion Taitei"* affair is described here not as a case of plagiarism but rather as an indication of the familiarity with which TDL-Disney was received into the local Japanese popular market. Although Disney defended its work as original, Tezuka Production, the company that controls the rights to the late author's work, said "Mr. Tezuka was an avid Disney fan who would have been flattered if his work had inspired 'The Lion King'" (cited in Pollack 1995: 32).

Cartoon characters, now a ubiquitous part of Japanese popular culture, are a successful marketing theme. One can even find them promoting serious services for adults, such as bank accounts. Mitsubishi Bank first put fluffy Sanrio characters on its credit cards and account books and then hired the Disney characters to do its promotion. TDL, of course, capitalizes on the Disney characters. As mentioned in Part I, the Disney Company has discovered that the Japanese see the park's Mickey as more effective and stronger than the original animated Mickey. Mickey Mouse is conceived as "the guy in the tuxedo," the performer, the entertainer, the emcee of TDL, and it is in this form that Mickey appears in TDL ads. Similarly, Kōrakuen regularly stages live shows featuring popular Japanese characters, including Goreinjā (Japan's Power Rangers) and Sailor Moon, the animated girl characters. If manga and animē characters are so popular, why not make them an overall theme at the park, as TDL does? The reply of Kōrakuen's managers to that question is noteworthy for understanding the cultural logic of the characters' market. According to Yamada Hiroya of Tokyo Dome's Amusement Department,

> Seramūn, Goreinjā, Doraemon, or Anpanman will be around only for a short while. In addition, these characters are trademarked, so we would have to pay a lot of money if we wanted to use them as themes. . . . I think, we have so much manga, so many characters, this is the problem. Heroes

come and go. Japan is the land of the trend. Can you count how many characters we have? So many. This is why we prefer to disperse our investments. We continually change the shows along with the themes. That is our theme: no theme. Have you seen the promotion for our latest attraction, Tower-Hacker? It's a manga-like ad drawn by the creator of *Akira*.

Further examples of Disney socialization of school-age children can be found in Disney educational books, Disney at a local community festival, and a school excursion to TDL. All three serve to illustrate the extent of TDL-Disney's reception and the dynamics through which it has been domesticated, imprinted with local cultural conventions in order to be consumed. Under the title "World Family," Disney offers various English-language learning products including videos, recorded tapes, CDs, and activity books. Another form of Disney education is the "Disney Discipline" (*Dizuniishitsuke*) series of colorful books aimed at pre-schoolers, which ask the young reader to identify the "naughtiest character" after looking at a picture of, say, Mickey-san, Minnie-chan, Donarudo-kun, and Pluto cheerfully walking in the rain with open umbrellas (Donald is splashing mud).

More interesting perhaps are the Disney extracurricular activities: the community festival and the school excursion. Visiting the local park one Saturday, my children and I were surprised to find ourselves in the middle of a community festival entitled "Nebārando no matsuri" (Neverland festival). Fashioned after the Disney animated version of *Peter Pan*, the festival, or sports day, included—in addition to the traditional host of food stands and other attractions—an activity course of five stations, each of them portraying a different theme from *Peter Pan's* Never-never land. At one station children could shoot arrows at wooden alligators; at another they could hit Captain Hook's head with a ball, and so on. The stations were decorated with illustrations copied from the Disney film (see Fig. 5). Those who managed to survive the queues received the ubiquitous stamp in a special *nōto* (notebook) designed for the occasion (see Fig. 6). Most of the participants were children of primary-school age escorted by their parents.

Matsuri, the Japanese festivals, are spread throughout the Japanese

Fig. 5 "Neverland" community festival

Fig. 6 Stamp notebook from the "Neverland" festival, showing a
map of the festival and two of the five activities, with the
stamps attesting the participant's completion
of the activities

calendar and play a significant role in making religion a social gathering. There has recently been a revival of local neighborhood and community *matsuri*, partly for touristic reasons (see Sadler 1969; Ashkenazi 1993; Raz 1992). Festivals and other events sponsored by local communities usually mark events in the traditional Japanese calendar, such as *bon-odori* dancing in August or Tanabata in July (see Bestor 1988; Sadler 1974, 1975, 1982), and are often staged in sacred spaces such as shrines (Littleton 1986; Akaike 1976). In recent years, urban festivals have proved enduring and yet flexible, thus becoming the focus of a great deal of attention from Japanese anthropologists (for a review, see Bestor 1990: 20). The Nebārando no matsuri that I observed was in fact a new kind of urban festival with borrowed themes in a traditional structure.

In an attempt to find out how many Disney-themed local festivals are held in Tokyo each year, I stumbled across a local ad on a message board outside the park. It invited neighborhood residents to the community center for a show entitled "Anpanman, Baikinman, and Mickey Mouse and His Big Monster" ("Anpanman to Baikinman, Mikki-mausu no okii na kaibutsu"). My children had already introduced me to Anpanman (an animated flying bun with a good heart and superpowers) who constantly fights Baikinman (literally, "germ man"). It was the first time, however, that I had realized Anpanman was powerful enough to get Mickey Mouse on his show. The two characters, both Japanese- and Disney-made, were to join forces in the dream world of Japan's children.

My last example of the early socialization of Disney is the school excursion (*shūgaku ryokō*). Traditionally, such excursions were (and still are) made to historical areas such as Nara, Kyoto, or Nikkō. Recently, however, TDL has become one of the most popular destinations. In 1988, some 1,171,000 of the park's visitors were students on such organized school outings (Brannen 1992: 217). The number was 1,049,000, including teachers, in 1994; this accounted for 7 percent of the total number of visitors to TDL that year (TDL Diary 1994–95). A detailed ethnography of such excursions is both beyond the scope of this study and unnecessary here. The very fact that TDL has become a popular destination for such excursions reflects how deeply it has penetrated Japanese society.

Although the students who visit TDL are conspicuous in their school uniforms, their actual consumption of and behavior in the park are quite similar to those of other visitors. The most unique characteristic of pupils' behavior in TDL is arguably their group activity (*hanka-tsudō*). The *han*, a small group comprising four or five classmates, is formed in every Japanese school at the beginning of each term (see also White 1990: 116–18; Duke 1988: 29–33). *Han* activities are mainly social rather than academic. They include cleaning, bringing food from the school's kitchen and serving it, and so on. In TDL, one can observe small groups of classmates—*han*—roaming around together. They usually have some prearranged assignments such as interviewing a *gaijin* (foreigner) and getting his or her autograph. *Han* also have some particular prescriptions designed to encourage teamwork. For example, although all students must be prompt, sometimes only one student per *han* is allowed to wear a watch. In a similar manner, another student gets to be the scribe, another carries the camera, another is chosen to be the treasurer. As Feiler (1991: 266; see also Teruhisa 1988) aptly observes, "Dependence on other people is not a genetic trait that the Japanese pass down through the blood, it is the logical outgrowth of deliberate pedagogical policies like these." The fact that *han* have become a general pedagogical instrument for inculcating teamwork in the workplace is well illustrated in Kondo's (1990: 80) discussion of *han* activities in the ethics center for company employees (Kondo translates *han* as "squad," which alludes to the term's military origin).

Perhaps the best way of sketching the TDL experience of students on school excursions would be to quote their own reflections. The following is a letter (translated by and cited in Feiler 1991: 270) written by a student to his teacher after such an excursion:

Dear Sensei,

I had a very nice time in Tokyo Disneyland yesterday. I enjoyed seeing Cinderella's Castle and having my picture taken with Mickey Mouse. I was glad it did not rain. But I am afraid I disobeyed one of your rules. You told us that we could not take more than 1,500 yen per person (about $15). My group, however, did not have enough money in our collection to buy each person a souvenir. Before I left home, my mother gave me 3,000 yen. I used some of this money so that all of our group members could buy the same T-shirt. Our shirts are very beautiful, and we are very happy today. I hope you are not angry. Now at least we have a pleasant memory.

Sincerely,

Tanaka Kumiko

Office Ladies, Burikko, and Disney

Keep it Cute
A motto pinned by Walt Disney over every animator's desk

—Bailey 1982: 75

Young Japanese women are a major market segment of TDL and the Disney Stores in Japan.[6] According to official OLC data (published in TDL 1995), women older than eighteen years invariably constitute more than 60 percent of the visitors. The customer profile of the Disney retail stores in Japan similarly shows that the largest age group (around 33 percent) is between 20 and 29 years old, and that 53 percent of the customers are single females (see Fig. 7). In the United States, the Disney Stores' major market consists of a different group—married people over 25 with children (The Disney Stores, pers. comm.). Since 1982 Kōdansha has published an expensive color bimonthly magazine called *Disney Fan* whose readership consists of young women aged 20–26.[7] Many American observers have noted with surprise the "inscrutable" zeal of young Japanese women toward things Disney. Jeannie Lo (1990: 43), an American woman who took a leave from Harvard to spend some months as an office lady at Brother Industries' Nagoya plant in 1986, was amazed at how OLs "cluttered their desks with toys and pins of Disney characters." Bruce Feiler (1991: 206–7), a teacher in an English school on his first date in Tokyo, was advised by an experienced Japanese friend that "Japanese girls around twenty years like Disneyland, so perhaps a (love hotel's) room with Mickey Mouse sheets would help the cause." An employee of Disney related the following story to me.

> Once I went downtown to meet some guys. We went into this restaurant. ... While I was introducing myself to everybody sitting around the table, one of the attendants came in and saw my *meishi* [name card]. She just

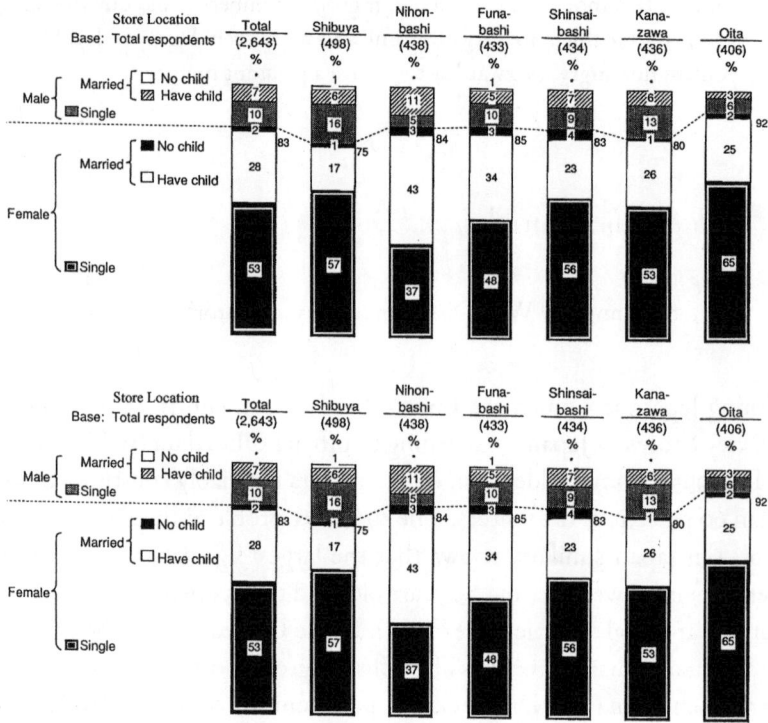

Fig. 7 Customer profiles of the Disney Stores, Japan
(top) gender and marital status; (bottom) age and gender

froze. She just—completely forgot where she was. And all she could do
was keep saying *kawaii! kawaii!* while staring at this card. Actually I had
to give her one of those cards. Just because it had a Mickey Mouse on it.

Danziger (1993: 60) states that "TDL is now ranked the country's
number one 'date course' (the ideal place to take a date). . . . A majority of Japanese women rated a visit to TDL the single greatest pleas-
ure-giving experience of their lives." I have heard stories of couples
who "got married because of TDL." To scrutinize this particular consumerist zeal for Disney, one has to enter the unique world of the
Japanese OL and her related cultural idioms of *kawaii* and *burikko*.
This section should be read as yet another example of the reception of

Disney, another angle from which to look at TDL in order to see the "Japan" behind it.

OLs are young women, usually in their twenties, who are hired as regular employees for office work. Their employment in the tertiary (service) industry has gradually increased since the 1960s. In 1990, 63.8 percent of all working women were employed in the tertiary industry; they accounted for 55.2 percent of the workforce in this sector (Iwao 1992: 157). Although OLs are usually hired as *keiyaku-shain*, they cannot expect promotion or seniority wages. They are known as *shokuba no hana* (flowers of the office)—"pretty to look at and decorative but insubstantial and transient" (Iwao 1992: 156). OLs form but one job category, however visible, in a fast-growing internal labor market for women workers in Japan. Other large job categories in that labor market are salesclerks, receptionists, and data-processing terminal operators. According to Shinotsuka Eiko's (1982; cited in Kumazawa 1996: 184) analysis of a list of job openings for women workers that appeared in the magazine *Torabayu* (from the French *travail*) in the early 1980s, the many glamorous jobs with English names stipulate age as the primary qualification (70 percent of the jobs are for women under 30), but only a handful of jobs specify education as a qualification.

The majority of OLs are employed for about four years and then usually marry. According to *Chere*, a fashionable young women's magazine, the average OL "would like to marry by the age of 30.8 and have her first child by 31.6 years of age" (Rosenberger 1995: 148). In 1990, 75.1 percent of Japanese women aged 20–24 were working—the peak of labor force participation for Japanese women (Iwao 1992: 163). Recently there has developed a new, slightly lower peak (71.7 percent) at ages 45–49, representing women who return to the workforce after their children have grown up. These are usually housewives who work as part-timers, a phenomenon found in TDL as well (see Fig. 8).

Many OLs remain at home with their parents as long as they are single (Iwao 1992: 165). They can therefore use their income primarily for shopping and consumption: clothing, hobbies, and vacations. A survey conducted by the Prime Minister's Office in 1989 on reasons for working found that the primary reason (57 percent) for women in their twenties

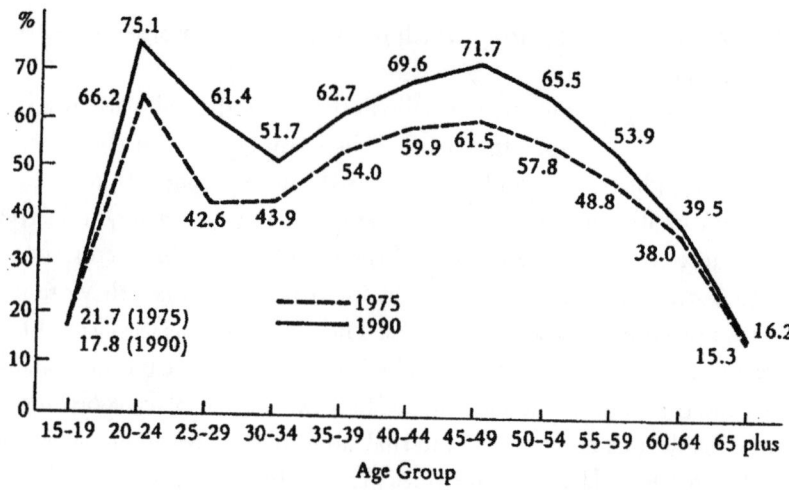

Fig. 8 Labor force participation rates for Japanese women

was "to make money to use freely" (Iwao 1992: 166). OLs therefore attract massive marketing efforts through the media, which in turn reinforce their image as easygoing, leisure- (and husband-)seeking "moratorium people." The rich imagery associated with the OL is artfully depicted in a manga book by Risu (1980), which was later translated into English. An important part of this image is the specific behavior and appearance code called *burikko*. *Buri* means pretense, *ko* is child. A *burikko* is a grown-up (usually a woman, often an OL) who acts like a child. As Merry White described it, "a caricature of a *burikko* girl has a high-pitched voice, giggles helplessly when addressed, and squeals '*kawaiiii!*' or '*iyaa!*'(I hate it) when asked her opinion on a boy, a new drink, or a cartoon on TV" (White 1993: 129). Consistent with the *burikko* behavior, young women have become avid consumers of things Disney, wearing Disney, going to TDL, and cluttering their desks with toys and pins of Disney characters. Disney can be used for *burikko* because it is *kawaii*. Western observers never fail to comment on this, seemingly unique, Japanese passion for things Disney. According to Brannen (1992: 225), "Japanese wear Mickey Mouse paraphernalia because they think it is cute (*kawaii*), not as an antiestablishment statement." Danziger (1993: 59) states that "the highest temple of cuteness (*kawaii*) is an

American import: Tokyo Disneyland." According to Katzenstein (1989: 135), "the Disney characters epitomize the cloying cuteness, called *kawaii*, so endearing to the Japanese."

Kawaii essentially means childlike; it celebrates "sweet, adorable, innocent, pure, simple, vulnerable, weak and inexperienced social behavior and physical appearance" (Kinsella 1995: 220). This style is not restricted to OLs, although it has certainly been elaborated by them. Several idioms—like *kawaiiko burikko* (or "mock cutie-pie," pretending to be a cute child)— distinctly refer to high-school girls and OLs. The Sanrio novelty company, which specializes in cute items, found in a market survey that "items sold to Japanese girls between the age of five and the time of marriage would be bought in America only by girls from four to seven years old" (White 1993: 126).

The *kawaii* style dominated Japanese popular culture in the 1980s, thus coinciding with the formative years of TDL's success. It inspired various fads (see Kinsella 1995; Shimamura 1991), including specialty goods (Hello Kitty), clothes (for example, knee-length schoolgirl socks), women's magazines (*Cutie for Independent Girls*), a top-rated animated television show with Chibi Maruko-chan as the terminally cute central character, pop music idols (most notably Matsuda Seiko), and a special style of handwriting (*burikko ji*, childish handwriting; extensively researched by Yamane 1986, 1990). Disney characters fitted neatly into this local consumerist realm of the *kawaii*. According to Kinsella (1995: 226), "The essential anatomy of a cute character consists in its being small, soft, infantile, mammalian, round, without bodily orifices, and nonsexual." In addition, the style should not be traditional Japanese but foreign—in particular American or European. Disney did all that and conquered a top place in the Japanese pantheon of the cute. *Kawaiiko burikku* pop idols posed while hugging fluffy Disney characters (notably Mickey Mouse). Matsuda Seiko, the reigning queen of *burikko* during the 1980s, wore a partial Minnie Mouse costume during her performance in the 1995 *Kohaku uta-gassen* (yearend television song contest). Many love hotels, internationally famous for their kitsch exteriors, feature themed "Disney rooms" with Mickey Mouse sheets, Disney wallpaper, and other paraphernalia. Disney as kitsch is readily assimilated into Japanese kitsch culture (see also Moeran 1993). Richie (1991: 44) suggests that "Japan found in Disneyland something in which a true fellow-feeling was discovered. . . recognized in it one of its own enduring qualities: This is a passion amounting to near genius for kitsch. . . . Japan embraced the biggest piece of kitsch in the West . . . broke off a chunk and brought it home to add to its collections."

The hybridization of Disney and Japan is best exemplified, in my opinion, in some of the paintings of Fukuda Miran (see Fig. 9). In inserting Disney kitsch from *Snow White and the Seven Dwarfs* into a kitsch landscape of Mount Fuji and combining it with ink on silk on a traditional hanging scroll, Fukuda has created a pastiche of Disneyfied Japan. It is a blend of painting conventions as well as of audience response. The art critic Yasuo Kamon (1995: 60) has written of these pictures that "the viewer often finds himself or herself laughing at them inadvertently. This laughter, however, is always directed at oneself, at the prejudices one brings to painting and art." Fukuda's paintings, like this study, acknowledge the consumerist magic of Disney while ultimately aiming for de-Disneyfication.

The childishness and innocence of *burikko* are an important part of the original Disney appeal. Sergei Eisenstein, in his insightful notes (published in French after his death) on Disney animation, summed it up as "blind purity . . . beyond good and evil" (1991: 22). Is there some internal quality in the Disney characters that makes them universally *kawaii*? My own intuition regarding this puzzle is that both Disney and *burikko* reveal forms of neoteny—a retention of youthful characteristics in the adult form. The physical evidence of neoteny includes a rounded face and cheeks, big round eyes, short and stubby limbs, softness, smallness, squeaky voice, and vulnerable weakness—the very characteristics described by the ethologist Konrad Lorenz (1981: 164–65) as the innate releasing schema for human parental care responses. The behavioral juvenilization accompanying this includes outgoing and playful friendliness and infantile speech. Mickey embodies all this; he "reflects a wish to recapture some aspect of lost childhood" (Lawrence 1986: 66). Mickey's speaking voice is that of a prepubescent child not entirely unlike the squeaky falsetto of some young Japanese women. Applying Lorenz's

Fig. 9 Fukuda Miran, *Suiboku Sansui*
(reproduced by permission of
Fukuda Miran)

schema to the evolution of Mickey Mouse, the biologist Stephen Jay Gould (1979) has shown that the image has been increasingly neotonized—the nose made thicker and shorter, the ears moving back, the eyes becoming much bigger, the limbs softer and puffier. At first, Mickey was very much a rodent. Only later did he become more anthropomorphic. In *Plane Crazy* (his first film) he went barefoot and barehanded, but by *Steamboat Willie* he wore shoes and had acquired white, four-fingered (a sign of incomplete development?) gloves.

Neoteny is a blatant social display of dependency and docility. In terms of ideology critique, this display can be interpreted as a symbol of social authority as well as of social revolt. Although described by Japanese media in terms of an exotic and longed-for world of individual fulfillment and by older-generation Japanese observers as "leisure-seeking moratorium people," the OLs are in fact caged in a social niche prescribed for them by patriarchal, middle-age Japanese society (see also Sievers 1983). Many of them resent their socially enforced moratorium, which prevents them from having their own careers while inevitably pushing them to marriage. Being "cute" is furthermore, as Kinsella (1995: 237) puts it, "an act of self-mutilation: posing with pigeon toes, dieting, acting stupid, squeaking and giggling" (see also Shimamura 1990). On the other hand, cuteness has also been viewed as a youthful rebellion against adulthood. "Rather than acting sexually provocative to emphasize their maturity, Japanese youth acted pre-sexual and vulnerable in order to emphasize their immaturity" (Kinsella 1995: 243; see also Silverberg 1991). At the end of the day, whether Mickey serves as an icon of imposed vulnerability or a symbol of anti-establishment attitude does not matter to OLC. What is important is that Mickey gets bought.

TDL and Middle Age

It is arguably with the middle aged, rather than with schoolchildren or unmarried women, that TDL's success rests. Middle-aged customers account for around 40 percent of TDL's visitors (TDL 1995: 5). Moreover, it is often the parents who decide when and how often a family will visit TDL. Since TDL's success depends on securing repeat visitors, it largely depends on catering to a middle-aged market. This section focuses on the repeaters and then moves to consider, for the first time, critical consumerist viewpoints on TDL.

OLC data (TDL 1995) suggest that the average repeater is most likely (65 percent) an adult from the Kantō district (40 percent from Tokyo itself). S/he has already been to TDL seven or eight times and arrives around 9:00–10:00 A.M. and leaves around 6:00–7:00 P.M., buys a snack and some stationery, eats a hamburger or a pizza for lunch, and probably does Splash Mountain. OLC realizes, of course, that getting the repeaters is its key to success. This is true for the U.S. Disney parks as well and, if Disneyland Paris is ever to succeed, must become true there as well. The main strategy for attracting the repeaters is new attractions. At TDL, for example, Cinderella's Castle Mystery Tour, Captain EO, and Big Thunder Mountain opened in 1986, 1988, and 1990, respectively. Each attracted long lines of eager repeaters as well as new visitors. Then came Splash Mountain (1992). The most recent addition is a whole new land, Toon Town, opened in May 1996. In the intervals between the opening of new rides, TDL offers its repeaters new events (such as the live show Pecos Goofy Goes West). The same strategy is also behind OLC's plans to build a second park, "Disney Sea," adjoining TDL's southeast side.

There are several major types of repeat visits in TDL: the family visit (around 35 percent of all visitors), the date (25 percent), the group visit (25 percent), the school excursion (7 percent), and the hospitality tour, or organized groups of workers from a particular company (7 percent). (The figures are my estimates, except for the last two, which are taken from TDL 1995). The ratios between the categories change on weekdays and weekends, vacations, and Starlight Express nights. Each type of repeaters has its own set of cultural and economic motivations for returning to TDL. In the following, I outline these motivations, first in regard to private repeaters (family, date, group) and then to non-private repeaters, the hospitality tours and school excursions. Although repeaters come from all age groups, the core group is arguably the middle-aged.

THE FAMILY

Parents visit TDL with their children for several reasons. In terms of cost, TDL was considered a good deal by many of my respondents. The following quotation is a collage of many typical explanations proffered by parents:

> It's true that Disneyland is not cheap—5,000 yen per ticket is expensive for an amusement park. But, everything considered, Disneyland is a good deal. You always get to do at least one or two of your favorite rides. A ticket to another amusement park, like Toshimaen or Kōrakuen, will be around 3,000 yen and of course you can't compare conventional-type rides to what Disneyland has. In addition to the rides, you can see at least one good show or the parade. They have good shows in Disneyland, and if you go to a show like this in Tokyo, it already costs about 2,000 yen. Parades are unique to TDL. Besides all that, you simply enjoy the walk inside TDL, the spacious atmosphere; it's very clean, impressive and safe.[8] To go for a whole-day tour in a place that interests your children is always more than 2,000 yen. In TDL you get all this—the rides, shows, and walk—in one place for 5,000 yen per ticket. That's a good bargain. You take the train from Tokyo, that's very efficient, quick and cheap, about 500 yen per round-trip ticket. You can also go there by car, and the parking is free.

Although this calculation seems extremely rational, it is also in part a rationalization. Although the TDL ticket does offer rides, shows, and parades, a family usually does all of that not on a singular outing, but over several days. Visitors therefore spend at TDL a sum equal to three or four regular outings in Tokyo. They come back to TDL because they like it and because there is nothing similar to it, despite its expense. Another often-cited reason for returning is the "plentitude principle." The following statement is typical of parents: "Of course, you cannot do everything in one day. We tried that on our first visit, and when we got home, we were exhausted. And this was on a weekday." These accounts are interesting for several reasons. They center on an economic, cost-and-benefit discourse—How much do we spend? What do we get in return?—and present the average Japanese parent as a rational consumer, which is in line with the conventional image of the Japanese (whose savings rate is one of the highest in the world). In addition, they illustrate the maturation of Japan's leisure culture. Parents are aware of their (many) leisure possibilities and plan ahead to make their visit more enjoyable.

Other replies focused on TDL's "cultural" meanings. Many parents said that "our children convinced us to go" and that "we go to Disneyland because there's nothing else like it around Tokyo or in Japan." The first reason relates to larger consumerist influences, discussed above, of Disney socialization and the importance of trends. The latter obliquely relates to TDL as a "foreign land." It is not that TDL is naively received as "America"; the Japanese consumer is more clever than that. I think that this remark conveys an appreciation of TDL as a total environment, complete-unto-itself (as an imagineer would say), a spacious, clean, and safe utopian space. And it's "fun."

There are arguably visitors for whom going to TDL is still a mini-pilgrimage to "America." Tokyoites with whom I spoke claim that such visitors are usually from the countryside, an impression that is in line with OLC data. They refer to this group of "naive repeaters" as *onoborisan* (literally, "Mr. Climber," or "people who 'come up' to Tokyo"). The name comes from the term *nobori*, which is applied to Tokyo-bound trains (trains leaving Tokyo are called *kudari*, "going down"). Even for *onoborisan*, however, TDL is gradually becoming a symbol of Tokyo—the big city—rather than of America. Examples for this come from distant places. In Ho Shao Shin's Thai film *Ton Ton's Summer Holiday*, a young village girl tells her boyfriend, as they dream about big city life, "I'd like to go to Disneyland" (meaning TDL, since they are talking of Tokyo). Tokyo's Disneyland has arguably become the "Japanese dream" for Asian *onoborisan*.

THE DATE

The Keiyō line, running from Tokyo station to TDL, usually carries many young couples and groups of three to five youngsters (*go-kon*, Japanese for "going out in company"). This is true particularly on weekdays, when young couples are the only passengers aboard that train after 10:00 A.M. These young people dress very similarly: sports shoes, jeans, windbreaker or leather jacket for the guy, and high heels or boots, nylon stockings, a miniskirt, black-vinyl coat, and small (very small) school-type *burikko* bag for the girl. Usually it is the girl who does the talking. TDL as a romantic destination is the perfect place for *burikko* display for many young women. I have heard many young men saying that they suggest going to TDL for a date "not because I like it or something, but I was told that suggesting Disneyland has the greatest chance of getting them to say yes" (i.e., to agree to go on the date). Many young women and OLs have confirmed this, adding: "If a guy suggests that we go to Disneyland, I know he's serious, because it's so expensive, it's for the whole day, it's fun so we don't have to worry about what to do and what to talk about, and obviously he's not expecting me to follow him to bed at night." According to John Van Maanen (pers. comm.), in southern California "there is a somewhat similar (older) teenage (middle-class, white) dating pattern wherein Disneyland represents a 'serious' date rather than a casual one—also, one suspects, because of cost as well as 'wholesome' environment suggesting to girls that their dates are perhaps less likely to expect to get laid following a visit." Kuenz (1993: 80) similarly observes how, "in spite of the park's sexlessness—or perhaps because of it, WDW is now the number one honeymoon destination in this country and may soon be also the number one site for marriage: Disney plans to open an on-site 'wedding pavilion' where, for anywhere from $17,000 to $100,000, couples can say their vows in the shadows of Cinderella's Castle." Although TDL does not yet offer such a service, it would surely become a major hit in the Japanese wedding market (Goldstein-Gidoni 1993), which is currently thriving with spectacular, high-tech and high-kitsch shows of "laser light extravaganza" (Feiler 1991: 256), rotating stages, and fireworks, which are exceeded in spectacle only by TDL's Electric Parades.

THE GROUP

Groups of Disney fans who return for a favorite ride or experience range from high-school students (girls, usually) to middle-aged housewives. Group members usually know precisely what they want to do in TDL. Akiko, a high-school TDL fan, said "I always do the same thing—Star

Tours and Splash Mountain." These dizziness machines, or "screamers" (as opposed to the "dreamers," the quieter thematic rides) are indeed the most popular in the park. Jun, a TDL fan in his twenties, says he "loves the sense of danger. To get off the ride with my tongue hanging out and say: I did it! I don't believe it, but it's over and I did it." This is the play element described as *illinx* by the French sociologist Roger Caillois (1961: 23): "The pursuit of vertigo . . . consists of an attempt to momentarily destroy the stability of perception and inflict a kind of voluptuous panic upon an otherwise lucid mind." Illinx-type activities, like skiing, motorcycling, dancing, and amusement park rides, involve the pursuit of a temporary disorder or sudden panic, the intentional suspension of bodily stability and clarity of perception. The desire for disorder, a drive that is normally repressed, is here given leeway to erupt—and then repressed again, proving that everything is in fact under control. In Victor Turner's (1969, 1982) terms, the amusement ride is a rite of passage whose middle phase consists of an anti-structure, a suspension of normative order (see also Katriel & Ness 1984). This is also captured in Csikszentmihalyi's (1975) notion of "flow." Such conceptualizations—as well as the international popularity of amusement parks—attest to the universal appeal of illinx.

Group visits to TDL are, however, also cultural performances. TDL gets worked into everyday life, becoming something of an expected and semi-programmed secular ritual anticipated like public holidays: "We always go to Disneyland before the end of summer"; "We try to go midwinter when the lines are short." This is, of course, true for other popular resorts as well. Visits become much like routines (for families and groups of friends), and the group develops its own ingenious strategies for visiting (we do Tomorrowland first, then cut across to Frontierland/Westernland, then eat at Plaza Pavilion, etc.). This is a logical extension of the rational consumerism described in the case of parents. With the advent of age, many fans replace Splash Mountain with Small World. Again, a similar approach is described by Van Maanen (pers. comm.) in the case of DL: "For urbanites with impoverished leisure sites, discomfort with seemingly unordered social scenes and distrust of surprise, DL is rewarding and it is always there, open and predictable. Peo-

ple in SoCal buy yearly passes as gifts as well as for personal use. The
elderly hang out on Main Street (viewed as a 'problem' by management)."

THE ELDERLY

Elderly people are usually neither repeaters nor Disney fans. An elderly
Japanese woman who went to TDL remarked that "I didn't understand
what the whole thing was trying to say. What impressed me was that the
fireflies were computerized. . . . You know, we used to have Japanese
pirates around the Inland Sea, but we are more familiar with those
mountain bandits who raided and stripped the travelers naked. I would
have understood [Pirates of the Caribbean] if they had these bandits on
the show" (cited in Notoji 1988: 8).

Elderly people are considered extremely conservative consumers, and
their consumption code is the most restricted. "Old age is characterized
by what we might call the 'consumption of tradition'" (Skov & Moeran
1995: 8). According to OLC, pressure from elderly visitors made them
open Hokusai, the only Japanese restaurant in World Bazaar. As far as
its advertisements are concerned, TDL is a temple of youth. Its numerous catalogues, guidebooks, and miscellaneous leaflets show only young,
good-looking customers. Old age is excluded from the Kingdom of
Dreams and Magic.

SCHOOL EXCURSIONS AND HOSPITALITY TOURS

My treatment of these two is quite brief since they are managed and
organized by institutions rather than individuals. I have already discussed the school excursion in the socialization section. Hospitality
tours are organized on Saturdays by companies, usually ones that sponsor a TDL attraction. According to Komuya (1989: 192–93), "OLC's
Members Section (Kai-in-gyōmu-ka, part of the Eigyō-bu, or Sales Division) organizes two clubs. The first is the Magic Kingdom Club for
corporations and government offices. Those who become members can
organize hospitality tours with discounted tickets. The second is the
Executive Club, which corporations join in order to use TDL as *settai*."

This reference to *settai* is interesting since it illustrates another (relatively hidden) facet of the domestication of TDL. *Settai* means business outings, company-sponsored entertainment for company guests. This is a common, often institutionalized practice that can amount to 5 percent of the company's annual operating expenses (Allison 1995: 16). Popular forms of *settai* include *"settai* golf," top-class hostess clubs in Akasaka or the Ginza, and expensive restaurants. *Settai* TDL illustrates the acceptance of the park into the leisure culture of companies. *Settai* TDL also throws into relief the use of the park as a programmed form of leisure (*rejā*) rather than individual play (*asobi*).

The Problem with Leisure: Rejā/Asobi and Infantile Consumerism

Rejā wa asobi to chigaimasu (Leisure and play are different).
> —IPA-Japan member, speaking at the
> 1995 Annual Meeting in Osaka

Amusement is the commodified negation of play.
> —Susan Willis, 1995

Is Disneyland an amusement park or a playground? For some observers, this distinction is critical. Disneyland is, undoubtedly, a controlled environment and a rational organization. Its managed onstage goes hand in hand with its managed backstage and the "managed heart" of its cast members. While appealing to most visitors, the Disney fixation with control bothers others, in Japan as well as in the United States. This section explores the critical reactions to Disneyland among some of its consumers. My exposition begins with the IPA-Japan (International Play Association)'s annual meeting, held in Osaka in December 1995, at which I was invited to give a paper on "the structure of play in Tokyo Disneyland." IPA is an international non-governmental organization, recognized by UNESCO and UNICEF with consultative status. Founded in Denmark in 1961, it currently has "national action groups" in nearly fifty countries. It is interdisciplinary and embraces members of all professions. IPA-Japan has several hundred members, but the hard core of activists contains about thirty–forty people. Members include academics, schoolteachers, labor union activists, and artisans, with a majority of white-collar, middle-aged professionals.

The Osaka meeting centered around Osaka municipality's plans for a new *kodomo no shiro* (literally, children's castle), a modern three-story activity center and children's museum. It was the first time that a municipality had sent official representatives to an IPA-Japan meeting and was willing to listen to the members' opinions. According to IPA member Sonoda Takaaki (associate professor of chemistry at Kyūshū University), this willingness was "mainly *tatemae*; the municipality promoted this new project under the slogan of 'residential participation,' and they merely wanted us to endorse their slogan." The standpoint of IPA members was that the museum had too much hardware (in the katakana version, *hādo*) and too little software (*sofuto*). In other words, its technological environment did not promote enough creative activity and free play. It provided *rejā*, but not *asobi*.

This opposition later became a major ideological premise of the IPA-Japan worldview. It was no coincidence that they chose *rejā*, a loanword written in katakana, to stand for activities that are designated as play but do not foster it in reality, or that are merely "fun" but do not have the added value of play. The word opposed to it, *asobi*, was made to stand for the Japanese tradition of children engaging in creative, free play. The word *asobi*, however, also carried with it a wide semantic array of "traditional" concepts, from outings, freedom, and indulgence to ritual worship (*kami-asobi*). It is a distinctly "Japanese" word, like *kokoro* (see Moriya 1989). Members explained that *rejā* is executed indoors and hinges on technology, for example, the *famicon* (family computer, same as Nintendo). *Asobi*, in contrast, is usually conducted outdoors, in natural settings and open spaces (*harappa*). Whereas *rejā* consists of prescribed activities, *asobi* promotes the imagination. IPA members spoke of *asobi* as a creative, unexpected activity in which a stick, for example, can turn into a pirates' sword and a cardboard box into the pirates' ship.

While opposing the American-import *rejā*, IPA members also fought what they considered the growing control in Japan over children's life. In an article entitled "Children's Spirit of Play and Creativity Being Withered by Adults' Management," IPA member Okuda Rikuku (1995:

30) typically laments that "Japanese children have lost their ability to play of their own free will. They lack creativity. A child asks a volunteer mother who works at an after-school playroom, 'What origami will you teach me today? Would you hurry because I have a piano lesson right after this.'"

IPA members argued that children's life in Japan is increasingly managed by parents who send them to *juku* (cram schools) and teachers who do nothing but follow the rigid curricula set by the Ministry of Education (a stance not uncommon among contemporary Japanese intellectuals). IPA-Japan members' paradigmatic opposition of *reja* versus *asobi* therefore entailed further dichotomies, such as control versus freedom, technology versus nature, and Americanization versus "traditional" Japan.

THE BIG NINTENDO

The meeting provided ample opportunities to discuss the meaning of TDL. At first, IPA members were careful to say what they thought was good about TDL. Sonoda told me that "from the point of the design, it is the best theme park in Japan. It looks like real. Other parks don't have this. I think this is the reason for its success." Tanpo, another IPA member and a furniture maker by profession, said that "the quality of the hardware is much higher compared with that in the regular Japanese park." According to Ogasawara Hirokata, an anthropologist, "It is the closest thing to virtual reality. It's animated." This praise, however, had in it the seeds of criticism, which was to follow quickly. TDL was *reja*. It was built on "play according to the manual" (*manyuaru-ka sareta asobi*) and on a totally controlled artificial environment which is the complete opposite of *harappa* (open space). According to Sonoda,

> Twenty years ago Japanese children played completely different games. Free play, in the street, with friends. . . . Today this has all changed. We sponsor here an exhibit of photographs [Haginoya 1995] that traces this change. Today, there's only mechanical leisure: Nintendo, Disneyland. Each of these is a technological environment, programmed and predictable, where the user does not have to show any creativity, only control of the machine.[9]

The complaint regarding overcontrol is also brought up by American visitors to WDW. Willis (1995: 1) cites academics who said that they were "bored during their entire Disney stay. . . . The trip was pleasant, but everything was so contrived." Similar criticisms were voiced by the Tokyo white-collar media professionals with whom I spoke. Meguro Keiki, an NHK (Japanese National Television) manager whom I interviewed in Tokyo, said: "When I go to TDL, I feel like I'm stupid, simpleminded, *onobori-san*. Like those people who love *Tora-san* movies. But this is mass culture, after all." Karen Klugman (1995: 106, 109) cites an American architectural engineer who confessed that his visit to WDW "was interesting, but once was enough. . . . I like my vacations to be more active. Like going to museums in Washington. They supply ten percent, we have to supply ninety. At Disney, it's ninety/ten the other way. Disney does the ninety. . . . I don't like to go somewhere where they chew the food for you."

These critical observations on the theme of control echo previous critiques, discussed at the end of Part II, of Disney's organizational culture. Some Disney visitors engage in unmasking the "laughter," in analyzing their own consumption of Disney, just as some Disney employees are bothered by their Disney smile. Many observers have suggested that control and predictability are the keys to the success of the Disney parks (Bryman 1995: 99) as well as to TDL's (Yoshimi 1996; Awata & Takanarita 1984: 140–222). For some Japanese writers, this line of analysis carries with it shades of criticism, reflecting a frustration that comes with the realization of the "fakeness" and how in fact the TDL magic works. According to Yoshimi (1996: 56, 63), TDL has "sold off the spirit of *matsuri*," replaced the carnivalesque with the predictable: "people never 'enjoy like crazy' in TDL; you merely take your part in the show, becoming two-dimensional as in a cartoon." Awata and Takanarita (1984: 140) similarly realize with disappointment that "TDL may look like a *matsuri*, but actually it is not. TDL is too clean, rich, pure, and anxiety-free." The authors conclude on an apocalyptic note: "Now Japan is a light (*karui*) culture, everything is light, trendy, playful, nothing ideological, nothing personal, light like Disney. But maybe, sooner or later, we will get tired of this lightness and look for another simulation" (1984: 228). More than ten years later, the Japanese have not grown tired of

TDL, which, according to Yoshimi (1996: 62), is still a synthetic, "hygienized" setting, similar to the "edited fairytales in the Disney films" (cf. Zipes 1994). This criticism (like its object, perhaps) is probably beyond time and place. More than 25 years ago, Schickel (1968: 327) called it "the Disney version": "[In the park], as in the Disney movies, the whole world and all man's striving for dominion over self and nature, have been reduced to a sickening blend of cheap formulas packaged to sell. Romance, Adventure, Fantasy, Science are ballyhooed and marketed: life is bright colored, clean, cute, safe, mediocre, and somehow poignantly inhuman."[10]

Perhaps the Disney version of amusement could be better illuminated by comparing it with Disneyland's most successful forerunner at the turn of the twentieth century: Coney Island. Located on the southwestern end of Long Island (New York), this amusement center flourished from 1895 until the years before World War I, its success coinciding with America's coming of age as an urban-industrial society. Coney Island was a true carnival city, with three enclosed amusement parks (Steeplechase, Luna Park, and Dreamland) as well as various sideshows along its main promenade, where the grotesque was prominently represented: midgets, giants, fat ladies, ape-men, and other freak shows (my description is based on the excellent book on Coney Island written by John Kasson [1978]). Walt Disney knew, of course, about Coney Island. He made it explicit that he wanted Disneyland to be different from those amusement parks, which were, in his words, "dirty, phony places run by tough-looking people" (Schickel 1968; cited in Spinelli 1992: 350). Besides his fixation with cleanliness, Walt Disney also wanted a controlled family entertainment. Disneyland was intended to be a complete contrast to Coney Island's freak shows and libertarian seashores, which emphasized the grotesque and the sexual, and its many attractions that encouraged visitors to break away from social control. Steeplechase, for example, installed a number of devices designed to catch patrons off guard in a way that would never be thought of in a Disneyland. Visitors entering Steeplechase from the ocean side had to "pass through the 'Barrel of Fun,' a huge, slowly revolving cylinder which frequently rolled patrons off their feet and brought strangers into sudden, intimate contact. The main lobby led customers inescapably to the Blowhole Theater, where concealed compressed-air jets sent hats flying and skirts shooting upward" (Kasson 1978: 61).

This carnivalesque spirit of release is cloaked, in Disneyland, by pixie dust. Steeplechase, very much like *matsuri*, provided a release from social control; Disneyland, in contrast, works hard to provide the illusion of control. At Steeplechase—as in the traditional Japanese ghost-house (*obakeyahiki*)—patrons were encouraged to play the fool; in Disneyland, guests are never an active part of the show. The presence of mirror attractions (such as the Laughing Gallery) at Steeplechase and their absence from Disneyland is no accident. Mirrors encourage reflexivity, as does playing the fool; together, they may very well destroy the performative illusion of Disneyland (see also Little 1993). Seeing his or her reflection in a mirror might also disturb a Disney costumed character (say, Goofy) in the act of symbolic typing.

As described above, acting as a cast member involves more than keeping up appearances: it often also involves maintaining an "emotional false consciousness," a term coined by Peter Freund (1990: 469) to describe a split between bodily displays (such as a smile) and awareness of internal, psycho-physical sensations (such as boredom or annoyance). Reflexivity (or "true" consciousness) is, therefore, a burden in Disneyland for both visitors and employees. Van Maanen (1989) mentions the term *go into robot*, used by cast members to describe keeping up appearances under stressful work conditions. Spinelli (1992: 283) cites an equivalent term used by cast members to describe patrons' behavior in the park: "checking their minds into the lockers in front." As one WDW cast member described it, "After a couple of rides, Guests almost seem as if they are in a cattle round up or something, or they are like sheep and they would simply mindlessly do things. . . . See, people are in a different environment and they sort of expect that they are going to be taken care of" (Spinelli 1992: 283).

The theme of infantilization, which is the flip side of overcontrol, therefore connects both cast members and guests. However, the critical remarks of IPA-Japan members also had, in this context, an additional *nationalist* overtone. According to one of them, "Americans exported Disney as a fantasy for the Japanese generation which distanced itself from the post-war ideal of 'America.' Disneyland is also a subtle mechanism of authority, you know. Read Dorfman about what Disney did in Chile. Disneyland works to keep us as children, to infantilize us." The ideological discourse of IPA-Japan members inevitably constructed TDL as *a priori* an *American* black ship of *rejā*. TDL was ideologically cast as the ambassador of American capitalism, spreading around Japan a smokescreen of infantile happiness and false consciousness.[11] As another member suggested: "TDL pretends to add new attractions, while in fact it remains the same. They have to make an impression of new attractions, so that visitors will keep flowing in. But this is only make-believe intended to make more money. They are just after the money. It's a capitalist machine."

The image of the infantile consumer is obviously partial and biased. As we saw in previous chapters, TDL has many types of consumers and gets worked into various forms of consumption—from the *aficionado* to the critical, from anti-establishment to traditional. TDL as a black ship of infantile leisure was an ideological facade created by IPA members. In addition, members ignored the fact that TDL is owned by a Japanese company, that some of its attractions are original and some have been changed in Japan, that its success is connected with the intrinsic changes that led the Japanese economy into its post-industrial stage in the 1980s, and that the spreading of "foreign lands" around Japan also reflects a kind of Japanese cultural imperialism. The image of TDL as a black ship—also conjured, although for other reasons, by Kōrakuen managers—provides an indication of its complex reception in Japan. The cultural imagery associated with TDL is varied, at times self-conflicting. TDL, as a recontextualized simulacrum, can accommodate all of this and more. In titling this study *Riding the Black Ship*, I offer the image of the black ship for reversal and deconstruction; it is an ephemeral label for the reflexive consumer designed to be a facade pointing at its own backstage.

TOON TOWN VERSUS DRAGON DUNES

Some IPA-Japan members, who were also play experts, had an additional substantive criticism of play in TDL, which extended beyond ideological facades. Concisely put, the argument criticized TDL for offering only "functional" play and no "social" play (see Senda 1992: 12–13 for definitions of these two developmental categories of play). The first, "functional" stage of play involves experiencing the play structure, for example, sliding down a slide. The final, "social" stage of play involves using the play structure as a medium, for example, playing tag on a slide. From the point of view of IPA members (as well as many developmental psychologists), the "social" stage is the more important one, since it promotes interpersonal communication and other forms of social competence. The rides in TDL simply do not allow for "social" play. As Ogasawara said, "You can slide down or swing on them, but that's it. They leave you socially incompetent."

Obviously, TDL is not supposed to foster "social" play. It is not the child's everyday playground but a special place to be visited once or twice a year. While agreeing with that observation, IPA members nevertheless claimed that a "good" park should also provide a setting for social play. Some of them mentioned their favorite example: Shōwa kinen kōen (Shōwa Memorial Park), located west of Tokyo near Nishi-Tachikawa station. Operated by the Parks and Recreation Foundation, this park comprises about 120 hectares (296 acres) and is advertised as the most up-to-date leisure spot in the Tokyo metropolitan area. In addition to the conventional-type water playland, woodland hobby house, and lakes, its special "social play" attractions include Foggy Woods (a maze filled with fog every 30 minutes), Rainbow Hammocks (a huge construction of interlinking hammocks for climbing and jumping), and Dragon Dunes (huge air-filled polyethylene dunes for the same purpose). In addition, there are no queues (because any child visiting the park can enter an attraction at will). Shōwa Memorial Park therefore eliminated the queues by giving up on *control*. Its visitors are not moved around (by "people-movers"), selected (at the gate and specific attractions), fed (with American fast food), or otherwise controlled. The visitors to Shōwa Memorial Park—my IPA-Japan respondents stressed—play by their own free will and on their own initiative, interact socially and physically, invent their own games while on the attraction, and often get dirty as a result. The park entrance fee is 400 yen per adult and 80 yen per child, which is about 10 percent of TDL's adult entrance fee and less than 3 percent of the children's fee.

The Disney imagineers are aware of and attentive to this line of criticism. One of TDL's imagineers noted that "interactive play is a big thing now. We recently introduced it in Toon Town, the bouncing house for example, though you would probably regard it as too small and too clockwork as well. OLC always asks us for more 'interactive' things, but when they see the designs, they say it's too dangerous, too unpredictable.[12] They say that guests will get dirty or might hurt themselves." The issue of social, or interactive, play thus brings us back to square one: control and predictability.

CHAPTER 7

TRAVELING THEORIES: ABOARD THE BLACK SHIP

Draw, partner: At the Japanese Disneyland outside Tokyo, children re-create America's cowboy myth.

—Photo caption in *Time Magazine*'s cover story "America in the Mind of Japan—Japan in the Mind of America" (February 10, 1992)

In *Sullivan's Travels*—a 1941 Preston Sturges film—Joel McCrea plays successful Hollywood director John L. Sullivan, an idealist who believes you cannot accurately direct a screen tragedy unless you live it first.[1] Disguising himself as a bum, Sullivan "goes native," as the anthropologists say, and sets off to see the United States from the bottom up. Soon he finds himself in a county prison, doing hard labor among chain-gang convicts. One of the most memorable scenes portrays the prisoners all dressed up and ready to be taken to a special treat: a Saturday night show. Crammed into the local movie theater, prisoners and wardens alike laugh themselves to tears in front of Disney cartoons. In the midst of the brutality and despair, the young director makes a valuable discovery—what the downtrodden need most is laughter.

Sullivan's Travels bear a superficial similarity to this author's traveling. Both of us went native in order to see things from the bottom up and rediscovered Disney as the site for personal/theoretical revelation. Sullivan's encounter with Disney, however, is very different from the encounter described in this study. A closer juxtaposition of the two could illustrate the problem of doing a cultural critique of TDL. Sullivan was a self-disguised tourist who carried the Hollywood melodramatic, modernist gaze into the world of the "less fortunate," framing Disney as an (exported) opiate for the masses. This author, in contrast, was a self-declared "barbarian in Asia" (following Michaux 1949), who trailed middle-class Japanese tourists into their imported "foreign land," otherwise known as Tokyo Disneyland.

Critics have seen the Disney scene from *Sullivan's Travels* as an illustration of Disney's contaminating power where "laughter is betrayed" (Kracauer 1950). The audiences may laugh, but Disney is not just a laughing matter. Disney has consistently attracted serious criticism, beginning with European social critics before World War II such as Benjamin and Adorno, who looked at Disney as the site for American cultural imperialism and a prototype of the American "culture industry." Walter Benjamin's reflections on film and mass culture were haunted by Disney, whose films "pioneer ways of disarming the destructive effects of technology through technologically-mediated laughter" (Hansen 1993: 32). In Max Horkheimer and Theodor Adorno's (1944: 138) chapter on the culture industry in *Dialectic of Enlightenment*, we read that "Donald Duck in the cartoons, like the unfortunate in real life, gets his beating so that the viewers can get used to the same treatment. . . . This 'iron bath of fun' administered by the culture industry does not inspire a conciliatory laughter that would echo the escape from power, but a *Schadenfreude*, a terrible laughter" (cited in Hansen 1993: 34).[2] At first, such deliberations might seem overburdened with ideology. Donald Duck? *Schadenfreude*? However, the sweeping global grasp of the Disney Company and its continuous economic success for the past fifty years inevitably lead to the conclusion that the question of Disney's cultural capital is worth pursuing. Recently, Benjamin's and Adorno's critiques of Disney were echoed in Fjellman's (1992: 3) assertion that WDW embodies the logic of Huxley's *Brave New World*, which "predicted that we might be tamed by desire and pleasure." Disney critique also erupted in Latin America with Dorfman and Mattelart (1975) and most recently resurged in

France with the opening, in 1993, of EuroDisney (aka Disneyland Paris), which suffered losses as well as a negative reception. Marguerite Duras likened it to a "cultural Chernobyl" (*International Herald*, December 6, 1991), and many French intellectuals expressed the view that it was another form of "creeping Americanism" (Van Maanen 1992).

This study began with the proposition that TDL is a case of cultural adaptation rather than cultural imperialism. The question was how Disney has been domesticated in Japan, a term suggested in order to convey, following Tobin (1992: 4), a process that is active, morally neutral, and demystifying. I have tried to show the local sides of globalization—to take, following the central metaphor of this book, the "black ship ride."[3] The ethnographic thrust was thus defined as reading Disney from below, from the Japanese point of view. Each of the preceding three parts has contributed a facet to this reading. Part I presented the onstage strategies of TDL through three of its "dreamers" attractions. These were read as three variations of cultural flow—Meet the World, explicitly Japanese in both content and style; Mystery Tour, implicitly Japanese in its uniqueness and audience reception; and Jungle Cruise, an adaptation of the American original whose cultural contents were preserved while its wrapping (spiel) was considerably changed.

Another form of cultural flow was described in Part II. Disney's American worlds and TDL share the basic distinctions and boundaries of the Disney organizational culture, such as regular/part-time and onstage/backstage. However, the specific contents are different and often reversed. Part-timers in TDL are trained in the Disney way and their service culture is "American," yet this Disney culture has been assimilated into a Japanese culture of behavior protocols and teamwork. The same applies, in reverse, to the world of regular employees. Here one could find glimpses of American corporatism in the midst of Japanese company life. Moving further into an ideology critique of the organization, I showed how the Disney Way is resisted both in America and in Japan, as illustrated by the reactions of part-timers to the smile factory. Global features of emotion management within service culture, such as symbolic typing, were described and linked to their Japanese conceptualizations, for example, those articulated through the "manual-*kokoro*" opposition, which later re-emerged as the "*rejā-asobi*" dichotomy.

Finally, Part III focused on domestication through consumption, offering a life-span view from which to link the passion for TDL-Disney with tourism, socialization, gender, and local forms of popular culture.

Obviously, not everything American automatically succeeds in Japan. It is interesting to compare the success of Disney with the failure, in Japan, of the world-famous television series *Dallas*. *Dallas* failed in Japan after being broadcast for six months. Liebes and Katz (1990: 130) report that Japanese focus group members, interviewed in Tokyo by Professor Iwao Sumiko, explained that they were unable to become emotionally involved in Dallas because of several inconsistencies. First, on the syntactic level, *Dallas* "violated their expectation of the genre of home drama" (Liebes and Katz 1990: 133). There was resentment that each episode was not complete in itself and did not end in a harmonious note. Second, on the semantic level, the narrative had many internal inconsistencies of plot and motivation.[4] Third, on the pragmatic level, the Japanese discussants said, "America was the model for postwar, not present-day Japan. We used to identify with America, but we do not any more" (Liebes & Katz 1990: 136). On the whole, they said, "*Dallas* doesn't give us a dream" (1990: 137).

In contrast to *Dallas*, Disney does all that. On the syntactic level, Disney fits into various local genres—from the *yūenchi* and *obakeyashiki* to *manga* and *animē*. It is self-consistent and complete unto itself, and the familiar semantics always have a harmonious note. In terms of television discourse, Disneyland is perhaps the perfect post-TV medium—free of prerequisites and long expositions, brief and easy to understand.[5] On the pragmatic level, Disney is not received as merely a window to "America," in the same way that *Dallas* was perceived. The domestication of Disney means that it gets worked into the everyday life of different age groups in different ways. "Disney" is part *kawaii*, part amusement, part illinx, part animation cinema, part family entertainment, and part domesticated "America."

The Culture Industry Revisited

It has been a long ride, moving through different lands and various themes. The "ride" metaphor works on several levels, conveying a sense of flow and transition. This study is neither on "Disneyland" proper nor on "Japan" alone. It was conducted in the margins, in the offstage zone between these two imaginaries. Properly speaking, it was conducted aboard the black ship. The notion of "ride" also conveys a temporary disruption of equilibrium, a consciously induced illinx of the theoretical scenery. Globalization as cultural imperialism—like all grand narratives—hinges on some affixed, unilateral order that needs to be shaken (see also Said 1981; A. King 1991; R. Robertson 1992; Spivak 1990). Aboard the black ship, our theories also travel. As Perry (1995: 51) concludes, "Insofar as globalization can be represented at all, it is through the contradictory pluralities of such enforced in-betweenness and the tactic of serious play to which it gives rise. . . . [Globalization can be] glimpsed, but not grasped." Does TDL (and this book) contain a general lesson about globalization? TDL can—perhaps—be grasped, but TDL is not the only case of or model for globalization. Perhaps globalization can only be glimpsed because it is actually a "ride," a dynamic process involving many actors, vehicles, and facades. Grand theories of either "world-systems" or "cultural adaptation" are often too abstract to provide a satisfactory account of who exactly is riding the ship, and how.

TDL has been constructed in this study as the site of theoretical revelation. My original intent was to frame the study of Disneyland in Tokyo as an opposition to what Sugimoto and Mouer (1981) call "the Great Tradition" of Japanese studies: the conventional worldview and orthodox research agenda of Japanology, which has focused on work and industrial relations rather than on leisure and the part-time service sector. Later, however, it transpired that the theoretical context of the study was more international than Japanological, and that the former needed as much opposition as the latter. Disneyland has been often described as the "post-modern" epitome of the culture industry in late capitalism.[6] Traveling with Disneyland to Tokyo offers the possibility of deconstructing these statements and exposing their blind spots. We need to look at our theories from the viewpoint of TDL, rather than read TDL within the framework of our theories.

The major theoretical theme that has been read into Disney, from Adorno to Fjellman, is the culture industry. Fjellman (1992: 410) describes

WDW as "presenting a 'scholastic program' for the naturalization of the commodity form." The notion of "scholastic program" goes back to Gramsci (1971: 103–4), who defined it as a "general conception of life" for the masses, disseminated through schooling, moral teaching, the mass media, and so on. In other words, we are talking about ideology. The hegemonic meta-message of our time, argues Fjellman (1992: 9), is that the commodity form is natural and inescapable; "our lives can be well lived (or lived at all) only through the purchase of particular commodities." WDW encapsulates this meta-message. It is "the teaching shrine for the corporate world of commodities" (1992: 17). To elucidate his point, Fjellman distinguishes between two prototypes of scholastic programs: the one described by Orwell in his *1984*, and the one that Huxley wrote about in *Brave New World*. Fjellman's point is that while we were watching for Orwell, Huxley rode into town, bringing *soma* (the opium of the brave new world) and wearing mouse ears. The same point was made more than ten years ago by Neil Postman in the context of television culture. "In America," argued Postman (1985: 155–56), "Orwell's prophecies are of small relevance, but Huxley's are well under way toward being realized. . . . In the Huxleyan prophecy, Big Brother does not watch us, by his choice. We watch him, by ours." In Disney's worlds, Fjellman argues, exhaustion and cognitive overload lead visitors into the bliss of Commodity Zen—the characteristic state of television culture and post-modern life in general. An ongoing hyperreality of pleasure captures the visitor's attention, deflecting it away from sustained critical thought about the "real world." As Fjellman describes it, this is management by carrot. Disney is not just offering entertainment: the company is also selling an antidote to everyday life.

This view of Disney's worlds is again problematized in TDL. To argue, along with Fjellman, that TDL sells *soma*, is to argue that TDL sells the same thing as WDW and DL—in other words, that TDL is a replicated 100 percent copy of the American parks. This view was indeed taken by several Japanese commentators. According to Yoshimi (1996: 56, 63), TDL has "sold off the spirit of *matsuri*"; Awata and Takanarita (1984: 140) similarly lament that "TDL may look like a *matsuri*, but actually it is not. TDL is too clean, rich, pure, and anxiety-free." These authors' characterization of TDL as the culmination of "light (*karui*) culture" in contemporary Japan echoes Fjellman's warnings about post-modern, corporate America.

This view, however, is only partial, since TDL is not a perfect copy of the original Disneylands. Japan has appropriated a large chunk of American kitsch and brought it home. The Japanese visitors to TDL are not simply naive recipients of Disney's *soma*. For the Japanese, TDL has also become a museum representing the commodification of "America"—a role usually played by the *depāto*, with which TDL shares a family resemblance. TDL has also become a lot of other things, as Part III set out to describe. TDL's Japanese visitors are also rational consumers, making their own choices, working Disney into their own everyday life. This, I would dare to suggest, applies just as well to many of Disney's American consumers.

TDL and Disney in general embody something different from the conventional "culture industry." The consumerist logic of Disney has no commitment to ideology. It is remarkably efficient when it comes to self-censoring attractions that are read as "ideological" by certain visitors. As Billig (1994: 155) argues,

> specific imagineered dreams can be always sacrificed on the altar of consumer satisfaction. For instance, women visitors might soon complain, via the questionnaire, about the Fantasyland[7] display in which the audio-animatronic pirate chases the audio-animatronic wench. . . . Professional calculations of profit and loss would then be computed. . . . Should the marketing graphs recommend change, there would be little to save today's racist or sexist images. They are expendable elements in the practical ideology of success.

In 1991 TDL, for example, scrapped a show featuring "three clowns in monkey costumes with colorful Filipino outer attire performing Filipino dances following a request from the Philippine Embassy in Tokyo, signed by Consul Erlinda Gavino" (*Japan Times*, October 10, 1991: 2[4]). The offending portion has been replaced by Chip and Dale, which—some would say—are also part of Disney's ideology. My suggestion is that if there is ideology in Disney's worlds, it is too often in the form of meta-messages read by observers.

The conventional culture industry is modified in Disneyland from two directions: first, Disney's own amazing ideological flexibility; and second, the different ways by which Disney is consumed and worked into everyday life. Conventional ideological readings of Disney as a culture industry therefore center on the text while neglecting the audiences. The culture-industry view, like the simulacrum, tends to be depopulated. The onstage ideological vacuum of Disneyland is not empty; it is filled with various cultural and consumerist interpretations made by intellectuals, repeaters, casual visitors, and committed sociologists. This study has attempted to repopulate the land of Disney by focusing on its vivid inhabitants—workers and consumers—whose life (obviously) extends before and after their visit to Disney.

The Black Ships of Glocalization

In the Introduction, I offered the term *glocalization* (borrowed from the discourse of international business and marketing) to stand for the local adaptation of global culture. I use this term in order to reclaim a cultural space that is found in between our structural binarisms of production/consumption, media/reception, onstage/backstage. In reclaiming this space, I am trying to make room for a plurality of negotiated meanings that undermine monolithic and bleak narratives of capitalist imperialism, either in the form of functionalist modernization or neo-Marxist dependency (world-systems, culture industry).

Ulf Hannerz (1989) sought to define glocalization within a "macroanthropology of culture." However, it seems to me that glocalization falls more naturally under the perspective of symbolic interaction, whose universe of discourse is located within a mezzo-world of negotiated meaning in between post-structuralism, semiotics, and phenomenology. One can link the recent theorizing about glocalization to the classical concerns of symbolic interactionists. Glocalization is what actually happens in social worlds, with the global commodity—the video, television, Hollywood, Coke, MTV, McDonald's—as the symbol that spins webs of interaction that become imbued with local meanings. Such glocalities are fluid, changing, emerging, always part of an interactive order.

Because of its fluidity, pinpointing glocalization is a difficult task. It is also a matter of perspective. There are those who would prefer to focus on the global processes—the production line of American culture, or the standardized scripts of service management, for example. To be sure, Disneyland contains these global elements. From a different perspective, however, these elements are neither the only ones nor the most essential. Onstage, TDL has no essence—it is an image processor; not an agent of Americanization but a simulated "America," showcased by and for the Japanese. It is an "America" to which the Japanese give meaning. Nationalist ideologies are part of this meaning but, again—not an essential part. TDL is not the place to look for national identity in its tribal, primordial, essentialist definition. "National identity" exists within specific fragments of TDL (Meet the World, for example), and it exists there in a playful, evasive manner. In that sense, TDL illustrates how our images of identity are becoming ever more transient, shallow, a matter of consumption.

Turning our attention to the backstage, we encounter again a play of perspectives and essences. Managers and business journalists would no doubt emphasize the ubiquitous catechism of the Disney Way—the manual. Yet in TDL one finds a plethora of manuals—not only the original Disney manuals, but also the traditional manuals of Japanese company life. In addition, the original Disney manuals have been changed through translation. In Japanese, DisneyTalk loses much of its magic. In a similar vein, while managers would tend to emphasize the success of the strong Disney culture in Japan, sociologists would offer a more sensitive and local discussion of the role of Japanese culture. Within such a sociological perspective, there is room for discussing alternative readings of individualism and subjectivity, even resistance. In a similar way, domestication through cultural consumption can be regarded as a counter-reaction to cultural imperialism.

The lesson here is that our discourses—academic and popular—are based on powerful images and preconceptions. Academics have their own reflex arc of smiles and laughters, and these may be as canned (Schickel's term) and horrendous (Adorno's) as those of cast members and Disney fans. Alarmist paradigms of globalization and of the black ships of cultural imperialism should always be examined from a position that is both nomadic and grounded. So situated, theories become, in the words of William James (1977), a pragmatic instrument, rather than answers to enigmas, in which we can rest.

Reference Matter

Notes

Introduction

1. The word *tabi* is a non-Sinified Japanese lexeme that "portrays an aesthetic and affective concept Japanese feel is uniquely theirs" (Ivy 1996: 36). The traditional meaning of *tabi* is exemplified through expressions such as *tabi-geinin* (itinerant players), *tabi-yakusha* (itinerant actor), or *tabi-garasu* (bird of passage; a wanderer). The traditional image of *tabi* had overtones of difficulty, sadness, perseverance, and great effort. Yanagita Kunio (cited in Shirahata 1995: 54) argued that "it is entirely due to a new culture that people began to travel (*ryokō*) for the purposes of pleasure." It was the difficulty and sadness of *tabi* that traditionally made it a symbol of life: the journey as life and life as a journey. Bashō's *Oku no hoso-michi* (The narrow road to the north) begins: "The years that come and go are travelers (*tabi-bito*)" (translated by Keene 1978: 100; cited in Shirahata 1995: 54). Marilyn Ivy (1996: 35–38) provides an intriguing discussion of the media use of *tabi* as a key image in Dentsū, Japan's 1970s "domestic tourism" campaign entitled "Discover Japan."

2. According to Bell (1973), post-industrial society begins when the workforce in tertiary industries (such as the service sector) exceeds 50 percent of the total workforce. By 1990, only one of every three employees and one of every five companies in Japan was in the manufacturing sector (Sano 1995: 40). The rise of the service sector was complemented by the exponential growth of leisure activities from 1980 to the 1990s (Harada 1994; Linhart 1988). According to Bell's original formulation, post-industrial society is also to be a leisure society. A similar process is often characterized in Japan as the shift from an "industrialized" to an "information-oriented" society and from hardware to software (Kakita 1984: 4).

3. The argument of appropriating or "domesticating" Disneyland in Japan was previously touched upon by Brannen (1992), Tobin (1992), and Yoshimoto (1994).

4. In summer 1853, four American "black ships" weighed anchor in what is now Tokyo Bay. Their hulls were huge and black, and two of them were belching smoke; to a contemporary Japanese witness, they were "floating sea fortresses." The U.S. East Indies Fleet, under the command of Commodore Matthew Perry, was an effective military display of might. It succeeded in putting an end to the long period of Japanese isolation, ultimately leading to the collapse of the Tokugawa shogunate and thus bringing feudalism in Japan to an end and prompting Japanese modernization. According to Sonoda Hidehiro, "the image that the Japanese have today of the black ships was formed in that year" (Umesao 1985: 182). Commodore Perry's ships, however, were not the original black ships. The expression *black ships* originally referred to the sailing ships that reached Japan from Europe. Most Portuguese trading ships were made from oak, which was particularly susceptible to woodworm. A black coating of pine resin, tar, hair, and pine shavings was supposed to prevent this (Umesao 1985: 181). These original black ships, loaded with the products of distant civilizations, conjured up a sense of the exotic rather than of military might. Because of the Tokugawa policy of isolation, they disappeared from Japanese waters during the seventeenth century, except for the annual arrival of Dutch sailing ships at Nagasaki.

5. "Modernization" and "world-systems" theories represent two different yet complementary axes in the worldview of globalization as cultural imperialism. The former stems from an evolutionist and positivist stance; the latter from a critical, neo-Marxist view of dependency. The "modernization thesis" argues that non-Western, "developing" countries are "modernized" by emulating the capitalist structure of Western democracy with its educational, technological, political, and medical systems. For the original suggestion, see Parsons 1966; Cogwill & Holmes 1972 offers a variation of this thesis in regard to aging; for critical discussions, see Webster 1984 and Roxborough 1979. The modernization perspective, as employed in "Japanology," produced numerous descriptions currently regarded as biased (Sugimoto & Mouer 1981). Following Japan's postwar economic boom, there has been a surge of socio-anthropological studies depicting and explaining the Japanese "development" from the village to the city and the company as a process of rapid "Westernization" (Vogel 1970; Cole 1971; Rohlen 1974; Masatsugu 1982; Hamilton & Biggart 1988). During the 1960s and the 1970s, Japan was regarded by many American Japanologists (and politi-

cians) as a symbol of peaceful modernization (in contest with the Soviet Union for "unaligned" nations) based on the presumed continuity of traditional values (Miyoshi and Harootunian 1991). The development of the Japanese educational system (DeVos 1973) and of the growing middle class with its pursuit of leisure and hence the growth of Japanese modern popular culture in general (Linhart 1988) were likewise considered the results of "Westernization"—here a synonym for "modernization" and perhaps also for "Orientalism" (Minear 1980).

Seen through the mirror of "modernization," third-world "developing" countries are considered to be passively and unreflexively (and often also "inconsistently") "modernized," or acculturated, into the Western world through identical cultural trajectories (Kumar 1978; Said 1978). Such criticisms produced the competing world-systems theory, which argues that Western capitalism hinges on the reproduction of the economic dependency of the third world (Wallerstein 1974; see also Tracey 1985; Fejes 1981; Mattelart 1979). These two competing theoretical agents of globalization—the modernization thesis and the world-systems theory—share a common blind spot: They both generalize and reproduce the image of the "acculturated" as passive recipients of Western, mainly American, cultural hegemony.

6. Cultural imperialism is, to be sure, part of global as well as local realities, as illustrated in studies of the international spread of the television series *Dallas* (Ang 1985; Liebes & Katz 1991), Hollywood ethnic cinema (Friedman 1991), or advertisement (Belk 1988).

7. Frank Stanek later became the executive vice president of MCA Enterprises International (a subsidiary of Universal; Paris 1988: 38). Ironically, in 1997 MCA was working to bring a Universal Studio Tour theme park to Japan. Negotiations for this huge project were being conducted with Nippon Steel and Osaka municipality.

8. Different figures have been cited regarding the royalties. Mary Yoko Brannen (1992: 231) claims that "the Walt Disney Company receives 7% of TDL's profits from admissions, food, and merchandise." Brannen does not cite a source for this figure. The 7 percent might represent an average of the 10 percent and 5 percent cited by my references. Mathematically, however, it would be a mistake to calculate such an average, since the profits from admissions and food and merchandise sales are far from being equal.

Chapter 1

1. In addition to the "general passport," which gives admission to all the attractions, visitors can purchase tickets for individual attractions. Attractions

are indexed according to their ticket's price. An "A" ticket was 100 yen in 1995–96, a "B" ticket was 200 yen, and so on up to the most expensive "E" ticket (500 yen). This follows the DL system.

2. *Jan ken pon* is a very popular children's game in Japan (and around the world). It is played between two or more people, often to decide who will go first in a game. The players say *'jan ken pon!'* in unison, and on the word *pon* they form with their hands one of three shapes: rock (*gu*), scissors (*choki*), or paper (*pa*). The rock (a fist) breaks the scissors (a "V" formed with the fingers), the scissors cuts the paper (open hand, palm up), and the paper wraps the rock. If there is a tie, players say together *ai, kode, sho!* and repeat the game, continuing until someone wins.

3. An example of ordinary polite language used by the guide is the frequent utterance "Minna-san, kochira desu" (Everyone, please step over here). The spiel does not, indeed cannot, contain words like *kochi dayo*, which mean "Get over here" in the plain/abrupt level of speech commonly directed at children (for more on discourse analysis of Japanese, see Ikegami 1989).

4. Pixie Dust, the dust from Tinker Bell's magic wand that enables Wendy and her brothers to fly with Peter Pan, is DisneyTalk for "the magic which enables people to let themselves be seduced into the fantasy and suspend disbelief" (Spinelli 1992: 279). It is used by Disney imagineers and designers to denote the stylish decor featuring Disney themes and characters. Its backstage use, however, can also be quite ironic and derogatory. Spinelli (1992: 279) quotes two examples: a former Jungle Cruise ride operator who said that his "training lasted two days but the pixie dust wore off in one week"; and a supervisor at one of the restaurants who said that pixie dust was the term for the litter used to clean up vomit. TDL employees were not familiar with this term.

5. This is a mistake. Main Street Cinema, showing six different vintage Disney cartoons simultaneously on separate screens, is also "complimentary." It is, like Meet the World, the Disney Gallery, and the live shows staged around the park, one of TDL's "services."

Chapter 2

1. There are about 300 frontline American employees, including face characters, costumed characters, dancers, and craftsmen, as well as about 30 Disney professionals working backstage as advisors and imagineers. Craftsmen such as glass-blowers and face-cutters (see next note) are sent from the Arribas Brothers Company, which provides such artists to DL and WDW as well. Frontline American cast members are hired by OLC as *keiyakushain*, or contract

employees, for six months. All those approached by me have been extremely careful, saying "I am a guest of this country," "I am not a Japanese citizen," "Talk to my boss." Their lives seem to be controlled by the company to a great extent. Some of them work sixteen hours per day and then return to apartments rented and maintained for them by OLC in Chiba City. Japanese language was evidently not part of their training before coming to Japan, and OLC preserves this situation. One of them told me over the telephone that "working in TDL is like living in an American resort." Some of the artists extend their six-month contracts. At least one of them had been married to a Japanese woman and later divorced her.

2. Face-cutters create and frame a silhouette of the customer's face while s/he waits in the Silhouette Studio located in the World Bazaar (called the Shadow Box in WDW Main Street, USA). The artists are employed by the Arribas Brothers Company and sent as contract employees from America to TDL.

Chapter 3

1. The postcard is a light-blue card with black printing signed by the Tokyo Disneyland Casting Center (written in katakana). The text accompanying the good news provides an indication of the meticulous instructions that await the new hire in the Disney manuals: "We are happy to inform you that you have received a job in TDL, so please call this number. If you don't call, it will be automatically canceled. The job is already yours, so if you call and the line is busy, try again. Tell the operator your name clearly and that you have this postcard. Looking forward to hearing from you."

2. The senpai-kōhai relation exists in almost every form of a Japanese dyad that is not collegial. It can be found in universities, corporations, and schools for martial arts. It denotes a relation of hierarchy—literally, the two concepts denote "the one who comes before (sen) and the one who comes after (go)." The senpai is not an official teacher (sensei) but a senior who becomes a guide—often a guide for life in general.

3. In May 1992, up to 3,000 French employees of EuroDisney reportedly quit over pay and working conditions. In January 1995, a report compiled by Jong Jarvis, an assistant professor of communications at Robert Morris College, indicated that French cast members were dissatisfied with many of the American working practices. These included exempting the park from established French labor laws, the requirement of American managers that English be spoken at all meetings (even if the vast majority of participants were French),

and insistence on American standards of dress and personal grooming (see also Van Maanen 1992: 27–28).

4. Hayashi (1988) suggests an explicit connection between the predisposition to *yarikata* as it appears, for example, in judo, kendo, the tea ceremony, and so on, and Japanese management protocols.

5. Reality is more complicated. The enterprise unions usually join a federation of a single industry (*tansan*), and several *tansan* assemble to form a national center. For example, Rengo, which started in 1989 as a national center, is a federation of 87 *tansan* (Karthaüs-Tanaka 1995: 82). The basic issues of wages and bonuses, however, are negotiated at the company level. For an ethnography of Japanese workers in protest, see Turner (1995).

Chapter 4

1. The OLs are an interesting example. They are hired as *seishain*, and their manuals are tremendously detailed and full of protocols. As *shain*, they are officially regarded as *shakaijin*, although in practice this group enjoys a kind of social moratorium. The OL completes her transformation into a true *shakaijin* only when she gets married.

2. Kondo (1982: 47) similarly argues that "to Westerners, who often prize the consistency of inner expression and outer feeling and the quality of 'sincerity,' Japanese ritualized behavior and polite language may seem a mask or charade—at worst, a betrayal of self." In reality, however, a Japanese person "may move with exquisite ease in the world of *tatemae* and remain exquisitely sensitive to the demands of *giri*, social obligation, but one's *honne* and *ninjō*, human emotion, never disappear. The tension is creative—and spiritual education can play on this tension" (Kondo 1982: 60). This exquisite ease with which one moves between public and private is no doubt enabled, in part, by the existence of elaborated *linguistic* discourses that discern and shift between these levels. Kondo's (1982: 143) example is the female workers in the shop, who "among themselves, spoke with a schoolgirl's informality, in a rough and boyish Japanese, but the moment a customer appeared, the most exquisitely polite language would flow effortlessly from their lips." This example is significant; it illustrates how language (intimate/honorific) becomes a marker for private and public realms, and in the process comes to stand *for* them. I am quoting from Kondo's Ph.D. dissertation rather than from her book (1990) since her attitude toward *tatemae/honne* later changed in an interesting way; in the book, these dual dimensions of selfhood become emphasized not as a social ontology in their own

right but rather as discursive modes of self-presentation that can challenge the Western idea of the "whole subject."

3. *Crafting Selves: Power, Gender, and Discourses of Identity in a Japanese Workplace* is the full title of Kondo's (1990) influential book. It deals with life on the shop floor of a small, family-owned artisanal factory, rather than with a large-scale service company. However, a comparison of Kondo and Hochschild can be justified on the grounds that (1) there are still almost no ethnographies of service culture in Japan; and (2) Kondo's and Hochschild's analyses of emotion management are very much in line. For example, one of Kondo's major *emic* concepts, the ideal of cultivating selfhood through work, is *sunao na kokoro* (which she translates as "the naive heart"). This "naive" heart, however, is the subject of much discipline and training—not unlike Hochschild's "managed heart."

4. For a discussion of cyclical versus linear time, see Leach 1971, 1976 and Hazan 1980, 1994.

5. The new operator failed in her *kimarimonku*. She should have used the slightly different expression *osewa ni natte orimasu.*

Chapter 6

1. *Undōkai* is a field day or a school sports day. October 10, for example, is a national holiday in Japan called "sports day," and schools schedule *undōkai* at this time, as well as at other times during the year. It is common for businesses to hold sports days also, featuring both serious athletic events and group games. I am somewhat stretching the meaning of *undōkai* in using it to refer to Mickey's *undōkai*.

2. There is an overtone of audience reception here. In the early Mickey Mouse and Silly Symphony films, Disney and his animators created a fantasy world, "freed from the burdens of responsibility, (where) events are open-ended, reversible, episodic, without obvious point. . . . The world is plastic to imagination and will." Then this world was replaced, around 1933, with an idealized world of moral tales. "This world has rules, and you better learn them or watch out" (M. Sklar 1975: 197). Ono is obviously referring to the "second stage" of Mickey cartoons. Such a preference may be linked to the prevailing Confucian-based moral worldview of Japan. Sergei Eisenstein (1991: 13), in contrast, was completely in favor of the first world, of which he writes with reverence: "What magical restructuration of the world according to its proper fantasy and proper arbitrariness! You tell the mountain: 'Move', and it moves. You tell the sun: 'Stop!', and it stops."

3. Suiho did not confess to this influence until just before his death (Kosei Ono, pers. comm.). For a discussion on the cultural meaning of *Norakuro*, see Yamaguchi 1990.

4. One of the animators who signed the original letter was Satōnaka Machiko, cartoonist, born in Osaka in 1948. Satōnaka later published an "open letter," based on the original letter, on the internet—http: //www.eccosys. com/SMN/opinions/sletter.html.

5. According to the *San Francisco Chronicle* (July 18, 1994, p. E1), "In interviews with eight Disney people who played important roles in producing *The Lion King*, three acknowledged some prior knowledge of Kimba." For pictures (GIF files) of "Kimba on a jutting rock" and additional Kimba art from Tezuka Studios, see http: //members.aol.com/~dragon456/kimba_gallery/index.html.

6. The Disney Stores are a new section of Walt Disney Company's Consumer Products Division. Disney Stores entered Japan without a partner, as they did all over the world. By the end of 1995 there were 27 Disney Stores in Japan. In 1995 these stores had over 7 billion yen in sales, which represents a 56 percent growth over 1994. Although World Bazaar's shops and the Disney Stores sell what seem to be the same Disney products, in fact they are strong competitors, owned and operated by different companies and buying their merchandise from different suppliers.

7. Figures about *Disney Fan* are from an interview I conducted with Honda Tadaakira, assistant editor of the magazine. *Disney Fan* is basically a heavily illustrated catalogue of new Disney merchandise and bargains. Eighty percent of its 80,000 bimonthly print run is sold through subscriptions. Kōdansha also publishes a Disney family activity magazine whose 150,000 copies are sold primarily in stands and stores. When I asked Honda to explain why a magazine like *Disney Fan* has been created in Japan (and not the United States), he simply replied: "because there are no OLs in the U.S."

8. John Van Maanen (pers. comm.) points out that in DL, some parents even "drop their children (as young as five or six) off at the main gate each morning during the summer (DL as a daycare center) since they figure, what better supervision can the kids get than DL. This is, however, viewed as a problem by management (and the Anaheim police department when unsupervised children are identified by park security and the cops are called)." No such phenomenon was found in TDL.

9. IPA-Japan members are not the only ones to criticize the social influence of the *famicon* (known as "Nintendo" in the U.S.). For a general discussion of how computer and video games are radically redefining patterns of interpersonal

communication and social abilities, see Provenzano (1991). For a discussion of computer games in the Japanese context, see Okuno 1995 and Takayama 1987.

10. Such views are overly stringent. The Disney magic apparently works for most people, whereas others remain immune or even become antagonistic. As Willis (1995: 1) asks, "Why are you so critical? Wasn't anything fun?" This is a question worth asking. If there is a "problem with pleasure," as Willis (1995) and Fjellman (1992: 3) suggest, this problem is not altogether Disney's, but is rather *ideologically read into* Disney—a tendency I have tried to avoid. Disney is made to stand for societal processes such as late capitalism, commodification, commercialization, simulation, and so on. In other words, Disney is reified. I return to this question in the conclusion.

11. One is tempted to draw here a connection to Asada Akira's (1991) term "infantile capitalism," which he coined to describe Japan's brand of capitalism as a frenzied state of competition among children, and a "childlike obsession with machines." Asada's infantile capitalism seems to pair rather well with Disney's smile factory. There is, however, a major difference between the two: the former seems to be about laissez-faire while the latter stresses control and management. I believe that Asada's term belongs to a different ride; I would love to hear his comments on TDL, though.

12. OLC has proved to be rather conservative on several occasions, the most recent of these being their refusal to build a Disney Studio Tour near TDL. A TDL imagineer recounted that "for several years, Disney has been presenting OLC with ideas for the new park, which Eisner (a film person basically) thought could be an MGM-style Studio, a movie park. But OLC finally said, thank you, we don't want it, it's too dangerous. It took them a pretty long time to decide, but finally they realized they were losing so much money because of it. . . . They wanted more of the same." According to a Japanese person who works as a conference interpreter in Disney presentations for OLC managers, "their attitude is one of playing safe, conventional. That's my general feeling. Refusing the MGM studio was one example."

Chapter 7

1. I am grateful to Norman Denzin for bringing this film to my attention.

2. Mickey Mouse (or Mickey Maus) was generally endorsed as a symbol of Americanization in Weimar. According to Hansen (1993: 34), the National Socialists included Mickey Maus in their campaign against the *Verniggerung* (negroization) of Germany, ironically (mis)interpreting Mickey's blackness and protruding white teeth (Storm and Dressler 1991).

3. It is a noteworthy feature of globalization that the word "ride" has been kept as a loanword in all of Disney's worlds (in Japanese, *raido*; in French, *le ride*), and subsequently has also been domesticated in the host language.

4. For example, "if Bobby and Pam elope, presumably against the wishes of their parents, how can they return to the parental ranch immediately after the honeymoon? If they are so rich, how is it that they set the table by themselves?" (Liebes and Katz 1990: 133).

5. See Neil Postman's (1985: 147–48) *Amusing Ourselves to Death* for a brisk articulation of the "ten commandments of television." See Wertheim 1995 for an analysis of Disneyland and the Disney films as a post-TV medium.

6. It is noteworthy to recall here Lash's (1990: 37) distinction between two types of post-modernism, one "mainstream" and the other "oppositional." Mainstream post-modernism furthers the hegemonic project of the new middle classes and promotes the values of consumer capitalism. This trend characterizes many recent cultural studies of Japan—books on kimono, marriages, tea, schooling, comics, and so on.

7. The scene Billig is describing seems to be taken from Pirates of the Caribbean, which is found in Adventureland rather than Fantasyland.

Works Cited

Abraham, K., & J. Medoff. 1984. "Length of Service, Terminations and the Nature of Employment Relations." *Industrial and Labor Relations Review*, October, 38(1).

Adams, J. 1991. *The American Amusement Park Industry*. Boston: Twayne.

Adler, S. 1983. "Snow White for the Defence: Why Disney Doesn't Lose." *American Lawyer*, Mar.: 32–35.

Akaike Noriaki. 1976. "Festival and Neighborhood Association." *Japanese Journal of Religious Studies* 3: 127–74.

Allen, Holly, & Michael Denning. 1993. "The Cartoonist's Front." *South Atlantic Quarterly*, special issue: The World According to Disney, ed. Susan Wills, 92(1): 89–119.

Allison, Anne. 1995. "Company Entertainment: Co-Mingling Play and Work." In T. Umesao, B. Powell, & I. Kumakura, eds., *Japanese Civilization in the Modern World XI: Amusement*, pp. 13–23. Senri Ethnological Studies, no. 40. Osaka: National Museum of Ethnology.

————. 1996. *Permitted and Prohibited Desires*. Boulder, Colo.: Westview.

Anderson, Laurel, & Marsha Wadkins. 1992. "The New Breed in Japan: Consumer Culture." *Canadian Journal of Administrative Sciences* 9(2): 146–54.

Ang, Ien. 1985. *Watching Dallas: Soap Opera and the Melodramatic Imagination*. London: Methuen.

————. 1996. *Living Room Wars: Rethinking Media Audiences for a Postmodern World*. London: Routledge.

Appadurai, Arjun, & Carol Breckenridge. 1988. "Why Public Culture?" *Public Culture* 1(1): 5–9.

Arakawa Sōbei. 1977. *Kadokawa gairaigo jiten* (Kadokawa loanword dictionary). Tokyo: Kadokawa.

Asada Akira. 1991. "Infantile Capitalism and Japan's Postmodernism: A Fairy Tale." *Boundaries 2*, special issue: *Japan in the World*, 18(3): 629–34.

Ashkenazi, Michael. 1993. *Matsuri: Festivals of a Japanese Town*. Honolulu: University of Hawaii Press.

Awata Fusaha & Takanarita Tōru (1984). *Dizuniirando no keizai gaku* (An economic study of Disneyland). Tokyo: Asahi Shinbunsha.

Baba Akiko. 1971. *Oni no kenkyū* (A study of oni). Tokyo: San'ichi.

Bachnik, Jane M. 1986. "Time, Space and Person in Japanese Relationships." In Joy Hendry & Jonathan Webber, eds., *Interpreting Japanese Society*, pp. 49–74. Oxford: JASO.

Bailey, Adrian. 1982. *Walt Disney's World of Fantasy*. New York: Everest House.

Baudrillard, Jean. 1983. *Simulations*. New York: Semiotext(e).

———. 1988a. *The Ecstasy of Communication*. New York: Semiotext(e).

———. 1988b. *America*. London: Verso.

———. 1993. "Hyperreal America." *Economy and Society* 22: 243–52.

Bauman, Zygmunt. 1992. *Mortality and Immortality and Other Life Strategies*. Cambridge, Eng.: Polity.

Befu Harumi. 1983. "Internationalization of Japan and Nihon Bunkaron." In H. Mannari & H. Befu, eds., *The Challenge of Japan's Internationalization: Organization and Culture*, pp. 232–66. Tokyo: Kodansha.

Bell, Daniel. 1973. *The Coming of Post-Industrial Society*. New York: Basic Books.

Belk, Robert. 1988. "Third World Consumer Culture." *Research in Marketing*, supplement no. 4, pp. 103–27.

Ben Ari, Eyal. 1986. "A Sports Day in Suburban Japan." In J. Hendry & J. Webber, eds., *Interpreting Japanese Society*, pp. 211–27. Oxford: JASO.

Best, J. 1989. *Images of Issues: Typifying Contemporary Social Problems*. New York: Aldine de Gruyter.

Bestor, Theodore C. 1988. *Neighborhood Tokyo*. Stanford: Stanford University Press.

———. 1990. "Lifestyles and Popular Culture in Urban Japan." In R. G. Powers & H. Kato, eds., *Handbook of Japanese Popular Culture*, pp. 1–33. New York: Greenwood Press.

Billig, Michael. 1994. "Sod Baudrillard! Or Ideology Critique in Disney

World." In S. Herbert & M. Billig, eds., *After Postmodernism: Reconstructing Ideology Critique*, pp. 150–72. London: Sage.

Birnbaum, Steve. 1989. *Walt Disney World: The Official Guide*. New York: Avon Books.

Blake, Peter. 1972. "Walt Disney World." *Architectural Forum*, no. 136, June, 24–41.

Blocklyn, Peter L. 1988. "Making Magic: The Disney Approach to People Management." *Personnel* 65: 28–35.

Boje, David M. 1995. "Stories of the Story-Telling Organization: A Postmodern Analysis of Disney as 'Tamara-Land.'" *Academy of Management Journal* 38(4): 997–1035.

Bornoff, Nicholas. 1991. *Pink Samurai: The Pursuit and Politics of Sex in Japan*. New York: Grafton Books.

Boyd-Barrett, J. O. 1982. "Cultural Dependency and the Mass Media." In M. Gurevitch et al., eds., *Culture, Society and the Media*. London: Methuen.

Brandtstadter, J. 1990. Development as a Personal and Cultural Construction. In G. Semin & K. Gergen, eds., *Everyday Understanding: Social and Scientific Implications*, pp. 83–130. Sage Publications.

Brannen, Mary Yoko. 1992. "'Bwana Mickey': Constructing Cultural Consumption at Tokyo Disneyland." In Joseph J. Tobin, ed., *Re-Made in Japan*, pp. 216–35. New Haven: Yale University Press.

Braverman, Harry. 1974. *Labor and Monopoly Capital*. New York: Monthly Review Press.

Bretherton, I., ed. 1984. *Symbolic Play: The Development of Social Understanding*. New York: Academic Press.

Bright, R. 1987. *Disneyland: Inside Story*. New York: Harry N. Abrams.

Brockway, Robert W. 1989. "The Masks of Mickey Mouse: Symbol of a Generation." *Journal of Popular Culture* 22(4): 25–34.

Bruner, Edward M. 1989. "Tourism, Creativity, and Authenticity." *Studies in Symbolic Interaction* 10: 109–14.

———. 1990. "Transformation of Self in Tourism." *American Anthropologist* 238–55.

Bryman, Alan. 1995. *Disney and His Worlds*. London: Routledge.

Butler, Ken, & Shū Kishida. 1992. *Kurofune gensō* (The black ship fantasy). Tokyo: Seidosha.

Caillois, Roger. 1961. *Man, Play and Games*. Trans. Meyer Barash. Glencoe, Ill.: Free Press.

Carey, Robert. 1995. "5 Top Corporate Training Programs." *Successful Meetings*, February, 56–61.

Cartwright, Lisa, & Brian Goldfarb. 1994. "Cultural Contagion: On Disney's Health Education Films for Latin America." In Eric Smoodin, ed., *Disney Discourse: Producing the Magic Kingdom*, pp. 169–81. London: Routledge.

Castoro, Amy. 1995. "A Passion for Service Excellence." *Credit Union Management*, June, pp. 28–31.

Chaney, David. 1979. *Fictions and Ceremonies*. London: Edward Arnold.

———. 1993. *Fictions of Collective Life*. London: Routledge.

Cohen, Erik. 1988. "Authenticity and Commoditization in Tourism." *Annals of Tourism Research* 15: 371–86.

Cole, R. E. 1971. *Japanese Blue Collar: The Changing Tradition*. Berkeley: University of California Press.

Cooley, Charles Horton. 1964. *Human Nature and the Social Order*. New York: Schocken.

Cowgill, D., and L. Holmes, eds. 1972. *Aging and Modernization*. New York: Appleton.

Cox, Miriam. 1964. *The Three Treasures: Myths of Old Japan*. New York: Harper & Row.

Crafton, D. *Before Mickey: The Animated Film, 1898–1928*. Cambridge: MIT Press.

Creighton, Millie R. 1991. "Maintaining Cultural Boundaries in Retailing: How Japanese Department Stores Domesticate 'Things Foreign.'" *Modern Asian Studies* 25(4): 675–709.

———. 1992. "The *Depāto*: Merchandising the West While Selling Japaneseness." In J. Tobin, ed., *Re-Made in Japan*, pp. 42–58. New Haven: Yale University Press.

———. 1994. "The Shifting Imagery of Childhood Amidst Japan's Consumer Affluence: The Birth of the 5 Pocket Child." In H. Eiss, ed., *Images of the Child*. Bowling Green, Ohio: Bowling Green State University Press.

Csikszentmihalyi, M. 1975. *Beyond Freedom and Anxiety: The Experience of Play in Work and Games*. San Francisco: Jossey-Bass.

Dale, Peter. 1986. *The Myth of Japanese Uniqueness*. London: Croom Helm.

Danziger, Charles. 1993. *The American Who Couldn't Say Noh*. Tokyo: Kodansha International.

Deal, T. E., & A. A. Kennedy. 1982. *Corporate Cultures*. Reading, Mass.: Addison-Wessley.

Debord, Guy. 1970. *The Society of the Spectacle*. Detroit: Black & Red.

Dentsū, Inc. 1991. *Images of Europe and America: A Survey of Japanese Consumer Attitudes.* Tokyo: Dentsū.

Denzin, Norman K. 1978. *The Research Act.* New York: McGraw-Hill.

———. 1991. *Images of Postmodernism: Social Theory and Contemporary Cinema.* London: Sage.

———. 1992. *Symbolic Interactionism and Cultural Studies.* Oxford: Basil Blackwell.

Der Derian, J., & M. J. Shapiro, eds. 1989. *International/Intertextual Relations: Postmodern Readings of World Politics.* Lexington, Mass.: D. C. Heath.

DeVos, George. 1973. *Socialization for Achievement.* Berkeley: University of California Press.

DeVos, George, & Changsoo Lee. 1980. *Koreans in Japan.* Berkeley: University of California Press.

Doeringer, Peter, & Michael J. Piore. 1985. *Internal Labor Markets and Manpower Analysis.* Armonk, N.Y.: M. E. Sharpe.

Doi Takeo. 1973. *The Anatomy of Dependence.* Tokyo: Kodansha.

Dorfman, Ariel, & Armand Mattelart. 1975. *How to Read Donald Duck: Imperialist Ideology in the Disney Comic.* New York: International General Additions.

Douglas, Jack. 1985. *Creative Interviewing.* Newbury Park, Calif.: Sage.

Drucker, Peter. 1992. *Managing for the Future.* New York: Dutton, Truman Talley Books.

Duke, Benjamin. 1988. *The Japanese School: Lessons for Industrial America.* New York: Praeger.

Duus, Peter. 1988. "Introduction." In S. Ishinomori, *Japan Inc*, pp. ix–l. Trans. Betsey Scheiner. Berkeley: University of California Press.

Eberts, Ray, & Cindelyn Eberts. 1995. *The Myths of Japanese Quality.* Upper Saddle River, N.J.: Prentice Hall.

Eco, Umberto. 1986. *Travels in Hyperreality.* London: Pan.

Economic Planning Agency. 1995. *White Paper on the National Lifestyle.* Tokyo: Printing Bureau, Ministry of Finance, Government of Japan.

Eisenberg, E. M., & H. L. Goodall, Jr. 1993. *Organizational Communication: Balancing Creativity and Constraint.* New York: St. Martin's Press.

Eisenstein, Sergei. 1991. *Walt Disney.* Strasbourg: Circé. (Also available as *Eisenstein on Disney*, ed. Jay Leyda, trans. Alan Upchurch [New York: Heinemann, 1988].)

Eisman, R. 1993. "Disney Magic." *Incentive*, September, 45–56.

Eliot, Mark. 1993. *Walt Disney: Hollywood's Dark Prince.* New York: Birch Lane Press, Carol Publishing.

Ewen, Stuart, & E. Ewen. 1982. *Channels of Desire*. New York: McGraw-Hill.

Falk, Pasi. 1993. *The Consuming Body*. London: Sage.

Featherstone, Mike. 1990. "Global Culture: An Introduction." *Theory, Culture and Society*, special issue: Global Culture, 7(2–3): 1–15.

———. 1991. *Consumer Culture and Postmodernism*. London: Sage.

Feiler, Bruce. 1991. *Learning to Bow: Inside the Heart of Japan*. New York: Ticknor & Fields.

Fejes, F. 1981. "Media Imperialism: An Assessment." *Media, Culture and Society* 3(3): 281–89.

———. 1984. "Critical Mass Communications Research and Media Effects: The Problem of the Disappearing Audience." *Media, Culture & Society* 6: 219–32.

Fields, George. 1983. *From Bonsai to Levi's*. New York: Macmillan.

———. 1988. *The Japanese Market Culture*. Tokyo: Japan Times.

Fine, G. A. 1984. "Negotiated Order and Organizational Cultures." In *Annual Review of Sociology* 10: 239–62. Palo Alto, Calif.: Annual Reviews.

Fjellman, Stephen M. 1992. *Vinyl Leaves: Walt Disney World and America*. Boulder, Colo.: Westview.

Francaviglia, Richard V. 1981. "Main Street USA: A Comparison/Contrast of Streetscapes in Disneyland and Walt Disney World." *Journal of Popular Culture* 15: 141–56.

Frank, Andre Gunder. 1967. "Capitalism and Underdevelopment in Latin America." *Monthly Review Press*.

Frank, Arthur. 1991. "For a Sociology of the Body: An Analytical Review." In M. Featherstone, M. Hepworth, and B. Turner, eds., *The Body: Social Process and Cultural Theory*, pp. 36–103. London: Sage.

Freeman, Richard B. 1989. "Bonuses and Employment in Japan." In idem, *Labor Markets in Action*, pp. 249–70. Cambridge: Harvard University Press.

Freund, Peter. 1990. "The Expressive Body: A Common Ground for the Sociology of Emotions and Health and Illness." *Sociology of Health and Illness* 12(4): 454–77.

Friedman, L. D., ed. 1991. *Unspeakable Images: Ethnicity and the American Cinema*. Urbana: University of Illinois Press.

Frost, P., M. Louis, & L. Moore, eds. 1985. *Organizational Culture*. Beverly Hills, Calif.: Sage.

Fusaho Awata 1988. "Disneyland's Dreamlike Success." *Japan Quarterly* 35: 58–62.

Gershuny, J., & S. Jones. 1987. "The Changing Work/Leisure Balance in Britain, 1861–84." In J. Horne et al., eds., *Sport, Leisure and Social Relations*. Routledge: London.

Giddens, Anthony. 1991. *Modernity and Self-identity: Self and Society in the Late Modern Age*. Cambridge, Eng.: Polity.

Goffman, Ervin. 1961. *Encounters*. Indianapolis: Bobbs-Merrill.

Goldstein-Gidoni, Ofra. 1993. "Packaged Weddings, Packaged Brides: The Japanese Ceremonial Occasions Industry." Ph.D. diss., Department of Anthropology and Sociology, School of Oriental and African Studies, University of London. Forthcoming—Richmond, Eng.: Curzon.

Goode, E., & Nachman Ben-Yehuda. 1994. *Moral Panics: The Social Construction of Deviance*. Oxford: Blackwell's.

Gordon, Andrew. 1985. *The Evolution of Labor Relations in Japan: Heavy Industry, 1853–1955*. Cambridge: Harvard University, Council on East Asian Studies.

Gottdiener, Mark. 1982. "Disneyland: A Utopian Urban Space." *Urban Life* 11: 139–62.

———. 1997. *The Theming of America: Dreams, Visions, and Commercial Spaces*. Boulder, Colo.: Westview.

Gould, Stephen Jay. 1979. "Mickey Mouse Meets Konrad Lorenz." *Natural History* 88(5): 30–36.

Gould, William B. 1984. *Japan's Reshaping of America's Labor Law*. Cambridge: MIT Press.

Graburn, Nelson. 1983. *To Pray, Pay and Play: The Cultural Structure of Japanese Domestic Tourism*. Aix-en-Provence: Centre des Hautes Etudes Touristique, France.

Gramsci, Antonio. 1971. "Notes on Italian History." In Quintin Hoare and Geoffrey N. Smith, eds., *Selections from the Prison Notebooks of Antonio Gramsci*. London: Lawrence and Wishart.

Grathoff, Richard H. 1970. *The Structure of Social Inconsistencies: A Contribution to a Unified Theory of Play, Game and Social Action*. The Hague: Martinus Nijhoff.

Haarmann, Harald. 1989. *Symbolic Values of Foreign Language Use: From the Japanese Case to a General Sociolinguistic Perspective*. New York: Mouton de Gruyter.

Haden-Guest, Anthony. 1972. *Down the Programmed Rabbit Hole: Travels Through Muzak, Hilton, Coca-Cola, Walt Disney and Other World Empires*. London: Hart-Davis, MacGibbon.

Haginoya Keiki. 1995. *Machi kara kieta kodomo no asobi* (Children's lost street playing). Tokyo: Taishu kan.

Hamilton, G., & N. W. Biggart. 1988. "Market, Culture, and Authority: A Comparative Analysis of Management and Organization in the Far East." *AJS* 94: S52–S94.

Handelman, Dan. 1986. "Charisma, Liminality and Symbolic Types." In E. Cohen, M. Lissac, and U. Almagor, eds., *Comparative Social Dynamics: Essays in Honour of S. N. Eisenstadt*. Boulder, Colo.: Westview.

———. 1990. *Models and Mirrors*. Cambridge: Cambridge University Press.

———. 1992. "Symbolic Types, the Body, and Circus." *Semiotica* 85 (3/4): 205–27.

Hannerz, Ulf. 1989. "Notes on the Global Ecumene." *Public Culture* 1(2): 66–75.

Hansen, Miriam. 1993. "Of Mice and Ducks: Benjamin and Adorno on Disney." *South Atlantic Quarterly*, special issue: The World According to Disney, ed. Susan Willis, 92(1): 27–63.

Harada Munehiko. 1994. "Towards a Renaissance of Leisure in Japan." *Leisure Studies* 277–87.

Harootunian, David. 1988. "Visible Discourses / Invisible Ideologies." *South Atlantic Quarterly* 87(3): 445–61.

Harvey, David. 1989. *The Condition of Postmodernity: An Enquiry into the Origins of Cultural Change*. Oxford: Basil Blackwell.

Hashimoto, M., & J. Raisian. 1985. "Employment Tenure and Earnings in Japan and the US." *American Economic Review* 75: 721–35.

Hayashi Shuji. 1988. *Culture and Management in Japan*. Trans. F. Baldwin. Tokyo: University of Tokyo Press.

Hazan, Haim. 1980. *The Limbo People*. London: Routledge and Kegan Paul.

———. 1994. *Old Age: Constructions and Deconstructions*. Cambridge: Cambridge University Press.

Heise, Steve. 1994. "Disney Approach to Managing," *Executive Excellence* Oct. 18: 18–19.

Henkoff, Ronald. 1994. "Finding, Training and Keeping the Best Service Workers." *Fortune*, Oct. 2, 110–15.

Hochschild, Arlie Russell. 1983. *The Managed Heart: Commercialization of Human Feeling*. Berkeley: University of California Press.

———. 1989. "Reply to Cas Wouters's Review Essay on *The Managed Heart*." *Theory, Culture & Society* 6: 439–45.

Holliss, R., & B. Sibley. 1988. *The Disney Story*. London: Octopus Books.

Horkheimer, Max, & Theodor W. Adorno. 1969 (1944). *Dialectic of Enlightenment*. Trans. John Cumming. New York: Herder & Herder.

Howard, Dennis R., & John L. Crompton. 1980. *Financing, Managing, and Marketing Recreation and Park Resources*. Dubuque, Iowa: Wm. C. Brown.

Ikegami Y. 1989. "Introduction: Discourse Analysis in Japan." *Text*, special issue, 9(3): 263–73.

Inohara Hideo. 1990. *Human Resource Development in Japanese Companies*. Tokyo: Asian Productivity Center.

Iriye Akira, ed. 1975. *Mutual Images: Essays in American-Japanese Relations*. Cambridge: Harvard University Press.

Ishinomori Shotaro. 1986. *Manga Nihon keizai nyūmon* (Comicbook: introduction to Japanese industry). Tokyo: Nihon keizai shimbun. (Also available as *Japan Inc*. Trans. Betsey Scheiner [Berkeley: University of California Press, 1988].)

Ito Mikiharu. 1995. *Tēma-pāku sangyō: kyōshū to sōzō-ryoku* (Theme park industry: nostalgia and creativity). Tokyo: Nihon keizai shinbun.

Ivy, Marilyn. 1988. "Critical Texts, Mass Artifacts: The Consumption of Knowledge in Postmodern Japan." *South Atlantic Quarterly* 87(3): 419–44.

———. 1993. "Formations of Mass Culture." In A. Gordon, ed., *Postwar Japan as History*. Berkeley: University of California Press.

———. 1996. *Discourses of the Vanisihing: Modernity, Phantasm, Japan*. Chicago: University of Chicago Press.

Iwao Sumiko. 1992. *The Japanese Woman: Traditional Image and Changing Reality*. New York: Free Press.

Iyotani Toshio. 1995. "Globalization and Culture." *Japan Foundation Newsletter* 23(3): 1–5.

James, William. 1977. "What Pragmatism Means." In John McDermott, ed., *The Writings of William James: A Comprehensive Edition*. Chicago: University of Chicago Press.

Jameson, Frederic. 1991. *Postmodernism, or, The Cultural Logic of Late Capitalism*. Durham, N.C.: Duke University Press.

Japan Almanac. 1993. Tokyo: Asahi Shinbun.

Japanese Corporate Decision Making. 1982. Tokyo: Japan External Trade Organization.

JMAM (Japanese Management Center). 1992. *Sutāto dassho shiriisu* ("Start dashing" series), Part I, *Shokuba no rūru * manā no jōshiki* (Office rules and commonsense manners). Tokyo: JMAM (a video cassette).

Johnson, David. 1981. "Disney World as Structure and Symbol: Re-creation of the American Experience." *Journal of Popular Culture* 15(1): 157–65.

Kakita Toshizumi. 1984. "Foreign-Capital Enterprises Operating in Japan's Service Industry." In *Dentsū Japan Marketing/Advertising Quarterly* 2(1): 4–13.

Kano Yasuhisa. 1986. *Tōkyō dizuniirando no shinso* (The true story of Tokyo Disneyland). Tokyo: Kindaiban geisha.

Kanter, Rosabeth. 1977. *Men and Women of the Corporation.* New York: Basic Books.

Kaplan, David, & Alec Dubro. 1986. *Yakuza: The Explosive Account of Japan's Criminal Underworld.* New York: Addison-Wesley.

Karasuyama Sekien. 1992. *Hyakki Yakō* (Night journey of "100 oni"). Originally a fifteenth-century scroll painted by Mitsunobu Tosa. Tokyo: Kokushokan kokai.

Karatani Kōjin. 1991. "The Discursive Space of Modern Japan." *Boundary 2,* special issue: Japan in the World, 18(3): 191–200.

Karthaüs-Tanaka, Nobuko. 1995. *How Japan Views Its Current Labor Market.* Leiden University: Netherlands Association of Japanese Studies.

Kasson, John F. 1978. *Amusing the Million: Coney Island at the Turn of the Century.* New York: Hill & Wang.

Kata Koji. 1979. *Kami-shibai shōwa-shi* (Shōwa history of *kami-shibai*). Tokyo: Obunsha.

Kato Akinori. 1994. "Package Tours, Pilgrimages, and Pleasure Trips." In Ueda Atsushi, ed., *The Electric Geisha: Exploring Japan's Popular Culture,* pp. 51–60. Trans. Miriam Eguchi. Tokyo: Kodansha International.

Kato Hideo, ed. 1959. *Japanese Popular Culture.* Tokyo: Tuttle.

Kato Hidetoshi, ed. 1973. *Japanese Popular Culture.* Westport, Conn.: Greenwood.

Kato Shuichi. 1974. *Zasshu bunka: Nihon no chisai kibō* (Hybrid culture: Japan's small hope). Tokyo: Kōdansha bunko.

Katriel, Tamar, & Sally Ann Ness. 1984. "Movement and Signification: Amusement Park Rides as Cultural Performance." *Recherches Semiotique / Semiotic Inquiry* 4(2): 177–94.

Katzenstein, Gary. 1989. *Funny Business: An Outsider's Year in Japan.* New York: Prentice Hall.

Kawai Hayao. 1988. "The Laughter of Oni." In idem, *The Japanese Psyche: Major Motifs in the Fairy Tales of Japan,* pp. 47–107. Dallas: Spring Publications.

Kawanishi Hirosuke. 1992. *Enterprise Unionism in Japan.* London: Kogan Page.

Keene, Donald. 1978. *World Within Walls: Japanese Literature of the Pre-modern Era, 1600–1867.* New York: Grove.

Kelly, John. 1982. *Scientific Management, Job Design, and Work Performance.* London: Academic Press.

Keown, Charles. 1989. "A Model of Tourists' Propensity to Buy: The Case of Japanese Visitors to Hawaii." *Journal of Travel Research,* Winter: 31–34.

Kerr, C. 1977. *Labor Markets and Wage Determination.* Berkeley: University of California Press.

King, Anthony D., ed. 1991. *Culture, Globalization and the World-System.* Binghamton: State University of New York.

King, Margaret. 1981. "Disneyland and Walt Disney World: Traditional Values in Futuristic Form." *Journal of Popular Culture* 15: 116–40.

————. 1983. "McDonald's and Disney." In M. Fishwick, ed., *Ronald Revisited: The World of Ronald McDonald.* Bowling Green, Ohio: Bowling Green University Popular Press.

Kinsella, Sharon. 1995. "Cuties Is Japan." In L. Skov & B. Moeran, eds., *Women, Media and Consumption in Japan,* pp. 220–55. Richmond, Eng.: Curzon.

Kinzley, W. Dean. 1991. *Industrial Harmony in Modern Japan: The Invention of a Tradition.* London: Routledge.

Klugman, Karen. 1995. "Under the Influence." In The Project on Disney, ed., *Inside the Mouse: Work and Play at Disney World,* pp. 98–110. Durham, N.C.: Duke University Press.

Komuya Kazumeki. 1989. *Tōkyō dizuniirando no keiei majikku* (Tokyo Disneyland's amazing management). Tokyo: Kōdansha.

Kondo, Dorinne. 1982. "Work, Family and the Self: A Cultural Analysis of Japanese Family Enterprise." Ph.D. diss., Department of Anthropology, Harvard University.

————. 1990. *Crafting Selves: Power, Gender, and Discourses of Identity in a Japanese Workplace.* Chicago: University of Chicago Press.

Koren, Leonard. 1990. *Success Stories: How 11 of Japan's Most Interesting Businesses Came to Be.* San Francisco: Chronicle Books.

Kracauer, Siegfried. 1950. "Sturges or Laughter Betrayed." *Films in Review* 1(1) Feb.: 11–13, 43–47.

Kraus, Richard G., & Joseph E. Curtis. 1986. *Creative Management in Recreation, Parks, and Leisure Services.* St. Louis: Times Mirror / Mosby.

Kuenz, Jane. 1993. "It's a Small World After All: Disney and the Pleasures of Identification." *South Atlantic Quarterly* 92(1): 63–89.

————. 1995. "Working at the Rat." In The Project on Disney, ed., *Inside the Mouse: Work and Play at Disney World*, pp. 110–63. Durham, N.C.: Duke University Press.

Kumar, K. 1978. *Prophecy and Progress: The Sociology of Industrial and Post-industrial Society*. Harmondsworth, Eng.: Penguin.

Kumazawa Makoto. 1996. *Portraits of the Japanese Workplace: Labor Movements, Workers, and Managers*. Trans. Andrew Gordon and Mikiso Hane. Boulder, Colo.: Westview.

Kunda, Gideon. 1994. *Engineering Culture*. Temple University Press.

Lash, Scott. 1990. *Theories of Postmodernism*. London: Sage.

Lawrence, Elizabeth A. 1986. "In the Mick of Time: Reflections on Disney's Ageless Mouse." *Journal of Popular Culture* 19 (2): 65–72.

Leach, Edmund. 1971. "Chronics and Chronos." In idem, *Rethinking Anthropology*, pp. 124–32. London: Athlone.

————. 1976. *Culture and Communication: The Logic by Which Symbols Are Connected*. Cambridge: Cambridge University Press.

Lee, Margaret J. 1993. *Consumer Culture Reborn: The Cultural Politics of Consumption*. London: Routledge.

Leibenstein, Harvey. 1987. *Inside the Firm: The Inefficiencies of Hierarchy*. Cambridge: Harvard University Press.

Leisure Industry Data (Rejā-sangyō shiryō). 1993. "Tēma-pāku no jūnen o furikaeru" (Theme parks' 10-years retrospective). No. 321 (June): 75–122.

————. 1994. "Amyūzumento bijinesu" (Amusement business). No. 333 (June): 65–92.

Liebes, Tamar, & Elihu Katz. 1990. *The Export of Meaning: Cross-Cultural Readings of "Dallas."* New York: Oxford University Press.

Linhart, Sepp. 1986. *"Sakariba*: Zone of Evaporation Beween Work and Home." In Joy Hendry & Jonathan Webber, eds., *Interpreting Japanese Society*, pp. 198–211. Oxford: JASO.

————. 1988. "From Industrial to Postindustrial Society: Changes in Japanese Leisure-Related Values and Behavior." *Journal of Japanese Studies* 14(2): 271–307.

Lipp, Douglas. 1994. *Tōkyō dizuniirando daiseikō no shinsō* (The truth about Tokyo Disneyland's great success). Trans. Kuchika Kimundo. Tokyo: NTT shuppan.

Little, K. 1993. "Masochism, Spectacle, and the 'Broken Mirror' Entree: A Note on the Anthropology of Performance in Postmodern Culture." *Cultural Anthropology* 8(1): 117–29.

Littleton, C. Scott. 1986. "The Organization and Management of a Tokyo Shinto Shrine Festival." *Ethnology* 25: 192–202.

Lo, Jeannie. 1990. *Office Ladies and Factory Women: Life and Work at a Japanese Company.* Armonk, N.Y.: M. E. Sharpe.

Longstreet, S. A. 1988. *Yoshiwara: The Pleasure Quarters of Old Tokyo.* Tokyo: Yenbooks.

Lorenz, Konrad. 1981. *The Foundations of Ethology.* New York: Simon & Schuster.

Mangajin. 1993. *Mangajin's Basic Japanese Through Comics.* Atlanta: Mangajin.

Marin, Louis. 1977. "Disneyland: A Degenerate Utopia." *Glyph* 1: 50–66.

Martin, Joanne. 1992. *Culture in Organizations: Three Perspectives.* Oxford: Oxford University Press.

Masanori Hashimoto. 1990. *The Japanese Labor Market.* Kalamazoo, Mich.: Upjohn Institute for Employment Research.

Masatsugu Mitsuyuki. 1982. *The Modern Samurai Society: Duty and Dependence in Contemporary Japan.* Amacom: American Management Association.

Matsuura Toshiyuki. 1989. "Amusement Park Business Zooms, Zips and Soars." *Business Japan* July: 113–16.

———. 1990. "Leisure Facilities to Expand in the Next Decade." *Business Japan*, July: 53–56.

———. 1993. "Current Trends and Developments in the Amusement Business." *Japan 21st*, July: 47–50.

———. 1994. "Roller Coasters Ride Out Recession." *Japan 21st*, July: 20–23.

Mattelart, Armand. 1979. *Multinational Corporations and the Control of Culture.* Brighton, Eng.: Harvester.

Mauss, Marcel. 1954. *The Gift.* Trans. I. Cunnison. Glencoe, Ill.: Free Press.

McCannell, Dean. 1974. "Staged Authenticity: Arrangements of Social Space in Tourist Settings." *American Journal of Sociology* 79(3): 589–603.

———. 1976. *The Tourist: A New Theory of the Leisure Class.* New York: Schocken.

McGuigan, Jim. 1992. *Cultural Populism.* London: Routledge.

Mead, George Herbert. 1932. *Mind, Self and Society.* Chicago: Chicago University Press.

Merkle, Judith. 1980. *Management and Ideology: The Legacy of the International Scientific Management Movement.* Berkeley: University of California Press.

Meyerowitz, J. 1984. "The Adult Child and the Childlike Adult." *Daedalus* 113(3): 19–48.

Michaux, Henri. 1949. *A Barbarian in Asia.* Trans. Sylvia Beach. New York: New Directions. (First published as *Un Barbare en Asie* [Paris: Gallimard, 1933].)

Miller, Roy A. 1977. "The 'Spirit' of the Japanese Language." *Journal of Japanese Studies* 3(2): 251–98.

———. 1982. *Japan Modern Myth: The Language and Beyond.* New York: Weatherhill.

Miller, Stephen. 1973. "Ends, Means, and Galumphing: Some Leitmotifs of Play." *American Anthropologist* 75: 87–97.

Minear, Richard. 1980. "Orientalism and the Study of Japan." *Journal of Asian Studies* 39: 507–17.

Minear, Richard, ed. 1974. *Through Japanese Eyes.* New York: Praeger.

Mino Hokaji. 1984. "Foresight the Success Key for Mitsui Real Estate: Interview with Hideo Edo." *Business Japan*, Feb.: 18–19.

Miyoshi, Masao, & Harry D. Harootunian, eds. 1988. *Postmodernism and Japan.* Special issue of *the South Atlantic Quarterly.* Durham, N.C.: Duke University Press.

———. 1991. *Japan in the World. Boundary 2,* special issue, 18: 3. Durham, N.C.: Duke University Press.

Moeran, Brian. 1983. "The Language of Japanese Tourism." *Annals of Tourism Research* 10: 93–108.

———. 1989. *Language and Popular Culture in Japan.* Manchester: University of Manchester Press.

———. 1993. "Cinderella Christmas: Kitsch, Consumerism, and Youth Culture in Japan." In D. Miller, ed., *Unwrapping Christmas,* pp. 105–33. Oxford: Oxford University Press.

Moore, Alexander. 1980. "Walt Disney's World: Bounded Ritual and the Playful Pilgrimage Center." *Anthroplogical Quarterly* 53: 207–18.

Morgan, David L., & Margaret T. Spanish. 1984. "Focus Groups: A New Tool for Qualitative Research." *Qualitative Sociology* 7: 253–70.

Moriya Takeshi. 1989. *Nihonjin to asobi* (The Japanese and play). Tokyo: Domesu.

Morris-Suzuki, Tessa. 1995. "The Invention and Reinvention of 'Japanese Culture.'" *Journal of Asian Studies* 54(3): 759–81.

Naff, Clayton. 1994. *About Face: How I Stumbled onto Japan's Social Revolution.* Tokyo: Kodansha.

Nakamura Osamu, Hideo Matsunaga, & Mari Kitaizumi. 1994. *A Bilingual Guide to the Japanese Economy.* Tokyo: Kodansha.

Nakamura Takafusa. 1981. *The Post-war Japanese Economy: Its Development and Structure.* Tokyo: Tokyo University Press.

Nakano Osamu. 1988. "A Sociological Analysis of the *shinjinrui.*" *Japan Echo* 15: 12–17.

Napier, Susan J. 1996. *The Fantastic in Modern Japanese Literature.* Nissan Institute / Routledge Japanese Studies Series. New York: Routledge.

National Defense Council for Victims of *Karōshi.* 1990. *Karōshi: When the Corporate Warrior Dies.* Tokyo: National Defense Council for Victims of *Karōshi.*

Nikkei Sangyō Shinbun (Nikkei industry magazine). 1991. *TDL's kaichō Takahashi Masatomo* (TDL's general president Takahashi Masatomo). Interview in the series *Shōgen Shōwa Sangyō-shi* (Testimonies about the industrial history of the Shōwa period).

Nitta Fumiteru. 1992. "Shopping for Souvenirs in Hawaii." In J. Tobin, ed., *Remade in Japan,* pp. 204–16. New Haven: Yale University Press.

Notoji Masako. 1988. "Cutural Boundaries and Magic Kingdom: A Comparative Symbolic Analysis of Disneyland and Tokyo Disneyland." Paper presented at the American Studies Association annual meeting, Miami Beach, October 27–30.

———. 1993. *Dizuniirando to-iu seichi* (The holy land called Disneyland). Tokyo: Iwanami shoten.

Oda Masahiko. 1983. *Compensation and Promotion: The Plight of Middle Managers.* Institute of Comparative Culture Business Series, Bulletin no. 95. Tokyo: Sophia University.

OECD (Organization for Economic Cooperation and Development). 1977. *The Development of Industrial Relations System: Some Implications of Japanese Experience.* Paris: OECD.

Ohmae Kenichi. 1991. *The Borderless World.* New York: Harper, Perennial.

Ohnuki-Tierney, Emiko. 1990. "The Ambivalent Self of the Contemporary Japanese." *Cultural Anthropology* 5(2).

Okonogi Keigo. 1978. "The Age of the Moratorium People." *Japan Echo* 5(1) (Spring).

Okuda Rikuko. 1995. "Children's Spirit of Play and Creativity Being Withered by Adults' Management." *PlayRights* 13(3) Sept.: 29–31.

Okuno Takuji. 1995. "Technology and Recreation: A Look at the Famicon and Personal Computer Communication." In Tadao Umesao, B. Powell, & I. Kumakura, eds., *Japanese Civilization in the Modern World XI: Amusement,* pp. 137–47. Senri Ethnological Studies no. 40. Osaka: National Museum of Ethnology.

O'Neill, John. 1985. *Five Bodies: The Human Shape of Modern Society.* Ithaca, N.Y.: Cornell University Press.

Ono Kosei. 1983. "Disney and the Japanese: Maintaining a Dream over Half a Century." *Look Japan,* July 10: 7–12.

Ouchi, William, and A. L. Wilkins. 1985. "Organizational Culture." *Annual Review of Sociology* 11: 367–412.

Paskal, Cleo. 1994. "Japanese Have New Designs of the World." *Japan Times,* Apr. 13: 13.

Paris, Ellen. 1988. "A Yen for Fun." *Forbes,* July 11: 38–39.

Parsons, Talcot. 1966. *Societies, Evolutionary and Comparative Perspectives.* Englewood Cliffs, N.J.: Prentice Hall.

Passin, Herbert. 1965. *Society and Education in Japan.* New York: Columbia University Press.

Perry, Nick. 1995. "Travelling Theory / Nomadic Theorizing." *Organization* 291: 35–54.

Peters, T., & R. Waterman. 1982. *In Search of Excellence: Lessons from America's Best-Run Companies.* New York: Harper & Row.

Piedra, José. 1994. "Pato Donald's Gender Ducking." In Eric Smoodin, ed., *Disney Discourse: Producing the Magic Kingdom,* pp. 148–69. London: Routledge.

Plath, David. 1964. *The After Hours: Modern Japan and the Search for Enjoyment.* Berkeley: University of California Press.

Pollack, Andrew. 1995. "Japan, a Superpower Among Superheroes." *New York Times,* Sept. 17: 32H.

Postman, Neil. 1985. *Amusing Ourselves to Death: Public Discourse in the Age of Show Business.* New York: Penguin.

Powers, Richard G., & Hidetoshi Kato, eds. 1990. *Handbook of Japanese Popular Culture.* New York: Greenwood.

The Project on Disney, ed. 1995. *Inside the Mouse: Work and Play at Disney World.* Durham, N.C.: Duke University Press.

Provenzano, Eugene F. 1991. *Video Kids: Making Sense of Nintendo.* Cambridge: Harvard University Press.

Rajchman, John. 1987. "Postmodernism in a Nominalist Frame: The Emergence and Diffusion of a Cultural Category." *Flash Art* 137: 40–53.

Raz, Jacob. 1992. "Tekiya and the Japanese Festival: Reverse, Disbelief and Performance." In idem, *Aspects of Otherness in Japanese Culture,* pp. 109–19. Tokyo: Institute for the Study of Languages and Cultures of Asia and Africa, Tokyo University.

Raz, Jacob, & Aviad E. Raz. 1996. "'America' Meets 'Japan': A Journey for Real Between Two Imaginaries." *Theory, Culture and Society* 13(3): 157–82.

Richie, Donald. 1991. "The 'Real' Disneyland." In idem, *A Lateral View: Essays on Contemporary Japan*, pp. 41–46. Tokyo: Japan Times.

————. 1995. "The Japanese Ghost." In idem, *Partial Views: Essays on Contemporary Japan*, pp. 80–87. Tokyo: Japan Times.

Risu Akizuki. 1980. *OL shinkaron* (The evolution of OL). Tokyo: Kōdansha. (Also available as *The OL Comes of Age*. Trans. Yuriko Tamaki. [Tokyo: Kodansha International, 1990].)

Ritzer, George. 1993. *The McDonaldization of Society*. Thousand Oaks, Calif.: Pine Forge.

Roberts, J. G. 1973. *Mitsui: Three Centuries of Japanese Business*. New York: John Weatherhill.

Robertson, Jennifer. 1989. "*Furusato* Japan: The Culture and Politics of Nostalgia." *International Journal of Politics, Culture and Society* 1(4): 494–518.

————. 1995. "Hegemonic Nostalgia, Tourism, and Nation-Making in Japan." In U. Tadao, H. Befu, & I. Shuzo, eds., *Japanese Civilization in the Modern World IX: Tourism*, pp. 89–104. Senri Ethnological Studies, no. 38. Osaka: National Museum of Ethnology.

Robertson, Roland. 1987. "Globalisation and Societal Modernisation: A Note on Japan and Japanese Religion." *Sociological Analysis* 47: 35–42.

————. 1992. *Globalization: Social Theory and Global Culture*. London: Sage.

Robertson, Roland, & Frank Lechner. 1985. "Modernisation, Globalisation and the Problem of Culture in World-Systems Theory." *Theory, Culture & Society* 2: 103–18.

Rohlen, Thomas. 1974. *For Harmony and Strength: Japanese White-Collar Organization in Anthropological Perspective*. Berkeley: University of California Press.

————. 1983. *Japan's High Schools*. Berkeley: University of California Press.

Rojek, Chris. 1993. "Disney Culture." *Leisure Studies* 12: 121–35.

Rosenberger, Nancy. 1995. "Antiphonal Performances? Japanese Women's Magazines and Women's Voices." In L. Skov & B. Moeran, eds., *Women, Media and Consumption in Japan*, pp. 143–70. Richmond, Eng.: Curzon.

Roxborough, Ian. 1979. *Theories of Underdevelopment*. London: Macmillan.

Ryuichi Nagao. 1991. "'*Amerika no seiki' no makugire wa chikai*" (The curtain is about to come down on the American century). *Chūōkōron*, Feb.: 80–93.

Sadler, Ann W. 1969. "The Form and Meaning of the Festival." *Asian Folklore Studies* 28: 1–16.

———. 1974. "At the Sanctuary: Further Field Notes on the Shrine Festival in Modern Tokyo." *Asian Folklore Studies* 33: 17–34.

———. 1975. "Folkdance and Fairgrounds: More Notes on Neighborhood Festivals in Tokyo." *Asian Folklore Studies* 34: 1–20.

———. 1982. "Carrying the *Mikoshi*: Further Field Notes on the Shrine Festival in Modern Tokyo." *Asian Folklore Studies* 31: 89–114.

Said, Edward. 1978. *Orientalism.* New York: Pantheon.

———. 1981. *The World, the Text and the Critic.* Cambridge: Harvard University Press.

Sano Yoko. 1995. "Customer-Driven Human Resource Policies and Practices in the Japanese Service Sector." *Human Resource Planning* 17(3): 37–53.

Sansom, George B. 1973. *The Western World and Japan.* New York: Vintage.

Sassen, J. 1989. "Mickeymania." *International Management*, Nov.: 32–34.

Sato, K., & Y. Hoshino, eds. 1984. *The Anatomy of Japanese Business.* London: Croom Helm.

Satō Tadao. 1973. *Nihon no manga* (Japanese comics). Tokyo: Hyōronsha.

Schickel, Richard. 1968. *The Disney Version.* New York: Simon & Schuster.

Schiller, H. I. 1973. *The Mind Managers.* Boston: Beacon.

Schilling, Mark. 1993. "Doraemon: Making Dreams Come True." *Japan Quarterly*, Oct.: 405–17.

Schodt, Frederik L. 1986. *Manga! Manga! The World of Japanese Comics.* Tokyo: Kodansha International.

———. 1994. *America and the Four Japans: Friend, Foe, Model, Mirror.* Berkeley, Calif.: Stone Bridge.

———. 1996. *Dreamland Japan: Writings on Modern Manga.* Berkeley, Calif.: Stone Bridge.

Senda Mitsuru. 1992. *Design of Children's Play Environments.* New York: McGraw-Hill.

Sengoku Tamotsu. 1985. *Willing Workers: The Work Ethics in Japan, England, and the US.* Trans. K. Ezaki & Y. Ezaki. New York: Quorum Books.

Shilling, Chris. 1993. *The Body and Social Theory.* London: Sage.

Shils, Edward. 1975. *Center and Periphery.* Chicago: University of Chicago Press.

Shimamura Mari. 1990. *Fanshii no kenkyū: kawaii ga hito, mono, kane o shōhai suru* (Research on fancy: cute controls people, objects, and money). Tokyo: Nesco.

———. 1991. "Kawaii!: The Cult of Cute Begins with Infancy, and Never Seems to End." *Japan Times Weekly* 31(1), Jan. 5: 1–3.

Shinotsuka Eiko. 1982. *Nihon no joshi rōdō* (Female labor in Japan). Tokyo: Tōyō keizai shinpōsha.

Shirahata Yozaburo. 1995. "Information Studies of Tourist Resources." In U. Tadao, H. Befu, & I. Shuzo, eds., *Japanese Civilization in the Modern World IX: Tourism*, pp. 51–65. Senri Ethnological Studies, no. 38. Osaka: National Museum of Ethnology.

Sievers, Sharon. 1983. *Flowers in Salt: The Beginnings of Feminist Consciousness in Modern Japan*. Stanford: Stanford University Press.

Silverberg, Miriam. 1991. "The Modern Girl as Militant." In G. L. Bernstein, ed., *Recreating Japanese Women, 1600–1945*, pp. 236–67. Berkeley: University of California Press.

Singleton, John. 1989. "*Gambaru*: A Japanese Cultural Theory of Learning." In J. Shields, ed., *Japanese Education: Patterns of Socialziation, Equality, and Political Control*. State College: Penn State University Press.

Sklair, Leslie. 1991. *Sociology of the Global System*. Baltimore: Johns Hopkins University Press.

Sklar, Martin A. 1975–76. *Walt Disney's Disneyland*. Walt Disney Productions.

Sklar, Robert. 1975. "The Making of Cultural Myths: Walt Disney and Frank Capra." In idem, *Movie-Made America: A Cultural History of American Movies*, pp. 195–221. New York: Vintage Books.

Skov, Lisa, & Brian Moeran. 1995. "Introduction: Hiding in the Light: From Oshin to Yoshimoto Banana." In L. Skov & B. Moeran, eds., *Women, Media and Consumption in Japan*, pp. 1–75. Richmond, Eng.: Curzon.

Smith, R. C., & E. M. Eisenberg. 1987. "Conflict at Disneyland: A Root-Metaphor Analysis." *Communication Monographs* 54: 367–80.

Smoodin, Eric, ed. 1994. *Disney Discourse: Producing the Magic Kingdom*. London: Routledge.

Spender, John Christopher. 1989. *Industry Recipes: The Nature and Sources of Managerial Judgement*. Oxford: Blackwell.

———. 1991. "Villan, Victim or Visionary: F. W. Taylor's Contribution to Organization Theory." Working paper. New Brunswick, N.J.: Rutgers University.

Spinelli, Maria-Lydia. 1992. "Fun and Power: Experience and Ideology at the Magic Kingdom." Ph.D. diss., University of Massachusetts, Amherst.

Spivak, Gayatri Chakravorty. 1990. *The Post Colonial Critic*. London: Routledge.

Stanlow, James. 1992. "'For Beautiful Human Life': The Use of English in Japan." In J. Tobin, ed., *Re-Made in Japan*, pp. 58–77. New Haven: Yale University Press.

Statler, Oliver. 1964. *The Black Ship Scroll: An Account of the Perry Expedition at Shimoda*. Tokyo: John Weatherhill.

Sterle, David, & Mary Duncan. 1973. *Supervision of Leisure Services*. San Diego: San Diego State University.

Stone, Kay. 1975. "Things Walt Disney Never Told Us." *Journal of American Folklore* 88: 42–50.

Storm, J. P., & M. Dressler. 1991. *Im Reiche der Micky Maus: Walt Disney in Deutschland, 1927–1945*. Berlin.

Strauss, Anselm. 1987. *Qualitative Analysis for Social Scientists*. New York: Cambridge University Press.

Sugimoto Yasuhiro & Ross Mouer. 1981. *Japanese Society: Stereotypes and Realities*. Melbourne: Monash University Press.

Suyuma Keiichi. 1968. *Nihon manga hyakunen* (100 years of Japaneae comics). Tokyo: Haga shoten.

Tadokoro Makoto. 1990. *Tōkyō dizuniirando no majikku shōhō* (The magic business of Tokyo Disneyland). Tokyo: Yell Books.

Taiyo (magazine). 1987. *Nihon no yūrei* (Japan's ghosts). Nihon no kokoro (Japan's heart), no. 57. Tokyo: Heibonsha.

Takahashi Yasuo. "You Can't Have Green Tea in a Japanese Coffee Shop." In Ueda Atsushi, ed., *The Electric Geisha: Exploring Japan's Popular Culture*, pp. 26–34. Trans. Miriam Eguchi. Tokyo: Kodansha International.

Takayama Hideo. 1987. "What Modern Japanese Games Reflect: Children, TV Games and Comics." *The Wheel Extended* (Tokyo: Toyota Publications), 18: 19–27.

Tanaka, Stefan. 1993. *Japan's Orient: Rendering Past into History*. Berkeley: University of California Press.

Tanaka Yasuo. 1981. *Nantonaku, kurisutaru* (Somehow, crystal). Tokyo: Kōdansha.

TDL. 1994–95. *TDL's Diary*. Chiba: OLC.

———. 1995. "TDL Dimensions and Fact Sheet." Maihama, Chiba: OLC Publicity Division.

Teruhisa Horio. 1988. *Educational Thought and Ideology in Modern Japan*. Tokyo: University of Tokyo Press.

Tezuka Osamu. 1979. *Boku wa mangaka: Tezuka Osamu jiden 1* (I am a cartoonist: vol. 1 of Osamu Tezuka's autobiography). Tokyo: Yamato Shobo.

Tobin, Joseph. 1992. "Introduction: Domesticating the West." In idem, ed., *Remade in Japan*, pp. 1–41. New Haven: Yale University Press.

Tobin, Joseph, David Y. H. Wu, and Dana Davidson. 1989. *Preschool in Three Cultures: Japan, China, and the US*. New Haven: Yale University Press.

Tokyo Dome Company. 1995. *Annual Report*. Tokyo: ToDo.

Tomlinson, John. 1991. *Cultural Imperialism*. London: Pinter Publishers.

Toufexis, A. 1985. "No Mickey Mousing Around." *Time*, Mar. 11: 40.

Tracey, M. 1985. "The Poisoned Chalice? International Television and the Idea of Dominance." *Daedalus* 114/4: 17–56.

Tsuromoki Yasuo. 1984. *Tōkyō dizuniirando o hadaka ni suru* (Stripping Tokyo Disneyland). Tokyo: Tsushinsha shuppanbu.

Tsurumi Shunsuke. 1987. "Comics in Postwar Japan." In idem, *A Cultural History of Postwar Japan, 1945–1980*, chap. 3. London: Kegan Paul International.

Tsurumi Yoshihiro. 1975. "Fried Chicken in Japan." Case 9-375-397. Cambridge: Harvard Business School Press.

Tsutsui, William Minoru. 1995. "From Taylorism to Quality Control: Scientific Management in 20th Century Japan." Ph.D. diss., Department of History, Princeton University.

Tung, Rosalie L. 1984. *Key to Japan's Economic Strength: Human Power*. Lexington, Mass.: Lexington Books.

Turner, Christena L. 1995. *Japanese Workers in Protest*. Berkeley: University of California Press.

Turner, Victor. 1969. *The Ritual Process*. Ithaca, N.Y.: Cornell University Press.

————. 1982. *From Ritual to Theater: The Human Seriousness of Play*. New York: Performing Arts Journal Publications.

Ueda Etsuko. 1994. "Your Japanese Guests." *Virtual Times: International Edition*. http://virtualtimes.com/writers/ueda/profile.htm.

Ueno Chizuko. 1987. *'Watashi' sagashi gēmu: yokubō shimin shakairon* (The search for "me" game: a social theory of desire for selfhood). Tokyo: Chikuma shobō.

Umesao Tadao (Ed.) 1985. *Seventy-seven Keys to the Civilization of Japan*. Union City, Calif.: Heian International.

Urry, John. 1988. "Cultural Change and Contemporary Holiday-Making." *Theory, Culture and Society* 5: 35–56.

————. 1990. *The Tourist Gaze*. London: Sage.

Van Maanen, John. 1989. "Whistle While You Work: On Seeing Disneyland as the Workers Do." Paper presented at the panel on the Magic Kingdom, American Anthropological Association annual meeting, Washington. D.C., Nov. 16.

————. 1991. "The Smile Factory: Work at Disneyland." In P. J. Frost, L. F. Moore, M. R. Louis, C. C. Lundberg, and J. Martin, eds., *Reframing Organizational Culture*, pp. 58–76. Newbury Park, Calif.: Sage.

————. 1992. "Displacing Disney: Some Notes on the Flow of Culture." *Qualitative Sociology* 15(1): 5–35.

Van Maanen, John, & Gideon Kunda. 1989. "'Real Feelings': Emotional Expression and Organizational Culture." *Research in Organizational Behavior* 11: 43–103.

van Wolferen, Karel. 1989. *The Enigma of Japanese Power*. New York: Knopf.

Vogel, Ezra. 1970. "Whither Studies of Urban Japan." In E. Norbeck & S. Parman, eds., *The Study of Japan in the Behavioral Sciences*, pp. 187–94. Houston: Rice University.

————. 1979. *Japan as Number One*. Berkeley: University of California Press.

Volkman, Toby Alice. 1990. "Visions and Revisions: Toradja Culture and the Tourist Gaze." *American Ethnologist* 17: 91–110.

Wakefield, N. 1990. *Postmodernism: The Twilight of the Real*. London: Pluto.

Walker, Derek. 1982. "Architecture and Theming." *Animated Architecture*, Dec.: 25–33.

Wallace, Mike. 1985. "Mickey Mouse History: Portraying the Past at Disney World." *Radical History Review* 32: 33–57.

Wallerstein, Immanuel. 1974. *The Modern World System*. New York: Academic Press.

————. 1990. "Culture as the Ideological Battleground of the Modern World-Systems." *Theory, Culture and Society* 7(2–3): 31–55.

WDW. 1986. *A Commemorative Disney Guidebook*. WDP.

Walter, E. V. 1988. *Placeways: A Theory of the Human Environment*. Chapel Hill: University of North Carolina Press.

Walthall, A. 1986. *Social Protest and Popular Culture in 18th-Century Japan*. Tucson: University of Arizona Press.

Warner, Malcolm. 1994. "Japanese Culture, Western Management: Taylorism and Human Resource in Japan." *Organization Studies* 15(4): 509–33.

Warren, Robert. 1993. "Theme Parks Flourish in Japan." *Japan 21st*, July: 35–41.

Wasserman, A. 1983. "Un and Loathing at EPCOT." *Industrial Design Magazine*, Mar./Apr.: 34–39.

Webster, A. 1984. *Introduction to the Sociology of Development*. London: Macmillan.

Wertheim, Michael. 1995. "The Disney Vision: Packaging History and the Fairy Tale in the Theme Park and the Animated Film." Honors essay presented to the Committee on Degrees in Social Studies, Harvard College, Mar.

White, Merry. 1990. *The Japanese Educational Challenge: A Commitment to Children.* Tokyo: Kodansha International.

———. 1993. *The Material Child: Coming of Age in Japan and America.* New York: Free Press.

———. 1995. "The Marketing of Adolescence in Japan: Buying and Dreaming." In L. Skov & B. Moeran, eds., *Women, Media and Consumption in Japan,* pp. 255–74. Richmond, Eng.: Curzon.

Wilkinson, Endymion. 1990. *Japan Versus the West: Image and Reality.* London: Penguin.

Willis, Susan. 1995. "The Problem with Pleasure." In The Project on Disney, ed., *Inside the Mouse: Work and Play at Disney World,* pp. 1–12. Durham, N.C.: Duke University Press.

Willis, Susan, ed. 1993. *The World According to Disney.* Special issue, *South Atlantic Quarterly* 92(1).

Wilson, Rob, & Wimal Dissanayake, eds. 1996. *Global/Local: Cultural Production and the Transnational Imagery.* Durham, N.C.: Duke University Press.

Wolfe, J. C. 1979. "Disney World: America's Vision of Utopia." *Alternative Futures* 2: 72–77.

Wouters, Cas. 1989. "The Sociology of Emotions and Flight Attendants: Hochschild's *Managed Heart.*" *Theory, Culture & Society* 6: 95–123.

Wren, Daniel. 1972. *The Evolution of Management Thought.* New York: Ronald.

Yamaguchi Masao. 1990. *Norakuro wa warera no tojidai hito* (Norakuro is our contemporary). Tokyo: Kōdansha.

Yamane Kazuma. 1986. *Hentai shōjo moji no kenkyū* (Anomalous teenage handwriting research). Tokyo: Kōdansha.

———. 1990. *Gyaru no kōzō* (The structure of the girl). Tokyo: Sekaibunkasha.

Yamazaki Masakazu. 1984. *Yawarakai kojinshugi no tanjō* (The birth of a softer individualism). Tokyo: Chūōkōronsha. (Also available as *Individualism and the Japanese: An Alternative Approach to Cultural Comparison.* Trans. Barbara Sugihara [Tokyo: Japan Echo, 1994].) See also Yamazaki Masakazu. 1984. "Signs of a New Individualism." *Japan Echo* 11(1): 8–18.

Yanagita Kunio. 1964. "Tanoshii seikatsu" (Fun life). In *Teihon Yanagita Kunio-shū* (Collected works of Yanagita Kunio), vol. 30. Tokyo: Chikuma shobō.

Yasuo Kamon (curator). 1995. "Art in Japan Today, 1985–1995." Museum of Contemporary Art, Tokyo.

Yoka kaihatsu sentā. 1973–1991. *Yoka handobukko* (Leisure handbook). Tokyo: Tsūshō sangyō chōsa-kai.

Yoshimi Shunya. 1996. "Yūenchi no yutopiā" (The utopia of amusment parks) and "Dizuniiirando ka suru toshi" (Disneyfication). In idem, *Riariti toransitō: jōhōshoni shakai no genza* (Realities in transit: the contemporary trend of info-consumer society), pp. 45–87. Tokyo: Kinokuniya.

Yoshimitsu Asano. 1970. *Rejā-sangyō* (Leisure industry). Tokyo: Nihon keizai shinbun.

Yoshimoto Mitsuhiro. 1989. "The Postmodern and Mass Images in Japan." *Public Culture,* Spring: 8–25.

———. 1994. "Images of Empire: Tokyo Disneyland and Japanese Cultural Imperialism." In Eric Smoodin, ed., *Disney Discourse: Producing the Magic Kingdom,* pp. 181–203. London: Routledge.

Yoshino Kosaku. 1992. *Cultural Nationalism in Contemporary Japan.* London: Routledge.

Yuki shobō. 1990. *Hishō kentei nikyū ni gokakusuru hon* (Secretaries' manual). Tokyo: Yuki shobō.

Zipes, Jack. 1994. *Fairy Tale as Myth, Myth as Fairy Tale.* Lexington, Ky.: The University Press.

Zukin, Sharon. 1991. *Landscapes of Power: From Detroit to Disney World.* Berkeley: University of California Press.

Index

Harvard East Asian Monographs

109. Ralph William Huenemann, *The Dragon and the Iron Horse: The Economics of Railroads in China, 1876–1937*

110. Benjamin A. Elman, *From Philosophy to Philology: Intellectual and Social Aspects of Change in Late Imperial China*

111. Jane Kate Leonard, *Wei Yüan and China's Rediscovery of the Maritime World*

112. Luke S. K. Kwong, *A Mosaic of the Hundred Days:. Personalities, Politics, and Ideas of 1898*

113. John E. Wills, Jr., *Embassies and Illusions: Dutch and Portuguese Envoys to K'ang-hsi, 1666–1687*

114. Joshua A. Fogel, *Politics and Sinology: The Case of Naitō Konan (1866–1934)*

115. Jeffrey C. Kinkley, ed., *After Mao: Chinese Literature and Society, 1978–1981*

116. C. Andrew Gerstle, *Circles of Fantasy: Convention in the Plays of Chikamatsu*

117. Andrew Gordon, *The Evolution of Labor Relations in Japan: Heavy Industry, 1853–1955*

118. Daniel K. Gardner, *Chu Hsi and the "Ta Hsueh": Neo-Confucian Reflection on the Confucian Canon*

119. Christine Guth Kanda, *Shinzō: Hachiman Imagery and Its Development*

120. Robert Borgen, *Sugawara no Michizane and the Early Heian Court*

121. Chang-tai Hung, *Going to the People: Chinese Intellectual and Folk Literature, 1918–1937*

122. Michael A. Cusumano, *The Japanese Automobile Industry: Technology and Management at Nissan and Toyota*

123. Richard von Glahn, *The Country of Streams and Grottoes: Expansion, Settlement, and the Civilizing of the Sichuan Frontier in Song Times*

124. Steven D. Carter, *The Road to Komatsubara: A Classical Reading of the Renga Hyakuin*

125. Katherine F. Bruner, John K. Fairbank, and Richard T. Smith, *Entering China's Service: Robert Hart's Journals, 1854–1863*

126. Bob Tadashi Wakabayashi, *Anti-Foreignism and Western Learning in Early-Modern Japan: The "New Theses" of 1825*

127. Atsuko Hirai, *Individualism and Socialism: The Life and Thought of Kawai Eijirō (1891–1944)*

128. Ellen Widmer, *The Margins of Utopia: "Shui-hu hou-chuan" and the Literature of Ming Loyalism*

129. R. Kent Guy, *The Emperor's Four Treasuries: Scholars and the State in the Late Chien-lung Era*

130. Peter C. Perdue, *Exhausting the Earth: State and Peasant in Hunan, 1500–1850*